I0112999

Financial Services and Preferential Trade Agreements

Financial Services and Preferential Trade Agreements

Lessons from Latin America

Mona Haddad and Constantinos Stephanou,
Editors

THE WORLD BANK
Washington, D.C.

© 2010 The International Bank for Reconstruction and Development / The World Bank
1818 H Street, NW
Washington, DC 20433
Telephone: 202-473-1000
Internet: www.worldbank.org
E-mail: feedback@worldbank.org

All rights reserved

1 2 3 4 13 12 11 10

This volume is a product of the staff of the International Bank for Reconstruction and Development / The World Bank. The findings, interpretations, and conclusions expressed in this volume do not necessarily reflect the views of the Executive Directors of The World Bank or the governments they represent.

The World Bank does not guarantee the accuracy of the data included in this work. The boundaries, colors, denominations, and other information shown on any map in this work do not imply any judgement on the part of The World Bank concerning the legal status of any territory or the endorsement or acceptance of such boundaries.

Rights and Permissions
The material in this publication is copyrighted. Copying and/or transmitting portions or all of this work without permission may be a violation of applicable law. The International Bank for Reconstruction and Development / The World Bank encourages dissemination of its work and will normally grant permission to reproduce portions of the work promptly.

For permission to photocopy or reprint any part of this work, please send a request with complete information to the Copyright Clearance Center Inc., 222 Rosewood Drive, Danvers, MA 01923, USA; telephone: 978-750-8400; fax: 978-750-4470; Internet: www.copyright.com.

All other queries on rights and licenses, including subsidiary rights, should be addressed to the Office of the Publisher, The World Bank, 1818 H Street, NW, Washington, DC 20433, USA; fax: 202-522-2422; e-mail: pubrights@worldbank.org.

ISBN: 978-0-8213-8273-8
eISBN: 978-0-8213-8312-4
DOI: 10.1596/978-0-8213-8273-8

Cover photo: Old Stock Exchange, Santiago, Chile; Richard Nowitz/National Geographic/Getty Images
Cover design: Naylor Design, Inc.

Library of Congress Cataloging-in-Publication Data
Financial services and preferential trade agreements : lessons from Latin America / Mona Haddad and Constantinos Stephanou.
    p. cm.
  ISBN 978-0-8213-8273-8 — ISBN 978-0-8213-8312-4 (electronic)
1. Financial services industry—Government policy—Latin America. 2. Latin America—Commercial policy. 3. Commercial treaties—Latin America. I. Haddad, Mona II. Stephanou, Constantinos, 1971- III. World Bank. IV. Title.
  HG185.3.L3H33 2010
  332.1098—dc22

2010016950

Contents

Boxes

Figures

Tables

Foreword

The financial services sector is one of the most important—though sometimes controversial—sectors covered by international trade agreements. It can influence macroeconomic conditions, given its close relationship with monetary and exchange rate policies. Moreover, at a microeconomic level, it provides a link between creditors and borrowers and serves as a vehicle for allocating resources. Financial sector activities may also involve sensitive policies such as social security (pension funds management), health (insurance), and personal savings.

This book deals with financial liberalization issues in the context of trade negotiations. The liberalization of trade and investment in financial services is only a subset of the broader financial liberalization agenda. The purpose of trade and investment liberalization is to increase financial market access and remove discriminatory and other access-impeding barriers to foreign competition. By contrast, the main purpose of financial liberalization is to remove distortions in domestic financial systems that impede competition and the allocation of capital to its most productive and profitable uses. In turn, financial liberalization can be divided into domestic financial reform and capital account opening, and there is a rich literature on its appropriate speed and sequencing.

The first part of the book covers the fundamental principles that affect trade liberalization in financial services at both the multilateral and the regional levels. It analyzes the various models of preferential trade agreements (PTAs) used by negotiators and the architectural differences of these models. The second part of this book provides concrete examples of how countries have negotiated these agreements by focusing on the specific country experiences of Chile, Colombia, and Costa Rica. These case studies provide the reader with a thorough understanding of how countries strategize, negotiate, and implement regional trade agreements in financial services.

The objective of this book is to provide applicable policy recommendations for developing countries that are currently negotiating or seeking to negotiate PTAs. The liberalization of financial services through trade agreements may bring about financial modernization domestically, but adopting a correct sequencing of reforms and openness is important. Moreover, complementary policies are needed, including adoption of international prudential standards, elimination of measures that may hamper private participation in the financial sector, and strengthening of the country's overall financial infrastructure.

Financial regulation issues are often not addressed in the context of trade in financial services negotiations. On the one hand, developing countries are responsible for strengthening their domestic regulatory environment when engaging in negotiations. They are also responsible for adopting measures to ensure that financial negotiations resulting from PTAs do not encourage vulnerabilities in their financial markets. Developed countries, on the other hand, can collaborate with their trading partners to improve financial regulation and strengthen the performance of the sector in developing countries.

The experiences of Chile, Colombia, and Costa Rica illustrate how countries that have the motivation to reform and engage in PTA negotiations can address the challenges of negotiations. These three countries embraced reforms and sought to negotiate PTAs with the United States— and are seeking to conclude negotiations with other developed countries— as part of their own strategic interests to further integrate with the world economy. They have managed to translate legitimate policy concerns into mutually acceptable provisions that take into account their economic and political reality. The experiences of these countries also show that although there are considerable differences in bargaining powers between developed and developing countries, developing countries are capable of defining limits in the concessions they are willing to make within

PTAs—especially when a strategic negotiating model is employed, offensive interests are aligned, and relevant and substantive provisions are included in the PTA text.

This publication comes at a time when the world is recovering from the biggest financial crisis since the Great Depression of the 1930s. Countries that were affected by previous financial crises and adopted corrective measures (including Chile and Colombia) were less severely affected by the present crisis. One of the main lessons is therefore that trade liberalization in financial services must coexist with strong and sound regulatory frameworks if these agreements are to contribute to developing countries' progress.

Marcelo Giugale
Director
Latin America and the
Caribbean Region
Poverty Reduction and
Economic Management
World Bank

Bernard Hoekman
Director
International Trade
Department
Poverty Reduction and
Economic Management
World Bank

Consolate Rusagara
Director
Financial Systems Department
Financial and Private Sector
Development Vice Presidency
World Bank

Acknowledgments

This book is the outcome of a 2006–07 policy research project, led by Constantinos Stephanou (senior financial economist, Financial and Private Sector Development Vice Presidency, World Bank), focusing on the experience of preferential trade agreements and financial services in selected countries in Latin America. Mona Haddad (sector manager, International Trade Department, World Bank) coedited the book. The main objective of the project was to draw useful policy lessons from experience that can be used to prepare policy makers involved in the liberalization of trade in financial services under future trade agreements. The project covers a topic that has become increasingly important with the proliferation of preferential trade agreements around the world and builds on prior work undertaken by the World Bank and other international organizations in recent years. This volume includes the background papers that were commissioned as part of the project dealing with different dimensions of this topic and with specific country case studies. The findings and policy implications are expected to be of interest to World Bank staff members and country clients as well as to the broader trade and development community.

The authors of the various chapters—María Angélica Arbeláez, Roberto Echandi, Andrés Flórez, Marilyne Pereira Goncalves, Mona Haddad, Martín

Molinuevo, Raúl E. Sáez, Natalia Salazar, Pierre Sauvé, and Constantinos Stephanou—would like to express their sincere gratitude to the numerous individuals who provided valuable input and are cited in the respective chapters. In addition, the team would like to thank Marco Arena, Stijn Claessens, Patricio Contreras, Augusto de la Torre, Norah Dihel, Carsten Fink, Juan Marchetti, Latifah Osman Merican, Pascual O'Dogherty, Sebastián Sáez, and Sherry M. Stephenson for their kind feedback and useful suggestions.

This project was financed by the Financial and Private Sector Development unit of the Latin America and the Caribbean Vice Presidency. The editing and publication of the book is a collaborative effort between the International Trade Department and the Financial and Private Sector Development Vice Presidency. Their crucial support is gratefully acknowledged.

Contributors

María Angélica Arbeláez (marbelaez@fedesarrollo.org.co), Associate Researcher, Fedesarrollo, Colombia

Roberto Echandi (rechandi@setic.org), Ambassador of Costa Rica at the European Union and former Costa Rican and Lead Negotiator to the CAFTA-DR-U.S. negotiation group on financial services

Andrés Flórez (aflorez@esguerrabarrera.com), Partner of Esguerra Barrera Arriaga law firm and former General Director of Financial Regulation, Colombian Ministry of Finance

Marilyne Pereira Goncalves (mgoncalves2@worldbank.org), Financial Sector Specialist, Financial and Private Sector Development Vice Presidency, World Bank

Mona Haddad (mhaddad@worldbank.org), Sector Manager, Poverty Reduction and Economic Management, International Trade Department, World Bank

Martín Molinuevo (martin.molinuevo@wti.org), Research Fellow, World Trade Institute, Bern, Switzerland

Raúl E. Sáez (rsaez@hacienda.gov.cl), Director of International Affairs, Ministry of Finance, Chile

Natalia Salazar (nsalazar@minhacienda.gov.co), Vice Minister of Finance and former Associate Researcher, Fedesarrollo, Colombia

Pierre Sauvé (pierre.sauve@wti.org), Director of Studies, World Trade Institute, Bern, Switzerland

Constantinos Stephanou (cstephanou@worldbank.org), Senior Financial Economist, Financial and Private Sector Development Vice Presidency, World Bank

Abbreviations

AFPs	*administradoras de fondos de pensiones,* or pension fund managers
AFS	Annex on Financial Services (GATS)
ALADI	Asociación Latinoamericana de Integración, or Latin American Integration Association
ANIF	Asociación Nacional de Instituciones Financieras, or National Association of Financial Institutions
ASEAN	Association of Southeast Asian Nations
Bancoldex	Banco de Comercio Exterior de Colombia, or Colombian Foreign Trade Bank
BCCR	Banco Central de Costa Rica
BTA	Bilateral Trade Agreement
BVC	Bolsa de Valores de Colombia, or Colombian Stock Exchange
CACM	Central American Common Market
CAFTA-DR-U.S.	Free Trade Agreement between Central America, the Dominican Republic, and the United States
CAN	Comunidad Andina, or Andean Community
CARICOM	Caribbean Community
CARIFORUM	Caribbean Forum of the African, Caribbean, and Pacific Group of States

CCSS	Caja Costarricense de Seguro Social, or Costa Rican Social Security Institution
CEPA	Closer Economic Partnership Agreement
CIS	collective investment scheme
COMEX	Ministerio de Comercio Exterior, or Ministry of Foreign Trade (Costa Rica)
CONASSIF	Consejo Nacional de Supervisión del Sistema Financiero, or National Council of Supervision of the National Financial System (Costa Rica)
CPI	Consumer Price Index
EC	European Commission
EFTA	European Free Trade Association
EPA	Economic Partnership Agreement
EU	European Union
FDI	foreign direct investment
Fogafin	Fondo de Garantias de Instituciones Financieras, or Financial Institutions Guarantee Fund (Colombia)
FONASA	Fondo Nacional de Salud, or National Health Fund (Chile)
FTA	free trade agreement
G3	Group of Three (Colombia, Mexico, and the República Bolivariana de Venezuela)
GATS	General Agreement on Trade in Services
GDP	gross domestic product
INS	Instituto Nacional de Seguros, or National Insurance Institute (Costa Rica)
Isapres	*instituciones de salud provisional*, or social security health providers
MAS	Monetary Authority of Singapore
MAT	marine, aviation, and transport
Mercosur	Mercado Común del Sur (Southern Cone Common Market)
MFN	most-favored-nation (treatment)
MOU	memorandum of understanding
NAFTA	North American Free Trade Agreement
NGO	nongovernmental organization
NPL	nonperforming loan
OECD	Organisation for Economic Co-operation and Development
PTA	preferential trade agreement

SAR	Special Administrative Region
SBIF	Superintendencia de Bancos e Instituciones Financieras, or Superintendency of Banks and Financial Institutions (Chile)
SP	Superintendencia de Pensiones, or Superintendency of Pensions (Chile)
SUGEF	Superintendencia General de Entidades Financieras, or General Superintendency of Financial Institutions (Costa Rica)
SUGEVAL	Superintendencia General de Valores, or General Superintendency of Securities (Costa Rica)
SUPEN	Superintendencia de Pensiones, or Pension Superintendency (Costa Rica)
SVS	Superintendencia de Valores y Seguros, or Superintendency of Securities and Insurance (Chile)
UPAC	*unidad de poder adquisitivo constante*, or constant purchasing power unit
URR	unremunerated reserve requirement
WTO	World Trade Organization

CHAPTER 1

Financial Services Liberalization, Preferential Trade Agreements, and the Latin American Experience

An Introduction

Mona Haddad, Pierre Sauvé, and Constantinos Stephanou

This volume chronicles the recent experience of governments engaged in liberalization of financial services in Latin America and the Caribbean. Its seven chapters aim at providing readers with an understanding of the process, substance, and likely effects of financial market opening through trade agreements in the region. The volume also aims at helping policy makers and negotiators, both within and beyond the region, better understand the complexities of financial services negotiations.

The volume fills an important gap in the literature on trade in services by focusing attention on the dynamics of trade and investment liberalization in a sector of considerable technical complexity and regulatory intensity—financial services. The subject is analyzed in a sample of countries (Chile, Colombia, Costa Rica) from a "first-mover" region in the financial services liberalization front, Latin America, and in the confines of one specific type of negotiating setting, preferential trade agreements (PTAs).

Despite the recent proliferation of PTAs featuring disciplines on services trade and investment, including in financial services, and despite the continued pursuit of market opening and rule making in services at the multilateral level under the aegis of the General Agreement on Trade in Services (GATS) of the World Trade Organization (WTO), services trade remains one of the most challenging subject matters in modern trade diplomacy. Its relative novelty—negotiations have proceeded in the sector for little over two decades—means that services negotiations continue to be characterized by considerable learning by doing and policy experimentation. Such characteristics heighten the relevance of this volume and its attempt to shed analytical light on the lessons derived from early attempts at addressing financial services liberalization in a trade policy setting.

A particularly helpful feature of this volume is the three in-depth country case studies, which offer useful analytical insights into the substantive content of the legal provisions governing financial market opening in the region and the evolution of those provisions over time and across negotiating settings (for example, multilateral versus preferential market opening). The common format of the case studies facilitates comparative analysis. All three are written by trade experts who led the negotiations of their respective countries in financial services. Of considerable interest are the chapters' descriptions of the background of financial policy reforms before, during, and (sometimes) after the negotiations; how each of the three governments organized the conduct of negotiations in the sector; the extent of preparatory work that governments undertook during negotiations, sometimes outsourced to experts in academia or consulting firms (as in the cases of both Colombia and Costa Rica); and the negotiating roadmaps that were put in place to help negotiators.[1] The case studies are complemented by other chapters dealing with the evolving architecture of trade and investment disciplines in financial services and the best way to prepare for negotiations in the sector.

Key Policy Messages

The volume aims to highlight key policy issues related to financial services trade negotiation, including the rationale driving liberalization, approaches, and negotiating paradigms as well as the implications of such negotiations.

Financial Services Liberalization versus Financial Liberalization
The liberalization of trade and investment in financial services is only a subset of the broader financial liberalization agenda. It is important to

situate trade and investment liberalization in financial services against this wider reform canvas and to appreciate what trade diplomacy is best suited to achieving while also acknowledging its inherent limitations. The purpose of trade and investment liberalization is to increase financial market access and to remove discriminatory and other access-impeding barriers to foreign competition. By contrast, the main purpose of financial liberalization is to remove distortions in domestic financial systems that impede competition and the allocation of capital to its most productive and profitable uses. In turn, financial liberalization can be divided into domestic financial reform and capital account opening, and a rich literature has arisen on its appropriate speed and sequencing. Seen this way, trade and investment liberalization in financial services is only part of overall financial liberalization, although in practice a strong overlap is typical in the manner and timing with which the two types of policy reforms are pursued.

The liberalization of trade in financial services is helpful to, but is not a panacea for, financial system modernization. Liberalization is desirable to serve the development needs of the domestic financial system by improving efficiency and the allocation of resources through healthy competition with foreign providers. However, the net benefits of liberalization will likely depend critically on the domestic market's perceived attractiveness, which will determine the extent to which foreign providers actually take advantage of the opportunity to enter. Thus, a government's commitment to complementary regulatory reforms—adoption of international prudential standards, elimination of financial repression measures, and strengthening of the enabling financial infrastructure (that is, creditors' rights, credit bureaus, collateral registries, accounting and auditing standards, payment systems, and the like)—may be of considerable importance not only in ensuring that liberalization does not destabilize the domestic financial system but also in attracting new foreign players. Many perceived barriers to entry are actually nondiscriminatory "doing business"–type problems that extend well beyond the traditional remit of trade and investment policy and cannot, therefore, be tackled solely in the context of a trade agreement.

Approaches to Financial Services Liberalization

Countries have achieved the liberalization of trade in financial services in three main ways: (a) unilaterally, by opening their financial systems to international competition in an autonomous manner in the context of domestic reform efforts; (b) at the multilateral level under the auspices of

GATS; and (c) on a reciprocal or preferential basis by concluding bilateral or plurilateral PTAs, of which free trade agreements (FTAs) are the most common type. Depending on the country context and circumstances, one or more of these approaches have been used to liberalize specific subsectors or modes of financial services provision.

Autonomous market opening remains the most common form of liberalizing trade and investment in financial services. Most developed countries have adopted such a strategy, progressively liberalizing their financial markets over a relatively long period. Many developing countries followed (or are following) the same path, although in some cases—such as Mexico—the advent of the Tequila Crisis in December 1994 led to or even accelerated the market-opening process. When the time came to negotiate GATS, these countries typically bound at (or below) the regulatory status quo in their schedules, consolidating the actual degree of openness prevailing at the time of the agreement's entry into force. Recent WTO accession countries (for example, Cambodia, China, and Vietnam) are the clearest examples of liberalization of trade in financial services in a multilateral context. Fewer examples generally exist of further (or de novo) liberalization stemming from PTAs, although Mexico (under the North American Free Trade Agreement, or NAFTA) and Costa Rica (under the Free Trade Agreement between Central America, the Dominican Republic, and the United States, or CAFTA-DR-U.S.) stand out as vivid examples to the contrary.

Broadly, three main reasons appear to underpin the decision of countries negotiating PTAs to include financial services disciplines and commitments in them. The first and typically most important reason is the existence of offensive negotiating interests in the sector and of asymmetric bargaining powers between the negotiating counterparts. This rationale should not be surprising: a trade agreement is essentially a mercantilist exercise, so the inclusion of certain sensitive sectors such as financial services reflects the perceived interests and negotiating strengths of the partners. In such cases, a country includes financial services commitments either because it is forced to do so by its more powerful negotiating partner (perhaps as a quid pro quo for securing market access in another sector) or because it has offensive interests in financial services and is able to pursue them in the markets of its trading partners—typically in a North-South PTA context. A second rationale is for a trade agreement to serve as a vehicle either to lock in recent unilateral liberalization or to advance the government's reform agenda in the sector by precommitting to future market opening, thereby overcoming any lingering resistance from domestic constituencies and providing a positive signal to foreign investors. This reason seems to have spurred financial services commitments undertaken by, for example, Costa Rica in CAFTA-DR-U.S., as described later in this volume. Finally, countries can decide to include financial services in PTAs more for long-term strategic interests or political reasons than for purely economic or commercial ones (notably, when a country has negligible exporting interests in the sector). The clearest examples of such cases involve plurilateral regional trading bloc initiatives, such as the Mercado Común del Sur (Southern Cone Common Market, or Mercosur) in Latin America.[2]

Trade and investment commitments in financial services need to be aligned with a country's financial system characteristics and policy objectives. Potential drawbacks to liberalization include regulatory sensitivities about further domestic financial market opening and the related fear of limiting "policy space" in the sector; potential distortions that could arise from giving preferential treatment to specific counterparts (especially in cases where first-mover advantages can be important, such as in markets characterized by high levels of concentration); strategic considerations (commitments made with one PTA counterpart can become a floor in multilateral or other bilateral trade negotiations); and administrative problems that arise from managing a complex web of financial services liberalization rules with different countries. By far, the most important factors until now have been regulatory sensitivities and strategic considerations, which have also been evident in the GATS negotiations and have fueled significant regulatory precaution about the scheduling of legally binding liberalization commitments. As the current global financial crisis illustrates, the process of market opening in financial services needs to be gradual to ensure financial stability and to promote orderly adjustment in a sector that is critical to broader economic performance.

The existence of different architectural approaches to the treatment of trade and investment in financial services suggests that there is no single model to which all countries should aspire. Diverse approaches are used to cover financial services in PTAs, ranging from general chapters on trade and investment in services at one extreme to a stand-alone, self-contained financial services chapter at the other extreme—each with its own characteristics, strengths, and potential weaknesses. In practice, specific PTA circumstances will largely determine the approach taken. The choice of negotiating template should be commensurate with a country's level of comfort or ambition with market opening in different modes of supplying financial services and various subsectors. However, international experience to date suggests that coverage of financial services by a dedicated chapter allows the parties to better tailor disciplines to the particularities of the financial sector, which may limit any unforeseen consequences deriving from its coverage under a trade agreement.

Impact of Financial Services Liberalization

International experience on the inclusion of financial services in PTAs remains too recent to allow an exhaustive evaluation of its effects on domestic financial systems and overall welfare. Although numerous studies have addressed the effects of foreign entry (particularly that of banks) flowing from unilateral liberalization, no comparable literature treats the effects of PTA-induced financial liberalization. Such effects do not appear a priori to be very significant—with a few exceptions, such as the opening of Costa Rica's previously state-owned insurance sector—because most PTAs seem to be primarily used to consolidate and lock in existing unilateral liberalization rather than to actively promote further (de novo) market opening and the process of domestic regulatory reform.

The lack of relevant data and methodologies to assess ex post (as opposed to estimate ex ante) effects remains an important constraint.[3] However, even if a commonly accepted methodology for quantifying effects was established, the short time span since the negotiation or entry into force of PTAs featuring detailed disciplines and market-access commitments in financial services (the earliest, and rather atypical, example being NAFTA in 1994) means that their contribution still cannot be fully assessed. In particular, financial services commitments and disciplines, including dispute settlement mechanisms, have not been put to the test during a prolonged market downturn (as may currently exist) or a significant revision of domestic financial system policy priorities, which is typically when constraints on policy space and regulatory sensitivities more fully reveal their binding nature.

Preparing for Financial Services Negotiations

Trade negotiators must be cognizant of important nuances between the two main negotiating templates. In particular, negotiators need to be aware of important differences in disciplines and commitments between the GATS and NAFTA templates as they relate to financial services if they are to avoid unintended consequences or to limit policy space beyond what is desired. Examples in NAFTA-type agreements include the definition of financial services suppliers as regulated financial institutions, the relationship between financial services and other chapters, the denial-of-benefits clause, limits to state aid and to preferential arrangements for state-owned financial institutions, restrictions on the imposition of capital controls, the adoption of ratcheting or standstill clauses, and the use of a negative list approach. The dispute resolution mechanisms adopted for financial services may also be crucial, given the limited degree of jurisprudence generated to date in the sector within trade agreements, be it at the WTO or under PTAs. Notwithstanding the overall architecture of the trade agreement, however, significant scope exists to maintain or introduce certain trade- and investment-restrictive measures, where needed, in financial services commitments or reservations.

Preparing for financial services negotiations is conceptually no different from preparing for negotiations in other sectors. In all trade agreements, demandeurs strive to enhance market-access opportunities for their services providers rather than to promote mutual recognition or the harmonization of prudential standards. Therefore, negotiators need to develop a strategy or roadmap for the negotiation process that allows them to classify offensive and defensive interests, identify "red lines," anticipate requests, and avoid surprises, as well as to ensure the coherence of positions by resolving internal inconsistencies that could weaken the negotiating stance.

Securing the active collaboration of financial sector officials in financial services negotiations is essential to trade negotiations. The financial services negotiating team typically includes, or relies on, financial sector officials—from the ministry of finance, central bank, deposit insurance agency, and supervisory agencies—in addition to trade and investment specialists. This composition is an inevitable consequence of the heavy regulation of the financial sector for prudential and market-conduct purposes, which thus requires a high level of technical expertise and regulations that fall outside the responsibilities of ministries in charge of trade. Cultural and institutional factors—historical involvement, degree of trust and knowledge, relative political power, and the like—are important determinants of whether financial or trade officials lead negotiations in the sector.[4] Given the regulatory complexities and sensitivities of the financial system, the input of financial sector officials—who will, after all, be tasked with implementing any commitments that are made—is critical. In most countries, this process is challenging because of the existence of institutional silos and bureaucratic turf battles as well as varying political interests. The creation of institutional collaboration mechanisms and the active participation of financial sector officials in the negotiations can greatly facilitate this process. Conducting a trade-related regulatory audit to identify suboptimal regulatory measures and the rationale behind trade- and investment-restrictive regulations in financial services can serve as a useful conduit for discussions between financial sector and trade officials and can help promote a collaborative interagency process within the government.

Developing a robust consultation process with nongovernmental stakeholders can also enhance the effectiveness of financial services negotiators. To be in a position to make informed and meaningful negotiating offers and requests, a country requires knowledge of the export potential or priorities of its domestic services suppliers. A country needs to feel confident of its ability to manage the regulatory, sectoral, and economy-wide implications of its own commitments. Strengthening processes of policy dialogue and consultations with key stakeholders in the private sector and civil society is of great importance in this context. The consultation process with the financial industry is typically extensive, although the one with civil society varies more widely across countries and tends to reflect the country's state-civil society traditions. Although the scope and frequency of such consultations can differ, they invariably represent an important means of securing greater transparency of regulatory practices and the underlying policy rationales of such practices and ensuring greater legitimacy of negotiated outcomes.

Structure of the Volume

This volume is structured around seven chapters: an introduction, an overview, and two parts. The first part (chapters 3–4) addresses a series of horizontal themes in the design, conduct, and assessment of the effects of trade and investment liberalization in financial services. The second part (chapters 5–7) then details three in-depth country case studies, focusing on the Chilean, Colombian, and Costa Rican experiences with financial services liberalization.

Following this introduction, chapter 2 by Marilyne Pereira Goncalves and Constantinos Stephanou provides a comprehensive overview of the volume's main findings and some of the key policy lessons. The chapter introduces readers to many of the conceptual and negotiating challenges arising in financial services and recalls the key elements of the existing multilateral architecture of rules governing financial services liberalization under the WTO's GATS. It does so to highlight key distinctions and convergences arising from the recent attempts at tackling financial market opening in PTAs and the motivations and policy rationales behind observed trends. The chapter summarizes the key findings of the country case studies featured in the volume, thus providing readers with an early appreciation of how cross-country differences in economic contexts, political economy, and level of financial market development ultimately shaped negotiated outcomes. It also features a useful comparative description of the nature and extent of liberalization commitments entered into by the countries under review and how these commitments differ both from one another and from each country's financial services commitments under GATS. Goncalves and Stephanou alert readers to the central importance of sound preparations for negotiations in the sector and describe how the countries reviewed in the case studies fared in this regard, issues that are taken up in greater depth in subsequent chapters.

In chapter 3, Pierre Sauvé and Martin Molinuevo tackle the issue of architectural differences in the treatment of trade and investment disciplines in financial services across a sample of PTAs from around the world. The chapter highlights how PTAs vary in their approach to crafting disciplines and scheduling trade and investment commitments in financial services, as well as some of the policy consequences likely to flow from the choice of negotiating architecture. The country case studies reviewed in this volume reveal how the choice of a stand-alone chapter governing all aspects (that is, trade and investment) of financial services trade liberalization and the adoption of a negative list approach to market opening first pioneered in NAFTA strongly influenced the agreements discussed.

In chapter 4, Pierre Sauvé, who served on Canada's services negotiating team in NAFTA, discusses how trade agreements in services offer a ready-made opportunity for governments to conduct an audit of domestic regulatory measures. The chapter tackles both the *why* and the *how* of conducting a trade-related regulatory audit in financial services. It highlights the manifold uses to which such an audit can be put: to inform the conduct of negotiations, to provide an analytical anchor for interagency coordination and external stakeholder consultations, to anticipate the requests of trading partners, to identify alternative and less trade- or investment-distorting means of securing compliance with key regulatory objectives, and, just as important, to help promote a culture of regulatory reform and regulatory impact assessment domestically long after trade negotiations are concluded.

The volume's country case studies are found in chapters 5 to 7, respectively, on Chile (by Raúl E. Sáez); Colombia (by María Angélica Arbeláez,

Andrés Flórez, and Natalia Salazar); and Costa Rica (by Roberto Echandi). To facilitate comparative analysis, all three case studies follow the same structure. They start off with a description of financial sector developments up to the onset of the PTAs under review, recalling how trade policy in financial services inserted itself into—and complemented—the broader (and longer-term) set of ongoing domestic reform efforts in the sector. The case studies also provide a brief depiction of the level and nature of international commitments in financial services entered into by each of the three countries at both the WTO and PTA levels. Each of the three chapters also devotes close attention to the critical twin processes of interagency coordination and external stakeholder consultations that each government has put in place to guide its negotiations in the financial sector.

A word of caution appears warranted in closing this introduction. Readers of this volume need to treat the principal policy lessons that derive from the experiences depicted in it with some measure of caution for three main reasons:

- Only a limited sample of country case studies is offered, and all from one specific region of the world. That region is characterized by close and highly asymmetric relations with a hegemonic power (the United States), which left the countries relatively little room to discuss potential offensive interests.
- All three countries were actively engaged in unilateral financial liberalization reforms and saw PTAs as a means to enhance this process.
- The time horizon over which to gauge the potential effects of the PTAs under review has been relatively short.

Despite the preceding caveats, the volume makes an important and welcome contribution to the literature in the field of services trade. Moreover, the richness of the country case studies and horizontal themes taken up in the volume and the analytical ease with which country experiences can be analyzed and compared should provide the trade policy community with a practical tool to guide future negotiations—and future generations of negotiators—in financial services in Latin America and the Caribbean and beyond.

Notes

1. For a fuller discussion of how best to prepare for services negotiations, see World Bank (2009).

2. A fourth, and more technical, reason for including financial services in a PTA would be to ensure that the agreement has substantial sectoral coverage and therefore constitutes a lawful exemption to the nondiscrimination requirement articulated in GATS article V (Economic Integration). This issue can be addressed by not carving out a priori financial services from the scope of the agreement.

3. Unlike the case with trade in goods, assessing the direct effects of including financial services in PTAs goes well beyond trade volumes to include various financial sector outcomes (depth, efficiency, stability, and so on). For a recent review of the literature on liberalizing trade in services, see Hoekman (2006).

4. For example, the ministry of finance led the negotiations process in the Chilean (Chile-U.S. FTA, Chile-European Community Association Agreement) and Colombian (Colombia-U.S. FTA) cases, but the ministry of trade led negotiations for Costa Rica (CAFTA-DR-U.S. FTA). In the case of the United States, the Office of the United States Trade Representative handles insurance negotiations, and the Treasury handles negotiations in other financial services.

References and Other Resources

Hoekman, Bernard. 2006. "Liberalizing Trade in Services: A Survey." Policy Research Working Paper 4030, World Bank, Washington, DC.

World Bank. 2009. *Preparing for Services Negotiations: A Practical Guide for Developing Countries.* Washington, DC: World Bank.

CHAPTER 2

Financial Services and Trade Agreements

An Overview

Marilyne Pereira Goncalves and Constantinos Stephanou

Many countries have made significant progress in liberalizing their domestic financial systems. Such progress can be achieved in three ways. First, it can be done unilaterally, when countries decide to open their financial systems to international competition, typically in the context of far-reaching domestic reforms. Second, countries can enter into preferential trade agreements (PTAs), either bilateral or plurilateral, in which the removal of barriers to trade and investment is negotiated on a reciprocal and preferential basis. Finally, specific commitments can be undertaken at the multilateral level within the framework of the World Trade Organization (WTO). These three channels are, of course, closely interrelated, and depending on the country context and circumstances, different combinations of these approaches have been used to liberalize specific subsectors or modes of financial

This chapter is based on Goncalves and Stephanou (2007) and Stephanou (2009). The authors would like to thank Pierre Sauvé for his excellent guidance and express their gratitude to Augusto de la Torre, Carsten Fink, Juan Marchetti, and Latifah Osman Merican for helpful comments and suggestions.

13

services provision. Therefore, although this overview chapter focuses on the experience of Latin American countries in the negotiation of PTAs, the international framework governing trade and investment in financial services is also considered. The case studies to follow pay closer attention to the interaction between unilateral and preferential liberalizations.

Overview of Trade in Financial Services: Liberalization of Trade in Financial Services and Financial Liberalization

In contrast to trade in goods, the main barriers to international trade in financial services are "behind-the-border" measures (that is, laws, regulations, and administrative procedures) that cause market-access impediments for or discriminatory treatment of foreign financial services providers. Examples of impediments include differential tax rates and unduly onerous prudential regulations, as well as restrictions on foreign equity participation in domestic financial institutions.[1] They also include limitations on the purchase of financial services abroad and on the remote supply of services by foreign providers. The lifting of such discriminatory barriers is what is typically understood by the liberalization of trade in financial services, and accordingly, the "hard law" of international trade agreements has so far focused primarily on these issues.

In addition to these direct and explicitly discriminatory barriers to international trade in financial services, a continuum of nondiscriminatory barriers—often with unintended adverse effects—exists. Such indirect barriers include those related to the coexistence of diverse national laws and regulatory standards and practices that may raise the cost of regulatory compliance and of doing business for foreign providers. Although the development and adoption of international standards and codes ("soft laws") by multilateral organizations[2] have facilitated the process of regulatory convergence and harmonization, these measures are often justified on the basis of the overarching objective of protecting the stability and integrity of domestic financial systems. Indeed, some commentators (see, for example, Claessens 2002) have argued that the gains arising from trade liberalization in financial services depend greatly on the quality of domestic regulation and the broader institutional environment, such as disclosure and transparency practices or rule of law. Yet some uncertainty exists about where necessary regulation stops and discrimination starts—that is, where the line should be drawn between trade-distorting measures and domestic regulation.

With this in mind, it is important to see the liberalization of trade in financial services in the context of an often broader financial liberalization agenda. The purpose of the former is to increase financial market access and remove discriminatory and other access-impeding barriers to foreign competition. By contrast, the chief purpose of the latter is to remove distortions in domestic financial systems—for example, interest rate and capital account controls, directed lending policies, restrictions on intrasectoral activities, and preferential treatment of publicly owned banks—that impede competition and the allocation of capital to its most productive and profitable uses. Financial liberalization can be conceptually divided into domestic financial reform and capital account opening, and a broad literature discusses its appropriate speed and sequencing. In that context, trade liberalization in financial services is part of overall financial liberalization, and in practice, strong overlaps typically occur between the two types of policy reforms.[3]

Also of note is that the liberalization of trade in financial services is helpful to, but is not a panacea for, modernization of the domestic financial system. Liberalization is desirable because it serves the development needs of the domestic financial system by improving efficiency and resource allocation through healthy competition with foreign providers. A substantial body of literature on the positive relationship between finance and growth[4] and on the spillover effects of foreign (particularly bank) entry[5] already exists, though there are also preconditions for the success of financial liberalization.[6] More specifically, the size of benefits from trade liberalization in financial services depends critically on the market's attractiveness (the "if you build it, will they come?" argument). Equally important are complementary regulatory reforms, such as the adoption of international prudential standards, the elimination of financial repression measures, and the strengthening of the financial infrastructure, which includes—among other things—accounting and auditing standards, payments and securities settlement systems, corporate governance frameworks, and creditor rights and insolvency regimes. Hence, neither the liberalization of trade in financial services nor financial liberalization implies the complete deregulation of the domestic financial system. Quite the contrary, stronger regulatory and supervisory frameworks are key complements to market-opening measures in that they preserve the integrity and stability of the financial system.[7]

The Multilateral Framework for Trade in Financial Services

The WTO's General Agreement on Trade in Services (GATS) represents the only legally binding framework of rules governing trade in services at the multilateral level.[8] It explicitly excludes any "services supplied in the exercise of governmental authority"[9] and defines four modes of supply for trade in services:

- Cross-border supply (for example, foreign providers supply a domestic market remotely)
- Consumption abroad (for example, domestic consumers purchase financial services while traveling abroad)
- Commercial presence (for example, the physical establishment of a foreign provider through a subsidiary, branch, or representative office for purposes of selling services in a host-country market)
- Temporary presence of natural persons (for example, the temporary entry of foreign individuals).

Commercial presence (mode 3) is considered the principal means of financial services delivery,[10] but the cross-border provision of services is becoming increasingly important in view of increased worldwide travel and e-commerce developments. The advent of e-finance has introduced additional complications to the preceding framework because whether the online provision of financial services by foreign providers belongs to mode 1 or 2 is not always clear.[11] By contrast, mode 4 is relatively less important in financial services because it is severely constrained by receiving countries' migration policies and chiefly relates to highly skilled experts or intracompany transferees in managerial positions. GATS consists of three core elements (see box 2.1), which are considered here: general obligations and disciplines; specific commitments; and consultation, dispute settlement, and enforcement.

The GATS framework, outlined in box 2.1, spells out the agreement's substantive disciplines and features a set of general obligations applicable to all services sectors of WTO members. The most important obligations are the following:

- *Most-favored-nation treatment* (article II), which requires extending liberalization measures in a sector to all WTO members equally on the principle of nondiscrimination.[12]
- *Transparency* (article III) with respect to the prompt publication, notification, and response to inquiries of relevant measures[13] (and their changes) and international agreements that affect trade in services covered by their GATS commitments.

An important exception to the GATS principles is found in article XII, which allows restrictions on trade in services commitments to safeguard

Box 2.1

GATS Framework on Financial Services

GATS Agreement (General Provisions on Services)

Modes of supply

- Cross-border supply
- Consumption abroad
- Commercial presence
- Temporary presence of natural persons

General obligations and disciplines

- Most-favored-nation treatment
- Transparency
- Recognition of services suppliers
- Restrictions to safeguard the balance of payments

Specific commitments

- Market access
- National treatment
- Additional commitments

Consultation, dispute settlement, and enforcement

Annex on Financial Services

Coverage and definition of financial services
Prudential carve-out
Financial services expertise in dispute settlement
Recognition of prudential measures

Schedules of Commitments

Hybrid-list approach
Scheduling by sector and subsector and by mode of supply
Market-access and national treatment limitations

Source: Adapted from Key 1997.

the balance of payments as long as such restrictions are proportional in scope, nondiscriminatory, consistent with the International Monetary Fund's Articles of Agreement, and temporary in nature.

GATS furthermore stipulates that members undertake specific commitments in their schedules on market access (that is, elimination of quantitative or juridical barriers to entry; article XVI) and national treatment (that is, nondiscrimination between domestic and foreign providers; article XVII).[14] Although the agreement does not define market access, it rules out six types of restrictions, unless inscribed in a member's schedule. These are restrictions on (a) the number of service suppliers, (b) the value of services transactions or assets, (c) the number of operations or quantity of output, (d) the number of natural persons supplying a service, (e) the type of legal entity, and (f) the participation of foreign capital. By contrast, no comparable typology exists for national treatment restrictions, so individual members must ensure that all potentially relevant measures are listed in sectors where commitments are scheduled. Members may also schedule additional commitments under article XVIII, such as those regarding qualifications, standards, or licensing matters. With regard to institutional provisions, covered measures are subject to both a consultation and a dispute settlement mechanism common to goods and services trade under the WTO. Members may use the latter to initiate an arbitration procedure to enforce the (legally binding) commitments undertaken by another member, which can ultimately result in trade sanctions equal to the commercial loss arising from the continued maintenance of a measure found in breach of the violating country's commitments.

GATS lists 12 annexes, which include additional or clarifying rules on specific sectors. The provisions on financial services are included in the Annex on Financial Services (AFS). The AFS defines *financial services* as "any service of a financial nature offered by a financial service supplier[15] of a Member. Financial services include all insurance and insurance-related services, and all banking and other financial services (excluding insurance)" (see annex 2A of this chapter for a detailed description). The AFS specifically excludes

(i) activities conducted by a central bank or monetary authority or by any other public entity in pursuit of monetary or exchange rate policies;
(ii) activities forming part of a statutory system of social security or public retirement plans; and
(iii) other activities conducted by a public entity for the account or with the guarantee or using the financial resources of the Government.[16]

This quotation implies that macroeconomic management and a potentially significant part of the financial sector (comprising development banks, mandatory pension funds that form part of the social security system in many countries, and the like) are not subject to WTO disciplines.

The AFS is also important because it includes a "prudential carve-out" clause that recognizes the right of WTO members to introduce and maintain measures "for the protection of investors, depositors, policy holders, or persons to whom a fiduciary duty is owed by a financial service supplier, or to ensure the integrity and stability of the financial system." Such measures can be subject to dispute settlement if they are viewed as a disguised restriction to scheduled liberalization commitments.[17] Because the AFS provides no definition or indicative list of prudential measures, domestic financial regulators are granted broad discretion in their choice of policies as long as they are not used as a means of avoiding the member's commitments and obligations under the agreement.[18]

Finally, the individual schedules of commitments describe the nature, extent, and timing of market-opening undertakings. Following protracted negotiations held after the Uruguay Round's conclusion in 1994, a new set of specific commitments on financial services was incorporated into GATS in the Fifth Protocol of December 1997 and entered into force in March 1999.[19] More than 56 WTO members improved or made legally binding commitments on market access and national treatment for the first time on financial services, which were attached to the Fifth Protocol.[20] As indicated in table 2.1, the specific commitments of WTO

Table 2.1   Sample Schedule of Financial Services Commitments

Sector or subsector	Limitations on market access	Limitations on national treatment
Horizontal commitments		
All sectors included in this schedule	Mode 4: unbound, other than for temporary presence, as intracorporate transferees, of essential senior executives and specialists	Mode 3: foreign investors may transfer their capital abroad 3 years after the date of entry
Sector-specific commitments: banking and other financial services (excluding insurance)		
Acceptance of deposits and other repayable funds from the public	Mode 1: unbound Mode 2: none Mode 3: foreign equity participation limited to 51% Mode 4: unbound, except as indicated in horizontal section	Mode 1: unbound Mode 2: unbound Mode 3: none Mode 4: unbound, except as indicated in horizontal section

Source: Authors' compilation.
Note: Modes 1 to 4 refer to limitations on liberalization commitments in the four modes of supply. *None* and *unbound* refer to full and no liberalization commitment, respectively, for a specific mode.

members are of two forms, horizontal (that is, applicable to all sectors in a schedule) and sector specific. The commitments range from full liberalization to full discretion to apply new restrictive measures in the future.

GATS sectoral commitments are scheduled on the basis of a so-called hybrid list approach, which combines elements of positive, or bottom-up, listing (identifying the sectors or modes of supply concerned) and negative, or top-down, listing (identifying the limitations and restrictions attached to specific commitments).[21] A group of mostly developed WTO members subscribed to an alternative scheduling mechanism, the Understanding on Commitments in Financial Services,[22] which relies exclusively on a negative list approach. Thereby, the participants aim at achieving deeper liberalization across a wider menu of issues in financial services. Some of the main provisions of the understanding are the following (see Grosso 2003):

- Standstill obligation, under which members agree not introduce any new nonconforming measures that are incompatible with their liberalization commitments
- Specific (and more liberal) market-access commitments by mode of supply, including for cross-border trade
- Extended scope of market-access commitments to include monopoly rights, new financial services,[23] and financial services purchased by public entities
- Extended scope of national treatment commitments to include access to payment and clearing systems operated by public entities; "normal" official funding and refinancing (but not lender-of-last-resort) facilities; and any self-regulatory body, securities, or futures exchange or market
- Commitment by members of "best efforts" to "endeavor" to remove or limit any adverse effects stemming from nondiscriminatory measures (for example, those related to differences in regulatory regimes) that might impede the ability of other members' suppliers to operate, compete, or enter the member's market.

GATS Commitments in Financial Services

When the members' regulatory situations at the time of the agreement's entry into force are compared, three different types of commitments can be distinguished. First, a few countries made use of GATS to credibly commit to future liberalization. Second, a large number of members, particularly countries that were also members of the Organisation for

Economic Co-operation and Development (OECD), consolidated the regulatory status quo in their GATS schedules. Finally, developing countries in particular opted to bind commitments below the regulatory status quo.

A number of reasons can explain the reluctance of some WTO members to take on binding commitments in financial services. These reasons include macroeconomic and regulatory weaknesses as well as strategic motivations: developing countries with limited export interests in financial services may have incentives to limit policy bindings, which they may be able to use in the future as negotiating chips.

Figure 2.1 depicts market-access commitments by modes of supply for various regional groupings of countries. An analysis of such liberalization commitments in financial services undertaken by countries in GATS should be viewed with caution for at least two reasons: (a) commitments do not always reflect the actual degree of liberalization prevailing at that time, and (b) modes and subsectors differ substantially in size within and across countries, which limits the usefulness of tables or liberalization

Figure 2.1   Market-Access Commitments by Modes of Supply

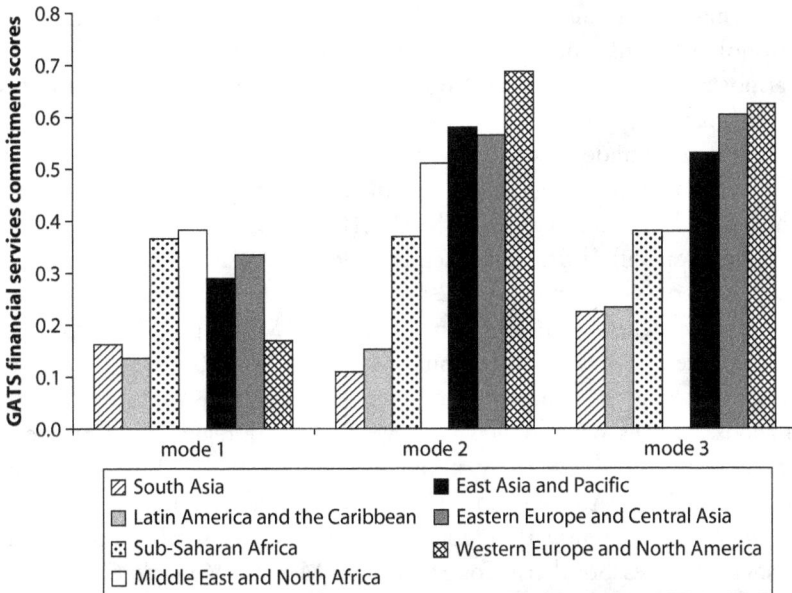

Source: Adapted from Valckx 2002b.
Note: These scores represent average market-access commitments by regional groupings (unweighted by size of country). See Valckx (2002b) for a description of the methodology used to assign scores.

indexes that—without including any weights of relative importance—compare the number of subsectors in which commitments were made. In fact, measuring both trade in financial services and the actual level of restrictiveness remains an important ongoing challenge.

Financial Services and Preferential Trade Agreements

Since the 1990s, the world economy has witnessed an unprecedented proliferation of PTAs. The WTO expects the number to reach 400 in 2010 if all negotiations currently under way are concluded; in comparison, only 50 such PTAs were notified as recently as 1990.[24] Almost every WTO member is party to at least one PTA, and Latin American and Caribbean countries have been particularly active in this regard.

Overview of Preferential Trade Agreements in Latin America and the Caribbean

According to the trade information database of the Organization of American States, Latin American and Caribbean countries entered into 33 PTAs between 1994 and 2007, primarily with trading partners within the Western Hemisphere, but also with the European Union (EU) and increasingly with countries in the Asia-Pacific region (see annex 2B for a chronological list of all recent PTAs in Latin America and the Caribbean).[25] As can be seen from annex 2B, many of these agreements cover financial services.

Liberalizing trade in services (including financial services) has also been of concern within subregional trading blocs, but progress has been limited. The Central American Common Market (CACM) is the only bloc that has developed specific rules and disciplines for financial services through a financial services chapter in its 2002 Treaty on Investment and Trade in Services. The Caribbean Community (CARICOM) adopted Protocol II on Establishment, Services, and Capital Movement in 1998 with the objective of achieving the complete elimination of restrictions to the movement of goods, services, people, and capital within the subregion; the Caribbean Single Market and Economy initiative supports these objectives. Both CARICOM and Andean Community (Comunidad Andina, or CAN) members are currently developing specific text on market opening in financial services. Southern Cone Common Market (Mercado Común del Sur, or Mercosur) member countries adopted the Protocol of Montevideo on Trade in Services in 1997, with the objective of achieving full liberalization of trade in services and an open regional market for services through periodic rounds of negotiations. Six such rounds have already taken place (see Gari 2004), and thus far, Argentina, Brazil, and Uruguay have ratified the protocol, which entered into force in December 2005.

Why Include Financial Services?

Broadly, there are three main reasons for countries to include financial services disciplines and commitments in their PTAs. The first—and typically the most important—reason is the existence of offensive interests in this sector and asymmetric bargaining powers in favor of the individual countries. This motive should not be surprising: a trade agreement is essentially a mercantilist exercise, so the inclusion of certain sensitive sectors such as financial services reflects the perceived interests and negotiating strengths of the partners. Therefore, a country includes financial services commitments either because it is forced to do so by the negotiating partner (perhaps as a quid pro quo for securing market access in another sector) or because it has offensive interests in financial services and is able to pursue them in the markets of trading partners, which is typically the case in the context of North-South PTAs (see annex 2B).[26] The second reason is to use such trade agreements as a vehicle either to lock in recent unilateral liberalization or to advance the government's reform agenda in this sector by precommitting to future market opening, thereby overcoming any lingering resistance from domestic constituencies and providing a positive signal to foreign investors. This motive seems to have been the case for financial services commitments undertaken by, for example, Argentina in GATS (Bouzas and Soltz 2005) and Costa Rica in the negotiation of the Free Trade Agreement between Central America, the Dominican Republic, and the United States (CAFTA-DR-U.S.) (see chapter 7 in this volume). Finally, countries can decide to integrate services, including financial services, in PTAs for strategic or political, rather than purely economic, reasons. The clearest examples of such cases involve plurilateral regional trading bloc initiatives, such as the CAN and Mercosur in the Latin American and Caribbean Region.[27]

Despite many reasons for including financial services in PTAs, a number of potential drawbacks exist. They consist primarily of (a) regulatory sensitivities about further domestic financial market opening and the related fear of limiting "policy space" in this sector, (b) potential distortions that could arise from giving preferential treatment to specific counterparts (especially in cases where first-mover advantage is important), (c) strategic considerations (commitments made with one PTA counterpart can become a floor in multilateral or other bilateral trade negotiations), and (d) administrative problems that arise from managing a complex web of financial services liberalization rules with different countries. By far the most important factors until now have been regulatory sensitivities and strategic considerations, which have also been evident in the GATS negotiations and scheduling of commitments.

From an empirical point of view, it is still too early for an exhaustive evaluation of the effects on domestic financial systems and overall welfare. Although numerous studies exist on the effects of foreign entry (particularly banks) from unilateral liberalization, no comparable literature analyzes the effects of PTA-induced financial liberalization. The effects do not appear a priori to be very significant, because most PTAs seem to be used primarily to consolidate and lock in existing unilateral liberalization, rather than to actively promote further market opening (see annex 2C). The lack of relevant data and methodologies to assess the actual effect ex post remains an important constraint.[28] Even if a commonly accepted methodology for quantifying effect was established, the short time span since the negotiation or entry into force of PTAs that include financial services (the earliest and rather atypical example being the North American Free Trade Agreement, or NAFTA, in 1994) means that their contribution still cannot be fully assessed. In particular, financial services commitments and disciplines, including dispute settlement mechanisms, have not been put to the test during a market downturn or a significant revision of domestic financial system policy priorities, which is typically when constraints on policy space and regulatory sensitivities more fully reveal their binding nature.

The Architecture of Preferential Trade Agreements

The way in which PTAs cover financial services is an important consideration for policy makers.[29] In particular, the lack of a carve-out for financial services does not necessarily mean that all disciplines of the agreement will apply to that activity. Notwithstanding the overall architecture of the trade agreement, significant scope remains to maintain or introduce restrictive measures, where needed, in financial services commitments or reservations. Past PTAs have followed one of two main approaches (or a mix of them) as follows.

GATS versus NAFTA template. PTAs have traditionally followed one of two distinct architectural models, based either on GATS or on NAFTA. As already noted, GATS-type agreements cover the supply of services through four distinct supply modes, whereas NAFTA-type agreements feature separate chapters dealing with cross-border trade in services (modes 1, 2, and 4 of GATS); investment (mode 3); and the temporary entry of businesspeople (mode 4), applying to all subject areas covered by the PTA, except (usually) financial services. In this last case, a self-contained chapter dealing with all modes of supply and matters related to financial services is included.

An important distinction in NAFTA-type agreements is that between regulated *financial institutions*, which are covered by the financial services chapter, and *financial services providers*, which might include unregulated financial institutions and are subject to the investment chapter of such agreements. This distinction implies different standards of treatment and protection for financial services providers in different countries depending on whether the country regulates its activities, a potentially important consideration for certain lending activities that can take place outside a bank (for example, factoring, leasing, or consumer financing). Such a distinction, as well as the associated possibility of differentiated rule making, does not arise under GATS-type agreements.

The scheduling of commitments under the two templates is also different. GATS-type agreements are based on a hybrid list approach to scheduling sectoral commitments, which combines elements of positive, or bottom-up, listing (identifying the subsectors and modes of supply concerned) and negative, or top-down, listing (identifying the limitations and restrictions attached to specific commitments). By contrast, NAFTA-type PTAs exclusively use a negative-list (or top-down) approach in which trade and investment in financial services are assumed to be free from discriminatory treatment, except for those nonconforming measures explicitly included in annexes. This approach obliges countries to list all nonconforming measures before an agreement's entry into force (or subject to mutually agreed longer time frames); otherwise, they are deemed to be fully and automatically liberalized—a so-called list-it-or-lose-it approach.

Implications of the two approaches. The architectural approach toward liberalization and regulatory disciplines in financial services is linked to the overall architecture found in PTAs and, in particular, their services and investment chapters. Countries that have followed the GATS approach for their general trade in services chapters have found it natural—and more familiar—to adopt the same approach toward financial services or to introduce a special chapter expanding on the GATS AFS. Similarly, countries that have previously relied on a NAFTA-like approach may have felt more at ease with a financial services chapter modeled after the latter agreement's separate disciplines on financial services (including for investment). Interestingly, some countries have adopted a range of architectural approaches in their PTA coverage of financial services, which can be attributed to different trading partners (particularly if these partners are large OECD countries), changes in policy priorities, timing issues, preference for preserving greater policy space in some market segments or modes in financial services, and so on.

As table 2.2 shows, each of these approaches has its own characteristics, benefits, and potential weaknesses. Although both the negative and hybrid list approaches can achieve the same level of liberalization, the former is sometimes considered more conducive to liberalization because it introduces a strong element of regulatory transparency and a potentially higher level of commitments. The detailed inventories of nonconforming measures that are appended to PTAs following a negative list approach, while technically more onerous to prepare, allow foreign investors and trade negotiators alike to obtain a comprehensive picture of a country's regulatory landscape. By contrast, only the measures that apply to the sectors, subsectors, and modes of supply entered in a country's schedule are listed under the hybrid approach, and such measures often differ from the regulatory status quo prevailing at the time the commitment is scheduled. Although neither of the two approaches inhibits the ability of host countries to preserve policy space, the hybrid approach has the advantage of affording greater latitude in determining the overall level of commitments and related regulatory conditions that might differ from actual practice, allegedly making it more flexible or "development friendly" than the negative list approach. However, as Fink and Molinuevo (2007) note and as the case studies in part 2 of this book underscore, the actual approach to scheduling commitments matters less than is commonly thought because the direction of causality between scheduling approaches and liberalization outcomes often runs both ways.

The majority of PTAs negotiated by countries in the Western Hemisphere have followed the NAFTA template, whereas GATS-type agreements have been more popular with European and Asian countries. The popularity of NAFTA-type agreements in the Western Hemisphere is partly explained by the role played by Canada, Mexico, and the United States in using the NAFTA template in their own subsequent PTAs. In its free trade agreements (FTAs) with Bolivia, Colombia, El Salvador, Guatemala, Honduras, Nicaragua, and the República Bolivariana de Venezuela, Mexico included financial services chapters that were almost identical to the rules and disciplines found under NAFTA. These agreements all opt for the negative list approach to scheduling commitments in financial services, with lists of reservations

Table 2.2 The Architecture of Financial Services in PTAs

Coverage of financial services in agreement	General chapter on trade in services	Dual coverage of investment in services	Separate coverage by services and investment chapters	Dedicated chapter on financial services
Description	• Chapter covers both cross-border trade and investment (mostly in the form of foreign direct investment) in financial services. • Agreement includes an extra chapter or annex on financial services, sometimes used for specific provisions.	• Financial services are covered by general chapters on trade in services and on investment. • Most agreements establish rules regarding the relationship between the two chapters. • Agreement includes an extra chapter or annex on financial services, sometimes used for specific provisions.	• Disciplines on financial services are split into separate chapters on cross-border trade in services and on foreign investment. • Separate chapter on financial services is used solely for specific provisions.	• All rules on cross-border trade and investment in financial services are found in a single chapter. • Great variation in the content of financial services chapter occurs across agreements. • Agreement may have a GATS- or NAFTA-like structure.
Examples	Lao PDR–U.S. Bilateral Trade Agreement, ASEAN–China Agreement on Trade in Services, China–New Zealand Free Trade Agreement, ASEAN Framework Agreement on Services	Australia–Thailand Free Trade Agreement, Japan–Malaysia Economic Partnership Agreement, U.S.–Vietnam Bilateral Trade Agreement, Mercosur	EU-CARIFORUM Economic Partnership Agreement, Australia–Singapore Free Trade Agreement	NAFTA, CAFTA-DR-U.S., Chile–U.S. Free Trade Agreement, Chile–EU Association Agreement, Singapore–U.S. Free Trade Agreement

(continued)

Table 2.2 *(continued)*

Coverage of financial services in agreement	General chapter on trade in services	Dual coverage of investment in services	Separate coverage by services and investment chapters	Dedicated chapter on financial services
Benefits	• Chapter incorporates financial services in a familiar and well-accepted GATS framework.	• Agreement can provide protection to foreign investors in financial services similar to that provided to investors in other sectors.	• No interpretational conflicts from overlapping disciplines occur. • Approach adds a transparency element from use of general chapters.	• Stand-alone chapter provides greater comfort to financial sector policy makers. • NAFTA variant is very flexible in terms of scheduling financial services commitments.
Weaknesses	• Chapter might not capture well the specificities or policy sensitivities of the financial services sector.	• Potentially conflicting overlaps may occur in the treatment of foreign investment in financial services, leading to legal conflicts. • Approach is complex for financial sector policy makers because of multiple chapters.	• Approach is complex for financial sector policy makers because of multiple chapters.	• Additional complexity is introduced by customization of financial services commitments.

Source: Adapted from chapter 3 in this volume.

Note: ASEAN = Association of Southeast Asian Nations; CAFTA-DR-U.S. = Free Trade Agreement between Central America, the Dominican Republic, and the United States; EU = European Union; GATS = General Agreement on Trade in Services; Mercosur = Mercado Común del Sur (Southern Cone Common Market); NAFTA = North American Free Trade Agreement.

included in separate annexes. Because of the experience acquired in negotiating this type of FTA and the influence of the United States, other Latin American and Caribbean countries have developed templates similar to NAFTA in their own FTAs. Panama, for instance, used the NAFTA template in negotiating its FTAs with El Salvador; Singapore; and Taiwan, China. And the financial services chapter of the Treaty on Investment and Trade in Services in the CACM is modeled on NAFTA and very similar to that agreement's financial services chapter in terms of coverage.

Recent agreements between Mexico and the EU and Chile and the EU, as well as agreements negotiated by the United States, have introduced some innovations to the traditional NAFTA and GATS templates that illustrate the iterative, learning-by-doing interaction between regional and multilateral negotiations in services (see Contreras 2008). FTAs concluded by the EU with Chile and Mexico mix in elements of GATS (positive list approach); NAFTA (provisions on the right of establishment and cross-border trade, as well as the standstill obligation for the EU-Mexico FTA); and the GATS Understanding on Commitments in Financial Services. In the case of FTAs negotiated by the United States, the relevant NAFTA chapter template still serves as the basis for the treatment of financial services, but provisions from GATS have also been incorporated.[30]

Moreover, an increasing number of countries seem to favor a dedicated financial services chapter. The main reason for its appeal is its flexibility with respect to the scheduling of commitments and obligations. This flexibility leaves financial sector policy makers in the "driver's seat" of financial services negotiations. Because policy makers are responsible for the implementation of any commitments made, such an approach allows them more control with regard to sensitivities in the regulatory system.

This impression is reinforced by the fact that the scheduling of commitments on financial services often shies away from a pure negative listing. Again, this wariness reflects countries' sensitivities to certain forms of trade, particularly cross-border commitments that might involve capital flows.

Rules and disciplines on financial services. This subsection provides a general overview of some of the main rules and disciplines applicable to financial services in Latin American and Caribbean PTAs but does not enter into the specificities of single agreements. Figure 2.2 maps the financial services–related trade commitments in Latin America and the

Figure 2.2 Map of Financial Services–Related Trade Commitments in Latin America and the Caribbean, Mid-2006

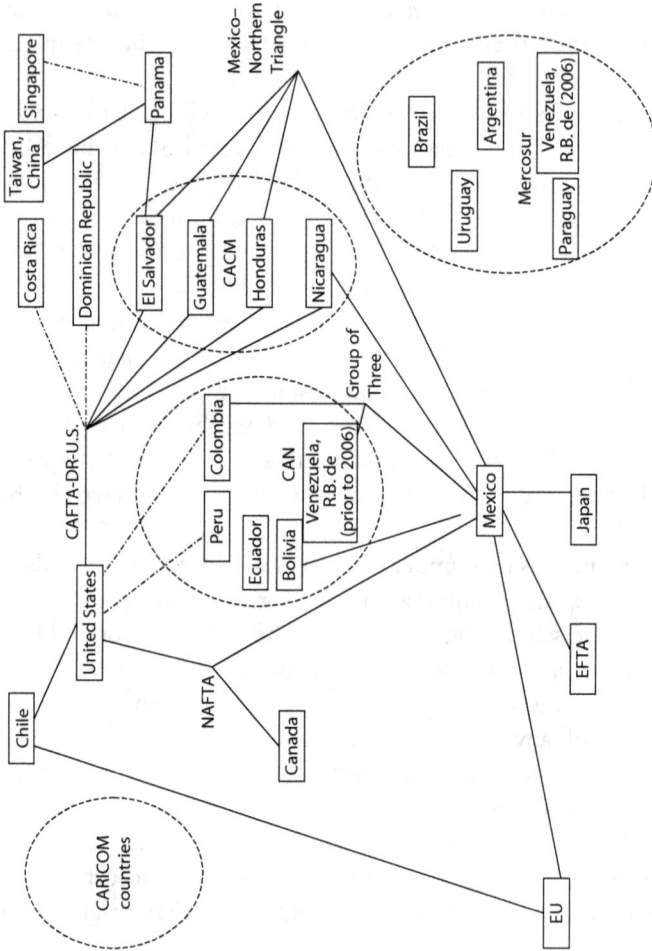

Source: Authors' analysis based on data from the Organization of American States SICE database.
Note: CACM = Central American Common Market; CAFTA-DR-U.S. = Free Trade Agreement between Central America, the Dominican Republic, and the United States; CAN = Andean Community; CARICOM = Caribbean Community; EFTA = European Free Trade Association; EU = European Union; Mercosur = Southern Cone Common Market. Lines indicate the existence of a financial services chapter or annex in a PTA between the relevant countries (dashed lines indicate that the agreement has not yet been ratified or implemented); ovals indicate the presence of a trade agreement for the creation of a common market or customs union.

Caribbean as of mid-2006. Figures 2.3 and 2.4 depict the financial serv-ices trade balance for 1997–2004 and foreign bank penetration for selected Latin American and Caribbean countries, respectively. The rules and disciplines contained in PTAs with regard to financial services have two main objectives: (a) to liberalize trade in financial services through the removal of discriminatory and market-access-impeding measures affecting foreign financial services suppliers and (b) to promote better regulatory practices (for example, on transparency)[31] while also allowing countries to regulate their financial services markets on prudential grounds. In particular, trade liberalization under the different PTAs entered into by Latin American and Caribbean countries is based on the nondis-criminatory principles of most-favored-nation (MFN) and national treat-ment, granting foreign suppliers of financial services the right to provide financial services through investment and cross-border trade and granting the elimination of market-access barriers. Countries may negotiate and

Figure 2.3   Financial Services Trade Balance for Selected Latin American and Caribbean Countries, 1997–2004

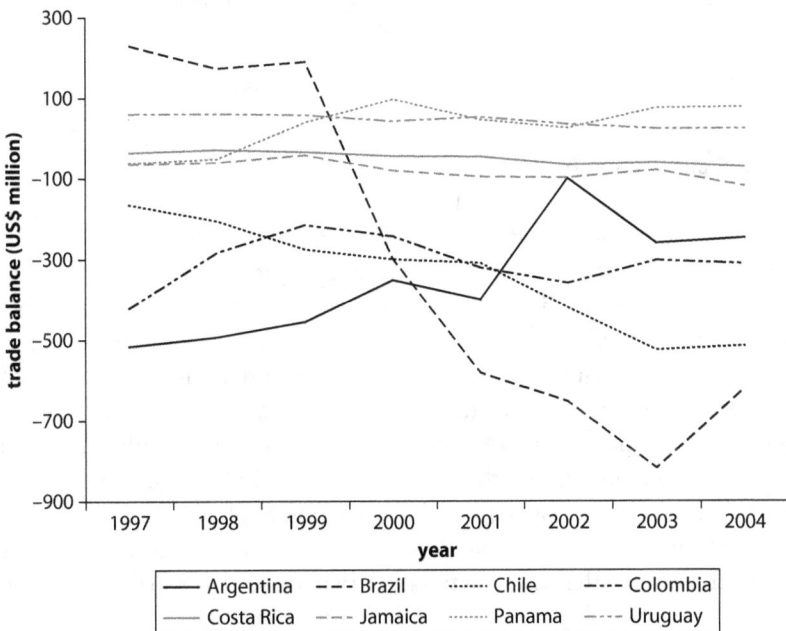

Source: Authors' analysis based on the IMF 2005.

Figure 2.4   Foreign Bank Penetration in Selected Latin American and Caribbean Countries, 2000–04

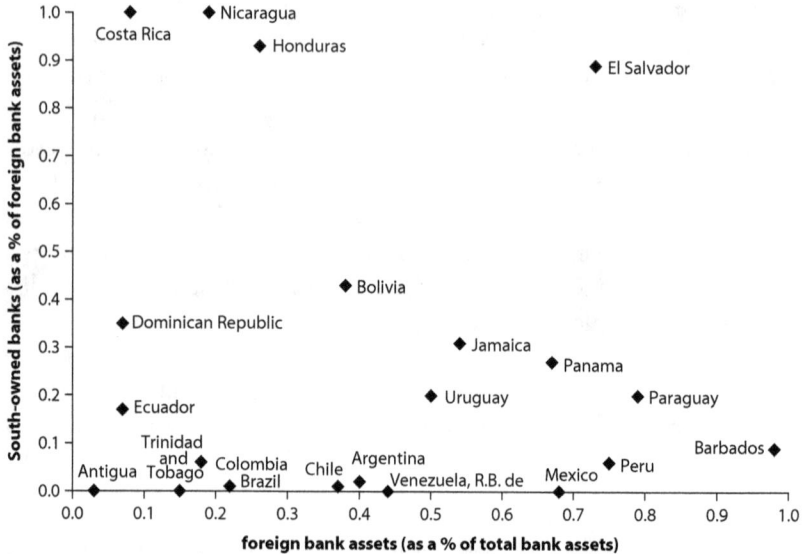

Source: Authors' analysis based on Van Horen 2006.
Note: A *foreign bank* is defined as having at least 50 percent foreign ownership. Figures reported represent averages over 2000–04 in each country. South-owned banks are foreign banks headquartered in a developing country.

include as part of their commitments nonconforming measures that limit the full application of these provisions.

National treatment—All PTAs include a provision on national treatment requiring that parties to the agreement grant to financial services and financial services suppliers from another party treatment no less favorable than that accorded to *like* financial services and financial services suppliers of national origin. The national treatment provision applies to both cross-border trade and investment in financial services and is either of general application (as in NAFTA-type agreements) or for only scheduled sectors, subsectors, and modes of supply (as in GATS-type agreements). The obligation does not require that measures applicable to foreign and national suppliers be identical. Rather, the focus is on the *effective* results of the treatment (that is, de facto rather than de jure national treatment).

MFN—The MFN obligation is included in most of the PTAs entered into by Latin American and Caribbean countries and is of general application under both NAFTA-type and GATS-type agreements. It requires that parties to the agreement grant immediately and unconditionally to financial services suppliers from another party the most favorable treatment accorded to any of their trading partners. Because national treatment and MFN treatment are of general application in NAFTA-type agreements, the better of the two treatments needs to be granted to financial services and services suppliers from the other party. The MFN provision in most NAFTA-type agreements also guarantees that any additional advantage flowing from an agreement subsequently entered into by a member with a third country is fully and automatically extended to all other members.

Market access—Market-access provisions refer to the conditions under which a foreign financial services supplier is allowed to enter and operate within a domestic market, and these provisions typically list a set of specific measures that parties cannot maintain or adopt without reserving them. Under GATS-type agreements, countries undertake specific market-access commitments in relation to the four modes of supply. By contrast, NAFTA-type agreements often do not contain a provision on market access per se but have a general provision on the right of establishment applicable to cross-border trade and investment, together with disciplines on nondiscriminatory quantitative restrictions as well as the right to nonestablishment (local presence), which is meant to encourage the cross-border supply of services. However, more recent agreements entered into by the United States include a market-access provision applicable to trade and investment in financial services along GATS lines.

NAFTA-type agreements, in common with the GATS Understanding on Commitments in Financial Services, sometimes include a standstill rule on existing nonconforming measures, which prohibits parties from adopting any law or regulation that would increase the level of nonconformity of its listed measures. The importance of the standstill rule relates to the depth of commitments undertaken by parties because it involves freezing the existing regulatory regime by undertaking a commitment not to make measures more nonconforming in the future. The existence of a standstill provision may have motivated countries in recent PTAs to bind their commitments at the level of the regulatory status quo. In addition, these agreements typically go a step further than the standstill rule by adding a "ratcheting" clause under which, when a party unilaterally amends a listed nonconforming measure, it automatically locks in the new liberalization and is prohibited from backsliding toward the original nonconforming measure.

New financial services—PTAs contain language requiring parties to permit financial services suppliers to offer new financial services of a type similar to services allowed for national suppliers under domestic law. The purpose of this provision is to allow innovative products introduced by financial institutions in their countries and approved by their home-country authorities to be introduced and sold abroad. However, host countries may, on prudential grounds, refuse to allow a particular service or a particular type of entity to provide any new financial services in its territory.

Transparency—All trade agreements entered into by Latin American and Caribbean countries contain general disciplines on transparency requiring the prompt notification or publication of measures affecting trade and investment in the sector. Transparency provisions also require that the authorization process be transparent and not unduly burdensome. In addition, more specific and detailed disciplines are developed in financial services chapters, such as the obligation to notify other parties of measures of general application that a party proposes to adopt (under NAFTA-type agreements). Some agreements extend such a prior notification obligation to "interested persons" with an opportunity for comments (for example, the Chile-U.S. FTA). Some financial services chapters also include the obligation to inform applicants of the decision concerning the application within a fixed period (for example, within 120 days in the case of NAFTA) and to provide them with information concerning the status of their application.

Recognition—Several PTAs contain provisions relating to the harmonization of standards applicable to financial activities and the setting up of arrangements designed to encourage mutual recognition of licensing and prudential standards. Indeed, NAFTA-type agreements consider the possibility for parties to recognize prudential measures adopted by another party or by a nonparty. As in GATS, any such mutual recognition can be extended on a preferential basis; that is, it is an accepted derogation from MFN treatment. PTAs entered into with the EU require parties to "endeavor" to implement and apply nonbinding international standards for regulation and supervision in the financial services sector and for dealing with money laundering. For example, the EU-Mexico FTA indicates that parties should implement international standards set by the Basel Committee, the International Association of Insurance Supervisors, and the International Organization of Securities Commissions.

Prudential safeguards—PTAs covering financial services typically feature provisions securing the right of governments to pursue domestic regulatory and macroeconomic policies. The prudential carve-out contained in these chapters recognizes the right of countries to adopt or maintain prudential measures for the following:

- Protecting investors, depositors, financial market participants, policy holders, policy claimants, or persons to whom a fiduciary duty is owed by a financial services supplier
- Maintaining the safety, soundness, integrity, or financial responsibility of financial services suppliers
- Ensuring the integrity and stability of a party's financial system.

As with GATS, prudential measures remain subject to dispute settlement under PTAs.

In terms of macroeconomic policies, another common feature of PTAs is the introduction of a provision guaranteeing the rights of countries to take actions to carry out nondiscriminatory monetary, credit, and exchange rate policies. Moreover, as under GATS, activities or services forming part of a statutory system of social security or a public retirement plan—as well as activities conducted by a public entity for the account of, or with the guarantee or use of, financial resources of the government (for example, an export credit agency)—are typically excluded from the scope of the financial services chapter, unless these activities are conducted in competition with a public entity or a financial services supplier.

Capital flows—PTAs incorporate provisions requiring governments to allow transfers of profits, interest, and other payments associated with an investment. GATS-type agreements instead require governments to allow capital flows when undertaking a commitment, but only to the extent that the movement of capital is an essential part of the service itself. Moreover, most agreements allow governments to impose restrictions on current or capital transactions in the event or the threat of serious balance-of-payments and external financial difficulties. In NAFTA-type agreements, parties may prevent or limit transfers through the equitable, nondiscriminatory, and good faith application of measures relating to the maintenance, safety, soundness, integrity, or financial responsibility of financial institutions or cross-border financial services providers. However, the broad definition of *investment* adopted in recent agreements, which has tended to include both foreign direct investment and short-term portfolio flows, has led to some friction in negotiations of provisions on the use of preexisting measures for "speculative" capital flows.[32]

Denial of benefits—Provisions on denial of benefits (also known as rules of origin) allow parties to a PTA to deny the benefits of the agreement to a financial services supplier that is not owned or controlled by nationals of the other party. These provisions can be important because their restrictiveness helps determine the extent of preferential treatment entailed in market-opening commitments undertaken by the parties.[33] Whereas the WTO framework defines *services suppliers* as a legal entity under majority ownership and effective control, denial-of-benefits provisions in NAFTA and NAFTA-type agreements (usually imported into the financial services chapter from the investment chapter) establish a double criterion of "domestic ownership or control" and "substantial business activities or operations." This definition strengthens the preferential nature of the commitments made by preventing the establishment of shell companies in the territory of a party by suppliers from third countries to take advantage of benefits arising from the agreement.

Dispute settlement—All PTAs include provisions submitting disputes arising from the agreement to arbitration, thereby allowing an increased degree of legal certainty for investors. An important feature of PTAs, also found under the AFS, relates to the obligation that panelists appointed to dispute panels have the necessary expertise relevant to the specific financial service under dispute, as well as expertise in financial services law or practice. Moreover, NAFTA-type agreements tend to include both investor-to-state and state-to-state dispute settlement mechanisms in financial services[34] and require that countries establish a roster of financial services experts who are willing to serve as panelists, some of whom may be nonparty nationals.

The application of trade policy disciplines in financial services can facilitate better regulatory practices (for example, transparency) and constrain the arbitrary abuse of policy space by the authorities (for example, through standstill or ratcheting clauses). However, the latter issue remains somewhat of a paradox. On the one hand, policy makers, especially in developing countries, need to maintain policy flexibility and some regulatory discretion to properly balance financial stability, economic efficiency, and social equity considerations that go beyond trade liberalization per se. On the other hand, they also need to provide credible assurances to foreign investors of a stable business environment by committing to increasingly liberalized (and costly to reverse) policy regimes.[35] Possibly, the regulatory status quo in financial services might not be the most appropriate level for countries to bind. The right answer might depend on countries' level of financial development, but little research or empirical analysis has been done on this topic.[36]

Negotiating Financial Services Liberalization

Preparing for financial services negotiations is no different from preparing for negotiations in other sectors. As previously mentioned, trade agreements are essentially mercantilistic exercises in which demandeurs strive to enhance market-access opportunities for their services providers rather than to promote mutual recognition or the harmonization of prudential standards. Thus, developing a strategy for the negotiation process that allows classification of offensive and defensive interests, identification of "red lines," anticipation of requests, and avoidance of surprises, as well as resolution of any internal inconsistencies that could weaken the negotiating stance, is important. Some good practices adopted by other countries to achieve this objective, specifically in the case of financial services, are summarized in the following section and described in greater detail in other chapters of this volume.

Negotiating Financial Services in PTAs: International Experience

The structure of the financial services negotiations team tends to be similar across countries, although its leadership tends to be country specific. In particular, the financial services negotiating team typically includes, or relies on, financial sector officials—from the ministry of finance, central bank, and deposit insurance and supervisory agencies—in addition to trade specialists. This composition is an inevitable consequence of the heavy regulation the financial sector, which requires a high level of technical expertise. Cultural and institutional factors—historical involvement, degree of trust and knowledge, relative political powers, and the like—are important determinants of whether financial or trade officials lead negotiations in the sector.[37] Leadership of the negotiating process will sometimes (though not always) determine the negotiating template, with ministries of finance and central banks typically opting for a dedicated financial services chapter to isolate the negotiations from other chapters and to keep them among financial sector specialists. However, even in such cases, such specialists need to interact with negotiators and stay abreast of developments of negotiations in related chapters.[38]

The consultation process with the private sector and civil society on financial services negotiations differs substantially across countries. As subsequent chapters show (see also annex 2A), the scope and frequency of consultations depend on the perceived importance and sensitivity of financial services in the overall PTA negotiations. The consultation process with the financial industry is typically extensive. It consists of measures ranging from information sessions with financial institutions and relevant associations to "side-room" participation by those actors during the negotiations and their feedback or commissioning of reports on negotiating positions. The process often includes, at least in the early stages, training on trade law concepts and principles to enhance understanding in the private sector of the full scope and business implications of the negotiations. The consultation process with civil society varies more widely across countries and tends to reflect the country's state–civil society traditions.[39]

Use of a trade-related regulatory audit in financial services can facilitate the negotiations and potentially generate positive spillovers in the consultation process and in domestic regulatory conduct and design (see chapter 4 in this volume). Use of such an audit was pioneered in the context of preparing the negative lists of nonconforming measures under NAFTA.[40] Conducting such an audit is useful in preparing for services negotiations (to master the sectoral intricacies); in ensuring that key regulatory objectives are met in the most efficient manner, in identifying antiquated or inefficient regulations, which can then yield useful negotiating currency; in encouraging the adoption of pro-competitive regulation (where feasible); and in deepening the dialogue and building trust both within the government (trade negotiators, line ministries, and sectoral regulators) and with key stakeholders. Therefore, the process of preparing an inventory of discriminatory and trade- and investment-impairing measures not only may help anticipate partner-country negotiating requests but also may serve as an exercise in regulatory transparency, thereby generating positive spillovers for the development and implementation of domestic regulation. However, although preparing the list of nonconforming measures is a useful starting point in financial services, it is usually not sufficient to locate all relevant measures, given the presence of nondiscriminatory measures (including measures of a prudential nature, which may nonetheless be unduly burdensome or possible disguised restrictions to trade).

Lessons from Latin America and the Caribbean

The inclusion of financial services in Latin American and Caribbean PTAs depends greatly on whether the agreement is North-South or South-South. Unsurprisingly, given their strong offensive interests, developed countries have been the main proponents of including financial services in North-South agreements. Most Latin American and Caribbean countries are net importers of financial services and have few—if any—perceived offensive interests linked to a demandeur or domestic constituency, both of which lessen the scope for striking reciprocal bargains within the sector. Conversely, the inclusion of financial services in most North-South agreements likely reflects the fact that the majority of foreign financial institutions in Latin American and Caribbean countries are headquartered in developed countries (see figure 2.2), as well as the relative (and asymmetric) bargaining powers between the negotiating counterparts. In fact, only two countries in the region have tended to include financial services chapters in South-South agreements: Mexico (primarily in the immediate post-NAFTA period[41]) and Panama (which is an offshore financial center and a net exporter of financial services).

Country Case Studies: Negotiating Team, Strategy, and Consultation Process

Part 2 of this book includes case studies of countries that recently participated in negotiations of a financial services chapter in the context of FTAs. These case studies indicate that each country's financial services–related strategy, negotiating structure, and process were shaped by initial conditions and historical experience. The main findings for three of the countries—Chile, Colombia, and Costa Rica—are summarized as follows.

Chile. Chile had unilaterally liberalized its domestic financial system following the 1982 crisis, and the country enjoyed strong macroeconomic and financial stability at the time of FTA negotiations. Its only previous financial services commitments were made in GATS, and the FTA with the United States was seen as an opportunity to set a precedent for agreements with other countries. Chile's authorities decided to negotiate a separate, self-contained financial services chapter independently of other areas (whenever possible) for the benefit of financial supervisors and market players, with the Ministry of Finance undertaking full responsibility for that chapter. The negotiating stance was aimed at locking in the status quo, both because the authorities were comfortable with the existing (very high) level of market openness and because they perceived FTAs as a third-best alternative for trade liberalization, behind unilateral and multilateral trade negotiations. The right to introduce capital controls and limitations on balance-of-payments transfers was the most politically sensitive issue, which a small team of specialists from the ministry and the Central Bank of Chile negotiated separately. Although the private sector was involved through meetings with financial industry associations and commissioning of a study on the FTA effects, no broad consultations were held with civil society or other stakeholders in the area of financial services.

Colombia. At the time of Colombia's FTA negotiations with the United States, the country's financial system was still recovering from the effects of the 1998 crisis, which had also disrupted the progressive market-opening process of the 1990s. Before the FTA, Colombia had made (limited) financial services commitments in GATS and within the Group of Three (with Mexico and the República Bolivariana de Venezuela). The Ministry of Finance led the negotiating process for the financial services chapter, in collaboration with financial supervisors. Because negotiations with the United States were initially scheduled to take place at the same time for several Andean countries, Colombia sought to reach common negotiating positions whenever possible (for example, on social security and collective investments). In particular, there was an exclusive emphasis on defensive interests and an attempt to prevent a nonlevel playing field that was perceived to arise from various U.S. demands (for example, insurance and bank branching and certain cross-border trade activities). The private sector was actively involved through side-room participation and preparation of relevant studies by financial industry associations. Public presentations also followed each negotiating round.

Costa Rica. Costa Rica enjoyed a high degree of market openness coupled with significant state ownership (particularly in the insurance sector) at the time of the CAFTA-DR-U.S. negotiations. The only previous financial services commitments that it had made were in GATS. Unlike in the other two countries, the Ministry of Commerce—with support from financial supervisors—took responsibility for preparing the negotiations roadmap in financial services. The five Central American countries had created a joint negotiating team vis-à-vis the United States, and a coordination protocol and common objectives for financial services were agreed. These were sufficiently flexible to accommodate offensive interests, although Costa Rica (which acted as the secretariat of the negotiation process) had only defensive interests in this sector. Given Costa Rica's institutional and cultural experience, extensive consultation mechanisms with the private sector and with civil society were used.

Summary of the Case-Study Findings

Figure 2.5 depicts the market share of foreign financial institutions in the domestic financial systems of Chile, Colombia, and Costa Rica at the time of the FTA negotiations. Figure 2.6 shows the changes in the international financial integration of Chile, Colombia, and Costa Rica for 1997–2004.

Financial services liberalization commitments compared to GATS. An analysis of market-access and national-treatment commitments scheduled in the financial services chapters for the previously mentioned sample of Latin American and Caribbean FTAs provides evidence of significant additional liberalization commitments when such FTAs are compared to

Figure 2.5   Market Share of Foreign Financial Institutions in the Domestic Financial Systems of Chile, Colombia, and Costa Rica at the Time of FTA Negotiations

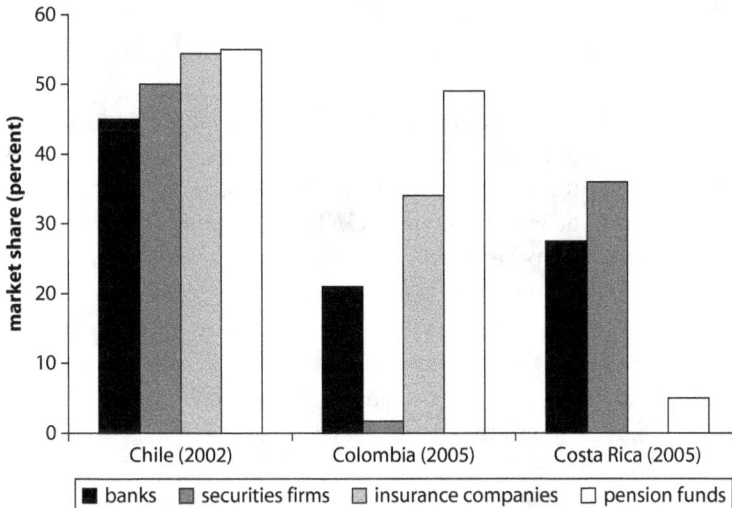

Sources: Authors' analysis based on de la Cruz and Stephanou 2006 as well as the case studies found in later chapters of this volume.

Note: Percentages are based on total assets for banks (credit institutions in the case of Colombia); number of foreign firms registered in the domestic stock market (Costa Rica) and total trading volumes (Chile and Colombia) for securities firms; total premiums (Chile) and life and nonlife assets (Colombia and Costa Rica) for insurance companies; and total mandatory pension assets under management for pension funds (the Costa Rican figure is an estimate). The foreign market share in the securities sector is likely underestimated, because many securities activities, such as trading, are actually provided (offshore and onshore) by banks.

Figure 2.6   International Financial Integration of Chile, Colombia, and Costa Rica, 1997–2004

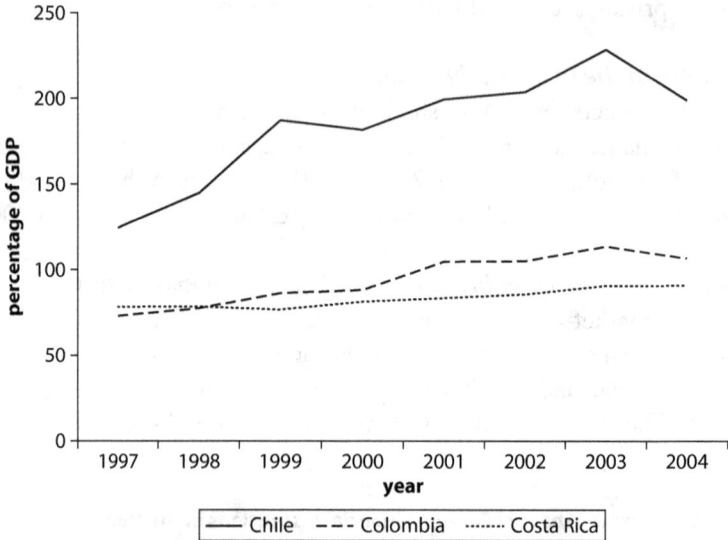

Source: Authors' analysis based on data from Lane and Milesi-Ferretti 2006.
Note: International financial integration is measured as the gross stock of a country's foreign assets and liabilities to GDP.

GATS. This finding is not unusual given the time elapsed and the (unilateral) market opening undertaken by these countries since the mid-1990s. Additional commitments tend to span all financial subsectors, including those that were not well covered in GATS, such as insurance, securities-related services, and other financial services. The same is true in modal terms, with significant new commitments—particularly in mode 2. Commitments are, in general, more extensive across all modes for FTAs involving the United States, particularly for mode 2. By contrast, mode 1 commitments, although better than what has been harvested to date under GATS, remain relatively modest (see figure 2.7).

Financial services liberalization commitments compared to the status quo. De novo liberalization—which has chiefly taken the form of precommitments to future market opening—is relatively rare for the sample of Latin American and Caribbean countries under review. An analysis of individual country experiences is much more difficult to undertake because of insufficient information on the regulatory status quo prior to, during, and after the implementation of such trade agreements. Apart

Figure 2.7   Market-Access Commitments: Proportion of Financial Services Committed by Chile, Colombia, and Costa Rica in GATS and Subsequent FTAs

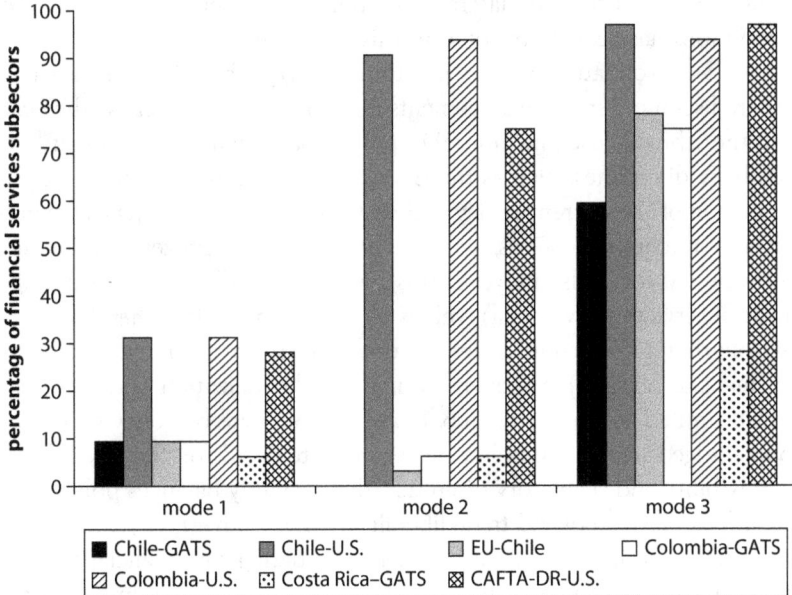

Source: Authors' representation.
Note: CAFTA-DR-U.S. = Free Trade Agreement between Central America, the Dominican Republic, and the United States; EU = European Union; GATS = General Agreement on Trade in Services. Three levels of market-access commitments are applied in this analysis by financial services subsector and mode: none (value of 0.0), partial commitment (value of 0.5), and full commitment (value of 1.0). Mode 4 commitments, as well as all national treatment commitments and horizontal restrictions, are excluded. All precommitments to liberalize additional subsectors or modes in future years are included.

from Costa Rica's insurance sector, which was opened for the first time because of the FTA with the United States, real liberalization appears to have mostly taken place in the cross-border provision of some insurance services, as well as in asset management and auxiliary financial services. Although limited data are available on the actual market size of these subsectors and modes, anecdotal evidence suggests they are relatively less important than core banking services. However, the abolition of numerical quotas (for example, an economic needs test) and certain juridical restrictions on forms of entry (for example, insurance branching[42]) might contribute to further liberalization in other subsectors under mode 3.

The findings of the case studies offer strong indications that, with few exceptions, PTAs are primarily used to consolidate and lock in existing unilateral liberalization rather to actively promote further market opening and the process of domestic regulatory reform. The fact that the countries under review appear to have already largely liberalized their domestic financial systems on a unilateral basis before their engagement in PTA negotiations has also contributed to this outcome.

Such a consolidation of the regulatory status quo and the application of certain disciplines in trade agreements remain important because they can limit the arbitrary use (and abuse) of policy space by host-country authorities. New disciplines, such as those on regulatory transparency, as well as the lock-in of the current policy regime through commitments and standstill and ratcheting clauses, enhance predictability, prevent potentially costly policy reversals, and can thus benefit both domestic and foreign financial services providers as well as local consumers. It is therefore conceivable that a PTA could influence the business environment (including for financial services) positively even if real liberalization commitments remain limited to the status quo. However, the issue of policy space is a double-edged sword, and policy makers need to decide on the level of policy flexibility and regulatory discretion that properly balances policy considerations that go beyond trade liberalization objectives per se. Linked to this issue is the need for policy makers negotiating the financial services provisions of PTAs to be cognizant of the important nuances in disciplines and commitments that might create unintended consequences or limit policy space beyond what was envisaged. The short time span since the entry into force of most PTAs means that their contribution—whether anticipated or unanticipated—still cannot be fully assessed.

Preferential nature of de novo liberalization commitments. An interesting additional finding of the case studies is that many de novo liberalization commitments are actually not preferential in nature. Although some commitments (for example, the abolition of an economic needs test for Chile) are country specific and benefit the financial services providers of the PTA counterpart, others (for example, permitting branching or opening the insurance industry to private providers for Costa Rica) were implemented through new "horizontal" regulations or laws that would apply to the entire industry and could actually benefit financial services providers from third countries. Therefore, unlike trade in goods, the extent to which financial services commitments were preferential was not primarily determined by rules of origin.[43] This result would seem to suggest that PTAs might not always create serious economic distortions, although much depends on whether the relevant liberalization commitments are actually preferential in nature.

Conclusions

A number of conclusions can be reached from the foregoing discussion and the case studies provided in succeeding chapters. First, the proliferation of PTAs in recent years, which is an ongoing phenomenon with global proportions, was associated with greater financial services liberalization commitments for many Latin American and Caribbean countries and led to an increasingly complex regional commitments map (or financial services "spaghetti bowl"). Most progress in financial services rule making and market opening in trade agreements—typically through a stand-alone financial services chapter—has been achieved by FTAs; by contrast, Latin American and Caribbean countries that have relied on the multilateral framework and on subregional customs unions for trade commitments in financial services have not made much progress to date.

Second, the inclusion of financial services in Latin American and Caribbean PTAs depends greatly on whether the agreement is North-South or South-South. As indicated in table 2.3, the main proponents of including financial services have been developed countries in North-South agreements. This finding is not surprising because most countries in the region are net importers of financial services and have few, if any, perceived offensive interests linked to a demandeur or domestic constituency, both of which lessen the scope for striking reciprocal bargains within the sector. Conversely, the inclusion of financial services in most North-South agreements likely reflects the fact that the majority of foreign financial institutions in Latin American and Caribbean countries are headquartered in developed countries, as well as the relative bargaining powers between the negotiating counterparts. Only two countries in the region have included financial services chapters in South-South agreements—Mexico (primarily in the immediate post-NAFTA period) and Panama (which is an offshore financial center and a net exporter of financial services). A more detailed comparison of financial services chapters under North-South and South-South PTAs, particularly when they involve the same country, would accordingly be an interesting follow-up research topic.

Table 2.3   Coverage of Financial Services by Type of FTA in the Latin American and Caribbean Region

Financial services chapter	North-South	South-South
Included	9	7
Not included	4	14

Source: Authors' compilation.

Third, an analysis of selected Latin American and Caribbean countries that have recently participated in PTAs yields evidence of significant additional liberalization commitments when these agreements are compared to GATS.[44] This finding is not unusual given the time elapsed and the (unilateral) market opening undertaken by these countries since the mid-1990s. Additional commitments tend to span all financial subsectors, including those that were not well covered in the first GATS round, such as insurance, securities-related services, and other financial services. The same is true in modal terms, with significant new commitments particularly in mode 2 (consumption abroad). Commitments are in general more extensive across all modes for FTAs involving the United States, particularly for mode 2. By contrast, mode 1 commitments, although better than what has been achieved to date under GATS, remain relatively more modest and are generally based on those found in the Understanding on Commitments in Financial Services.

Fourth, de novo liberalization—which has chiefly taken the form of precommitments to future market opening—is relatively modest for the sample of Latin American and Caribbean countries under review. Apart from Costa Rica's insurance sector, real liberalization appears to have mostly taken place in the cross-border provision of some insurance services, as well as in asset management and auxiliary financial services. Although available data on the actual market size of these subsectors and modes are limited, anecdotal evidence suggests they are relatively less important than core banking services. However, the abolition of numerical quotas (for example, an economic needs test) and certain juridical restrictions on forms of entry (for example, insurance branching) might also contribute to further liberalization in other subsectors under mode 3.

This finding is a strong indication that, with a few exceptions, PTAs are primarily used to consolidate and lock in existing unilateral liberalization rather than to actively promote further market opening and the process of domestic regulatory reform. The fact that the countries under review appear to have already largely liberalized their domestic financial systems on a unilateral basis before their engagement in PTA negotiations has also contributed to this outcome. In fact, an inverse relationship may exist between de novo liberalization and a country's initial conditions in terms of actual market openness—as evidenced when comparing Chile and Costa Rica—but the sample is probably too small to draw any firm conclusions. More work needs to be done in this area, in both expanding the number of countries and collecting relevant data on actual market size by subsector and mode, to fully corroborate these assertions.

Fifth, many de novo liberalization commitments in FTAs are actually not preferential in nature. Although some commitments are country specific and benefit the financial services providers of the FTA counterpart, others were implemented through new horizontal regulations or laws that would presumably apply to the entire industry and could actually benefit financial services providers from third countries. This finding may suggest that PTAs might not create important first-mover advantages or serious economic distortions in financial services, although much depends on the specific nature of liberalization commitments. This somewhat counterintuitive finding needs to be further corroborated by additional research.

Sixth, no evidence supports NAFTA- or GATS-type agreements with respect to the achieved liberalization in financial services. A review of the FTAs analyzed seems to favor the negative list approach and broader rules and disciplines embedded in NAFTA-type agreements (the most widely used in Latin America and the Caribbean), primarily on grounds of heightened regulatory transparency. However, this finding can be largely attributed to the U.S. involvement in such agreements. In addition, even NAFTA-type agreements have tended to use a hybrid list for financial services commitments. In fact, both models have introduced new features in recent years that borrow from each other, revealing signs of convergence around a more hybrid approach.

Seventh, consolidation of the regulatory status quo and the application of certain disciplines in trade agreements remain important because they can limit the arbitrary use (and abuse) of policy space by the authorities. New disciplines such as those on regulatory transparency, as well as the locking in of the current policy regime through commitments and standstill and ratcheting clauses, enhance predictability, prevent potentially costly policy reversals, and can thus benefit both domestic and foreign financial services providers and local consumers. Thus, a PTA could conceivably have a significantly positive influence on the business environment even if real liberalization commitments remain limited to the status quo. However, the issue of policy space is a double-edged sword, and policy makers need to decide on the level of policy flexibility and regulatory discretion that properly balances policy considerations that go beyond trade liberalization objectives per se. Linked to this issue is the need for policy makers negotiating the financial services provisions of PTAs to be cognizant of the important nuances in disciplines and commitments[45] that might create unintended consequences or limit policy space beyond what was envisaged.

Finally, it is probably too early to judge the outcomes of PTAs on domestic financial systems and overall welfare in Latin American and

Caribbean countries. The lack of relevant data and analysis available to assess their ex post impact—or to support the decision-making process ex ante—remains an important constraint. Additionally, even if a commonly accepted methodology for quantifying the impact was established, the short time span since the negotiation or entry into force of many PTAs means that their economic consequences—whether anticipated or unanticipated—still cannot be fully assessed. In particular, financial services commitments and disciplines, including dispute settlement mechanisms, have not been put to a test during a market downturn or a significant revision of domestic financial system policy priorities, which is typically when constraints on policy space kick in.

Annex 2A: GATS Definition of Financial Services

Article 5 of the GATS Annex on Financial Services provides the agreement's definition of financial services. The article reads as follows:

a) A financial service is any service of a financial nature offered by a financial service supplier of a Member. Financial services include all insurance and insurance-related services, and all banking and other financial services (excluding insurance). Financial services include the following activities:

Insurance and insurance-related services

   i. Direct insurance (including co-insurance)
      A. Life
      B. Non-life
  ii. Reinsurance and retrocession
 iii. Insurance intermediation, such as brokerage and agency
  iv. Services auxiliary to insurance, such as consultancy, actuarial, risk assessment, and claim settlement services

Banking and other financial services (excluding insurance)

   v. Acceptance of deposits and other repayable funds from the public
  vi. Lending of all types, including consumer credit, mortgage credit, factoring, and financing of commercial transactions
 vii. Financial leasing
viii. All payment and money transmission services, including credit, charge and debit cards, travelers cheques, and bankers drafts
  ix. Guarantees and commitments

x. Trading for own account or for account of customers, whether on an exchange, in an over-the-counter market, or otherwise, the following:

A. Money market instruments (including cheques, bills, certificates of deposits)

B. Foreign exchange

C. Derivative products including, but not limited to, futures and options

D. Exchange rate and interest rate instruments, including products such as swaps, forward rate agreements

E. Transferable securities

F. Other negotiable instruments and financial assets, including bullion

xi. Participation in issues of all kinds of securities, including underwriting and placement as agent (whether public or privately) and provision of services related to such issues

xii. Money broking

xiii. Asset management, such as cash or portfolio management, all forms of collective investment management, pension fund management, custodial, depository and trust services

xiv. Settlement and clearing service for financial assets, including securities, derivative products, and other negotiable instruments

xv. Provision and transfer of financial information, and financial data processing and related software by suppliers of other financial services

xvi. Advisory, intermediation and other auxiliary financial services on all the activities listed in subparagraphs v) through xv), including credit reference and analysis, investment and portfolio research and advice, advice on acquisitions and on corporate restructuring, and strategy.

b) A financial service supplier means any natural or juridical person of a Member wishing to supply or supplying financial services, but the term "financial service supplier" does not include a public entity.

c) "Public entity" means:

i. A government, a central bank or a monetary authority, of a Member, or an entity owned or controlled by a Member, that is principally engaged in carrying out governmental functions or activities for governmental purposes, not including an entity principally engaged in supplying financial services on commercial terms.

ii. Or a private entity, performing functions normally performed by a central bank or monetary authority, when exercising those functions.

Annex 2B: Financial Services in Latin American and Caribbean PTAs

Table 2B.1 illustrates the coverage and treatment of financial services in Latin American and Caribbean PTAs. The table includes only customs unions, common markets, and post-NAFTA FTAs up to mid-2006; nonreciprocal and partial-scope agreements are excluded. The dates of signature and implementation for customs unions and common markets refer to the financial services–related aspects of the relevant protocols. The 2002 Central America–Panama FTA has not been included because only the normative part of the agreement has been concluded to date.

Annex 2C: Liberalization Commitments in Financial Services for Selected Countries

Tables 2C.1, 2C.2, and 2C.3 (pages 56–66) show the financial liberalization commitments for the three Latin American countries under review in this chapter. Table 2C.1 shows the commitments for Chile. Colombia's and Costa Rica's commitments are shown in tables 2C.2 and 2C.3, respectively.

Table 2B.1 Coverage and Treatment of Financial Services in Latin American and Caribbean PTAs, as of Mid-2006

Trade partners	Date of signature	Date of entry into force	Coverage of financial services	Financial services model
Free trade agreements				
NAFTA (Canada-Mexico-U.S.)	August 1992	January 1, 1994	Specific financial services chapter	NAFTA
Costa Rica–Mexico	April 5, 1994	January 1, 1995	No specific chapter on financial services	
			Excluded from chapter on cross-border trade in services	
Group of Three (Colombia–Mexico–Venezuela, R.B. de[a])	June 13, 1994	January 1, 1995	Specific financial services chapter	NAFTA
Bolivia-Mexico	September 10, 1994	January 1, 1995	Specific financial services chapter	NAFTA
Canada-Chile	December 6, 1996	July 5, 1997	No specific chapter on financial services	NAFTA
			Excluded from chapter on cross-border trade in services	
			Covered in chapter on investment	
Mexico-Nicaragua	December 18, 1997	July 1, 1998	Specific financial services chapter	NAFTA
Central America–Dominican Republic	April 16, 1998	Costa Rica–Dominican Republic: March 7, 2002; El Salvador–Dominican Republic: October 4, 2001; Guatemala–Dominican Republic: October 3, 2001; Honduras–Dominican Republic: December 19, 2001	No specific chapter on financial services	NAFTA
			Covered under chapters on investment and trade in services	
CARICOM[b]–Dominican Republic	August 22, 1998	Not yet implemented	No specific chapter on financial services	NAFTA
			Covered under annex on trade in services	

(continued)

51

Table 2B.1 *(continued)*

Trade partners	Date of signature	Date of entry into force	Coverage of financial services	Financial services model
Chile–Mexico	October 1, 1998	August 1, 1999	No specific chapter on financial services Excluded from chapter on cross-border trade in services Covered under chapter on investment	
Central America–Chile	October 18, 1999	Costa Rica: February 15, 2002; El Salvador: June 3, 2002	No specific chapter on financial services Excluded from chapter on cross-border trade in services	
Israel–Mexico	April 10, 2000	July 1, 2000	Services not covered	
Mexico–Northern Triangle (El Salvador–Guatemala–Honduras)	June 20, 2000	El Salvador and Guatemala: March 15, 2001; Honduras: June 1, 2001; Mexico: March 14, 2001	Specific financial services chapter	NAFTA
European Union–Mexico	October 2000	March 2001	Specific financial services chapter	GATS (plus Understanding and NAFTA)
EFTA[c]–Mexico	November 2000	Mexico, Norway, and Switzerland: July 1, 2001; Iceland: October 1, 2001	Specific financial services section	GATS (plus Understanding and NAFTA)
Canada–Costa Rica	April 23, 2001	November 1 2002	Financial services excluded, but obligation to develop provision for trade in services and investment to be added in the future	
Panama–El Salvador	March 2002	April 2003	Specific financial services chapter	NAFTA
Chile–European Union	November 2002	February 2003	Specific financial services chapter	GATS (plus Understanding)

Agreement	Date signed	Entry into force	Services coverage	Model
Chile–Korea, Rep. of	February 15, 2003	April 1, 2004	No specific chapter on financial services / Excluded from chapter on cross-border trade in services / Covered under chapter on investment	NAFTA (plus Understanding and AFS)
Chile–United States	June 6, 2003	January 1, 2004	Specific financial services chapter	
EFTA[c]–Chile	June 26, 2003	December 1, 2004	Not covered by chapters on investment and services	NAFTA
Panama–Taiwan, China / Mexico–Uruguay	August 21, 2003 / November 2003	January 1, 2004 / July 15, 2004	Specific financial services chapter / No specific chapter on financial services / Excluded from chapter on cross-border trade in services / Covered under chapter on investment	
CARICOM[b]–Costa Rica	March 9, 2004	Barbados, Suriname, Trinidad and Tobago: 2006	Services not covered	
CAFTA-DR-U.S.[d]	August 5, 2004	El Salvador: December 2004; Honduras and Guatemala: March 2005; Nicaragua: October 2005; United States: July 2005	Specific financial services chapter	NAFTA (plus Understanding and AFS)
Japan-Mexico	September 17, 2004	April 1, 2005	Incorporates GATS Annex on Financial Services	GATS
Brunei Darussalam–Chile–New Zealand–Singapore	2005	Not yet implemented	Obligation to negotiate a financial services chapter 2 years after entry into force of the agreement	

(continued)

53

Table 2B.1 *(continued)*

Trade partners	Date of signature	Date of entry into force	Coverage of financial services	Financial services model
Guatemala–Taiwan, China	September 22, 2005	July 1, 2006	No specific chapter on financial services Excluded from chapters on cross-border trade in services and investment	
Chile–Panama	2006	Not yet implemented	Financial services may be incorporated 2 years after entry into force of the agreement	
Chile–China	2006	Not yet implemented	Services not covered by the agreement	
Panama–Singapore	2006	Not yet implemented	Specific financial services chapter	NAFTA
Nicaragua–Taiwan, China	2006	Not yet implemented	—	
Peru–United States	April 2006	Not yet implemented	Specific financial services chapter	NAFTA (plus Understanding and AFS)
Chile–Peru	August 22, 2006	Not yet implemented	No specific chapter on financial services Excluded from chapters on cross-border trade in services and investment Obligation to negotiate a financial services chapter 1 year after entry into force of the agreement	
Colombia–United States	Not yet signed	Not yet implemented	Specific financial services chapter	NAFTA (plus Understanding and AFS)

Customs unions and common markets

Agreement	Date signed	Status	Financial services coverage	Model
Mercosur's Protocol of Montevideo[e] (Argentina; Brazil; Paraguay; Uruguay; Venezuela, R.B. de[a])	December 17, 1997	December 7, 2005	Covers services generally (annex on financial services includes only specific commitments)	GATS
CAN's Decision 439[f] (Bolivia; Colombia; Peru; Ecuador; Venezuela, R.B. de[a])	December 1997	Not yet implemented	Covers services generally	NAFTA
CARICOM's Protocol II[b]	July 1998	Not yet implemented	Covers services generally; drafting of a specific financial services chapter in progress	
CACM's Treaty on Investment and Trade in Services[g] (El Salvador, Guatemala, Honduras, Nicaragua)	March 2002	Not yet implemented	Specific financial services chapter in treaty	NAFTA

Source: Authors' analysis based on data from the Organization of American States SICE database.

Note: — = not available. AFS = Annex on Financial Services; GATS = General Agreement on Trade in Services; NAFTA = North American Free Trade Agreement; Understanding = Understanding on Commitments in Financial Services.

a. The República Bolivariana de Venezuela notified its intention to withdraw from the Andean Community and the Group of Three free trade agreement and as of July 4, 2006, has acceded to the Southern Cone Common Market (Mercado Común del Sur, or Mercosur).

b. Caribbean Community (CARICOM) member countries are Antigua and Barbuda, The Bahamas, Barbados, Belize, Dominica, Grenada, Guyana, Haiti, Jamaica, Montserrat, St. Kitts and Nevis, St. Lucia, St. Vincent and the Grenadines, Suriname, and Trinidad and Tobago.

c. European Free Trade Association (EFTA) member countries are Iceland, Lichtenstein, Norway, and Switzerland.

d. Member countries of the Free Trade Agreement between Central America, the Dominican Republic, and the United States (CAFTA-DR-U.S.) are Costa Rica, the Dominican Republic, El Salvador, Guatemala, Honduras, Nicaragua, and the United States.

e. Mercosur (Mercado Común del Sur, or Southern Cone Common Market) member countries are Argentina, Brazil, Paraguay, and Uruguay.

f. Comunidad Andina (CAN, or Andean Community) member countries are Bolivia, Colombia, Ecuador, and Peru.

g. Central American Common Market (CACM) member countries are El Salvador, Guatemala, Honduras, and Nicaragua (later joined by Costa Rica).

Table 2C.1   Chile's Financial Services Trade Liberalization Commitments

Sector	Main commitments under GATS (1999)		Improvement in commitments compared to GATS			
			Chile–U.S. FTA (2004)		Chile–European Union FTA (2003)	
	Market access	National treatment	Market access	National treatment	Market access	National treatment
Horizontal (only those most relevant for financial services)						
All sectors (including financial services)	Mode 3: Limitations on juridical form of establishment and authorization criteria (including an economic needs test for financial services suppliers) Mode 4: No commitments, except for transfers of natural persons related to mode 3 and subject to various criteria	Mode 3: Foreign investors may transfer abroad their capital after 3 years from entry;[a] at least 85% of staff employed locally by enterprises with more than 15 employees must be Chilean Mode 4: No commitments, except for natural persons listed in market access	Mode 3: Lifting of numerical restrictions (including an economic needs test) on establishment of financial institutions (including mandatory pension funds); some juridical form restrictions on financial institutions that are mandated by existing legislation are also removed (see below)	Mode 3: At least 85% of staff employed locally by enterprises with more than 25 employees must be Chilean	Mode 3: No economic needs test for suppliers in financial services subsectors where commitments were made	Mode 3: At least 85% of staff employed locally by enterprises with more than 25 employees must be Chilean
Financial services specific						
Insurance and insurance-related services	Mode 1: No commitments except for foreign reinsurance providers (including brokers), subject to enrollment with, and requirements of, domestic supervisor	Mode 1: Same as for market access except that reinsurance premiums are subject to tax of 6% Mode 2: No commitments	Mode 1: Liberalization of sale and brokerage of MAT insurance (*no later than 1 year after entry into force of agreement*) and consultancy, actuarial,	Mode 1: Same as for market access Mode 2: Same as for market access Mode 3: No more than a minority of the board of	Modes 1 and 2: Liberalization of sale and brokerage of MAT (*1 year after entry into force of agreement*)	Modes 1 and 2: Same as for market access Mode 3: Same as for market access

Sector	Limitations on market access	Limitations on national treatment
	Mode 2: No commitments Mode 3: Liberalization of direct life and nonlife insurance and of reinsurance and retrocession (including brokerage) subject to restrictions on form of establishment and on enrollment with domestic supervisor Mode 4: Only commitments of horizontal schedule and risk assessment services Mode 2: Liberalization of all insurance and insurance-related services except mandatory insurance services or those related to the social security system Mode 3: Liberalization of insurance branching (*no later than 4 years after entry into force of agreement*) subject to regulation, and of services auxiliary to insurance	Mode 3: Same as for market access Mode 4: Only commitments of horizontal schedule directors of a U.S.-owned financial institution may be composed of Chilean nationals or residents (except for insurance brokerage and claims settlement) subject to supervision in the country of origin Mode 3: Liberalization of sale and brokerage of MAT (subject to enrollment with, and requirements of, domestic supervisor); of voluntary pension savings plans by life insurance companies (*as of March 1, 2005*) subject to supervisory authorization; and of claim settlement and auxiliary insurance services
Banking and other financial services	Mode 3: Liberalization of acceptance of deposits; lending (except factoring); financial leasing; issue and operation of Modes 1, 2, and 4: Liberalization of provision and transfer of financial information, financial data processing	Mode 3: Same as for market access Mode 4: Only commitments of horizontal schedule Modes 1, 2, and 4: Same as for market access Modes 1 and 3: Same as for market access Mode 3: Liberalization of voluntary pension savings plans (*as of March 1, 2005*), subject to supervisory Mode 3: Same as for market access; national treatment for factoring

(continued)

Table 2C.1 (continued)

Sector	Main commitments under GATS (1999)		Improvement in commitments compared to GATS			
			Chile–U.S. FTA (2004)		Chile–European Union FTA (2003)	
	Market access	National treatment	Market access	National treatment	Market access	National treatment
	credit cards; guarantees and commitments; participation and custody of securities; some advisory, intermediation, and other auxiliary financial services; and asset management (except collective investment schemes and pension funds), subject to restrictions on form of establishment, transfer of control, and operations (particularly for nonbank securities services providers) Mode 4: Only commitments of horizontal schedule		(subject to prior authorization as required), and advisory (subject to regulatory and registration requirements as required) and other auxiliary financial services except intermediation and credit reference and analysis (the latter service can be provided in the future) Mode 1: Liberalization of investment advice and portfolio management services (excluding custodial and trustee services) by financial institutions (except trust companies) for domestic collective investment	Mode 2: Same as for market access Mode 3: Same as for market access; no more than a minority of the board of directors of a U.S.-owned financial institution (except stockbrokers and securities agents) may be composed of Chilean nationals or residents; national treatment for U.S. investors in mandatory pension funds	authorization, banking-related advisory and other auxiliary services; provision and transfer of financial information and data processing; securities risk-rating activities, subject to supervisory authorization, and various trading operations and fund management activities by nonbank securities services providers	

schemes when they invest in securities traded abroad

Mode 2: Liberalization of all banking and other financial services

Mode 3: Liberalization of factoring; all payment and money transmission services; trading; money broking; management of collective investment schemes (subject to regulations on form of establishment); voluntary pension savings plans (*as of March 1 2005*); settlement and clearing services; financial information transfer and data processing; and all advisory, intermediation, and other auxiliary services

Sources: Authors' interpretation based on information provided by the World Trade Organization and the Office of the United States Trade Representative, Contreras 2008, Contreras and Yi 2004, and Sáez 2006.

Note: FTA = free trade agreement; GATS = General Agreement on Trade in Services; MAT = international maritime transport, international commercial aviation, and goods in international transit. Modes 1 to 4 refer to the four modes of supply. The table does not include other disciplines or provisions on payments and capital movements.

a. The limitation is two years in the case of foreign investors who participate in the financial services sector.

Table 2C.2 Colombia's Financial Services Trade Liberalization Commitments

Sector	Main commitments under GATS (1997)		Improvement in commitments under Colombia-U.S. FTA	
	Market access	National treatment	Market access	National treatment
Horizontal (only those most relevant for financial services)				
All sectors (including financial services)	Mode 3: Economic needs test might be required for domestic and foreign financial entities; limitations exist on juridical form of establishment; supply of financial services requires prior government authorization and is subject to relevant regulations. Mode 4: No commitments exist except for natural persons who are managers, legal representatives, or technical specialists.	Mode 3: Special conditions exist on privatization of state-owned entities exclusively offered to Colombian nationals; at least 80% and 90% of ordinary and specialist staff members, respectively, who are employed locally by enterprises with more than 10 employees must be Colombian. Mode 4: No commitments exist except for natural persons listed in market access.	Mode 3: Lifting of numerical restrictions and of an economic needs test on establishment of financial institutions (including mandatory pension funds); removal of some juridical form restrictions on financial institutions that are mandated by existing legislation (see below)	Mode 1: Foreign investors may make portfolio investments in securities only through a foreign capital investment fund. Mode 3: No more than a minority of the board of directors of a foreign-owned financial institution may be composed of nationals or residents.
Financial services specific				
Insurance and insurance-related services	Mode 1: Liberalization of reinsurance and retrocession and of direct insurance concerning foreign trade operations Mode 2: No commitments	Mode 1: National treatment for reinsurance and retrocession Mode 2: No commitments Mode 3: National treatment for all insurance and insurance-related services	Modes 1 and 4: Liberalization of sale and brokerage of MAT and space launching and freight insurance subject to registration requirements	Modes 1 and 4: Same as for market access, except a foreign national resident in Colombia for less than 1 year may not supply insurance agency services

Sector	Limitations on market access	Limitations on national treatment
(insurance, continued)	Mode 3: Liberalization of all insurance and insurance-related services except life insurance Mode 4: Only commitments of horizontal schedule *(no later than 4 years after entry into force of agreement)*, sale and brokerage of reinsurance and retrocession, and sale of services auxiliary to insurance Mode 2: Liberalization of all insurance and insurance-related services except mandatory insurance services or those related to the social security system or when the policy holder, insured, or beneficiary is a state entity *(no later than 4 years after entry into force of agreement)* Mode 3: Establishment of insurance branches subject to regulatory requirements *(no later than 4 years after entry into force of agreement)*; liberalization of life insurance	Mode 2: Same as for market access Mode 3: Same as for market access Mode 4: Only commitments of horizontal schedule
Banking and other financial services	Mode 1: No commitments Mode 2: No commitments Mode 3: Liberalization of all banking and other financial services except asset Modes 1, 2, and 4: Liberalization of provision and transfer of financial information, financial data processing, and	Mode 1: No commitments Mode 2: No commitments Mode 3: Same as for market access Modes 1, 2, and 4: Same as for market access Modes 1 and 3: Same as for market access

(continued)

Table 2C.2 *(continued)*

	Main commitments under GATS (1997)		Improvement in commitments under Colombia–U.S. FTA	
Sector	Market access	National treatment	Market access	National treatment
	management; payment and money transmission services; settlement and clearing services for financial assets; and trading for own account or for account of customers of money market instruments, foreign exchange, and interest rate instruments Mode 4: Only commitments of horizontal schedule	Mode 4: Only commitments of horizontal schedule	advisory and other auxiliary financial services except intermediation and credit reference and analysis (the latter service may be provided in the future) Modes 1 and 3: Liberalization of investment advice and portfolio management services (excluding custodial and trustee services) by financial institutions for domestic collective investment schemes subject to registration requirements *(no later than 4 years after entry into force of agreement)* Mode 2: Liberalization of all banking and other financial services subject to registration requirements *(no later than 4 years after entry into force of agreement)*	Mode 2: Same as for market access Mode 3: Same as for market access

Mode 3: Establishment of bank branches subject to regulatory requirements; liberalization of invest-ment advice and portfolio management services (including execution and custodial services for foreign investments) by financial institutions for domestic mandatory pension funds subject to regulatory requirements *(all of the above no later than 4 years after entry into force of agreement)* and of all remaining banking and other financial services not already covered in GATS

Sources: Authors' interpretation based on information provided by the World Trade Organization and the Office of the United States Trade Representative and Arbeláez, Flórez, and Salazar 2006.

Note: FTA = free trade agreement; GATS = General Agreement on Trade in Services; MAT = international maritime transport, international commercial aviation, and goods in international transit. Modes 1 to 4 refer to the four modes of supply. The table does not include other disciplines or provisions on payments and capital movements.

Table 2C.3   Costa Rica's Financial Services Trade Liberalization Commitments

Sector	Main commitments under GATS (1997)		Improvement in commitments under CAFTA-DR–U.S.	
	Market access	National treatment	Market access	National treatment
Horizontal (only those most relevant for financial services)				
All sectors (including financial services)	Mode 3: Limitations on juridical form of establishment for financial services providers Mode 4: No commitments except for entry and temporary stay of (at most 2) senior executives and supervisors of an enterprise	Mode 4: Same as for market access		Mode 3: No more than a minority of the board of directors of a foreign-owned financial institution may be composed of nationals or residents
Financial services specific				
Insurance and insurance-related services	Modes 1, 2, 3, and 4: No commitments	Modes 1, 2, 3, and 4: No commitments	Mode 1: Liberalization of sale and intermediation of MAT and space launching and freight insurance, sale and intermediation of reinsurance and retrocession, sale and intermediation of services necessary to support global accounts (for multinationals), and sale of services auxiliary to aforementioned insurance lines (*no later than date of entry into force of the agreement*); liberalization of all remaining insurance	Mode 1: Same as for market access Mode 3: Same as for market access Mode 4: Same as for market access

64

Sector	Limitations on market access	Limitations on national treatment
	intermediation and services auxiliary to insurance and of surplus lines[a] (*no later than July 2007*) Mode 3: Establishment of insurance representation offices (*no later than July 2007*); liberalization of all insurance and insurance-related services (*no later than Janury 2008*) except compulsory auto and occupational risk insurance (*to be liberalized no later than January 2011*) and social security–related insurance services Mode 4: Liberalization of all insurance and insurance-related services (except compulsory auto, occupational risk. and social security–related insurance services) subject to registration requirements Mode 1: Liberalization of investment advice and portfolio management services (excluding custodial and trustee services) by foreign financial institutions (except trust companies) for domestic collective investment schemes (which includes mandatory and voluntary pension funds) subject to registration requirements	Mode 1: Same as for market access Modes 1 and 4: Same as for market access Mode 2: Same as for market access Mode 3: Same as for market access Mode 4: Same as for market access
Banking and other financial services	Modes 1 and 2: Liberalization of provision and transfer of financial information and financial data processing Mode 3: Liberalization of acceptance of deposits, lending of all types, financial leasing (except for commercial banks and	Modes 1 and 2: Same as for market access Mode 3: Same as for market access Mode 4: Only commitments of horizontal schedule

(continued)

Table 2C.3 *(continued)*

	Main commitments under GATS (1997)		Improvement in commitments under CAFTA-DR-U.S.	
Sector	Market access	National treatment	Market access	National treatment
	nonbank financial companies that are legally prohibited to undertake this activity), credit card services, provision and transfer of financial information, and financial data processing Mode 4: Only commitments of horizontal schedule		Modes 1 and 4: Liberalization of advisory and other auxiliary financial services excluding intermediation Mode 2: Liberalization of all banking and other financial services subject to registration requirements Mode 3: Liberalization of all remaining banking and other financial services not already covered in GATS Mode 4: Liberalization of provision and transfer of financial information and financial data processing	

Sources: Authors' interpretation based on information provided by the WTO and the Office of the United States Trade Representative and Echandi 2006.

Note: CAFTA-DR-U.S. = Free Trade Agreement between Central America, the Dominican Republic, and the United States; GATS = General Agreement on Trade in Services; MAT = international maritime transport, international commercial aviation, and goods in international transit. Modes 1 to 4 refer to the four modes of supply. The table does not include other disciplines or provisions on payments and capital movements.

a. *Surplus lines* are defined (as of January 2008) as "insurance coverage not available from an admitted company in the regular market."

Notes

1. See Sauvé and Steinfatt (2001) for country-specific examples of barriers to financial services trade.

2. International standard setters include, among others, the World Bank, the International Monetary Fund, the Basel Committee on Banking Supervision, the International Association of Insurance Supervisors, the International Organization of Securities Commissions, and the Organisation for Economic Co-operation and Development.

3. Trade in financial services is often linked to capital movements, notably in the context of the establishment of a commercial presence that requires inward direct investment. Certain types of cross-border financial transactions may also involve capital movements and, hence, require some measure of capital account opening as an inherent part of services provision. In addition, countries often seek to promote greater policy coherence by opening domestic financial markets to foreign competition in the context of broader financial reform efforts.

4. See Demirgüç-Kunt and Levine (2008) for a recent overview of the evidence.

5. See Clarke and others (2003) for a review of the literature.

6. For more on these preconditions, see, for example, IMF (2007).

7. Such reforms go well beyond trade policy and cannot, therefore, be tackled solely in the context of a trade agreement per se.

8. Strictly speaking, the Code of Liberalization of Capital Movements (which also covers direct investment and establishment) and Code of Liberalization of Invisible Operations (which covers services)—which have been in existence since the 1960s—are earlier examples of binding legal instruments for promoting progressive liberalization among member governments of the Organisation for Economic Co-operation and Development. However, they are not treaties or international agreements in the sense of international law, as is the case for WTO agreements.

9. The definition of *governmental authority* for financial services is described later in this section.

10. According to Harms, Mattoo, and Schuknecht (2003, 30), who estimated the relative size of different modes and subsectors in financial services using U.S. data, "establishment trade is three-and-a-half times greater than cross-border trade for imports and more than twice as large for exports."

11. Although no universally agreed-on criteria exist, some WTO members have based the distinction between modes 1 and 2 on whether one or two jurisdictions are involved in the provision of a financial service and whether the service was provided as a result of direct online, cross-border solicitation.

12. Permissible departures from most-favored-nation obligations include one-time exemptions (usually based on preexisting reciprocity provisions) taken

when a country's initial schedule of commitments, economic integration agreements (to the extent that they do not result in a more restrictive market-access situation for services suppliers from countries outside such agreements), and prudential standards (including mutual recognition) enter into force.

13. Such measures include laws, regulations, rules, procedures, decisions, and administrative actions.

14. In contrast to the trade agreement on goods (the General Agreement on Tariffs and Trade), national treatment was not made a general obligation in GATS, because it would have meant that granting market access would be the equivalent of establishing free trade, and governments wanted to proceed more gradually in opening their services markets.

15. A *financial service supplier* is defined as "any natural or juridical person of a Member wishing to supply or supplying financial services," excluding public entities.

16. If a member allows any of activities (ii) or (iii) to be conducted by its financial services suppliers in competition with a public entity or a financial services supplier, "services" shall include these activities.

17. This prudential clause has not yet been tested in dispute settlement, and its coverage is still uncertain, especially because countries may have different perceptions on this issue for historical reasons. For example, European countries with a universal banking tradition could argue that traditional line-of-business restrictions (that is, separation of banking, securities, and insurance) cannot be justified on prudential grounds.

18. GATS explicitly recognizes the right of member states, and especially of developing countries, to regulate the supply of services within their territories in pursuit of national policy objectives as well as to conduct negotiations on the basis of progressive liberalization. In fact, GATS does not preclude any particular form of government involvement in the domestic financial system, such as directed or preferential lending schemes, as long as it is nondiscriminatory in nature and is administered transparently and objectively.

19. For a summary of this framework, see Kireyev (2002) and Tamirisa and others (2000).

20. Brazil, Jamaica, and the Philippines have not yet ratified the Fifth Protocol to GATS, so their current commitments are those dating to the Uruguay Round.

21. See chapter 3 on architectural approaches for more details in the context of PTA negotiations.

22. No countries in the Latin American and Caribbean Region have yet signed the understanding, which represents one of the most frequent requests made by developed countries in the current Doha Round of multilateral trade negotiations.

23. Section D.3. of the understanding provides, "A new financial service is a service of a financial nature, including services related to existing and new products or the manner in which a product is delivered, that is not supplied by any financial service supplier in the territory of a particular Member but which is supplied in the territory of another Member."

24. See Crawford and Fiorentino (2005); Roy, Marchetti, and Lim (2006); and World Bank (2005) for a description of recent trends and potential drivers.

25. The World Bank (2005) also reports that, on average, Latin American and Caribbean countries belong to eight different PTAs, which is the highest number among developing countries.

26. All Latin American and Caribbean Region free trade agreements (including those not yet implemented), starting with the North American Free Trade Agreement, have been categorized either as North-South (that is, including at least one developed country) or as South-South.

27. A fourth, more technical reason for including financial services in a PTA would be to ensure that the agreement has substantial sectoral coverage and therefore constitutes a lawful exemption to the nondiscrimination requirement articulated in article V of GATS. This issue can be addressed by not carving out a priori financial services from the scope of the agreement.

28. Unlike trade in goods, assessing the direct effect of including financial services in PTAs goes well beyond trade volumes to include various financial sector outcomes, such as depth, efficiency, and stability (see Hoekman 2006).

29. This section is partly based on chapter 3 of this volume.

30. Examples include the adoption of a positive list approach for the cross-border supply of financial services and the treatment of potentially sensitive information, as well as the introduction of a binding—as opposed to "best endeavors" as in NAFTA—market-access provision listing the types of restrictive measures that parties cannot adopt or maintain with regard to investors or providers of another party.

31. Marconini (2006) defines four main aspects of domestic regulation in PTAs: transparency (contact points, publications, notifications, and the like); governance (tribunals, prior comments, reviews and appeals, authorization, and so on); requirements; and recognition.

32. For example, in the case of the Chile-U.S. FTA, the two parties agreed in an annex that measures adopted by Chile (such as applying a restriction on payments and transfers) could be subject to dispute settlement by U.S. investors. Different types of claims were identified to distinguish between short-term and longer-term capital flows, with restrictions on the latter being more punitive for Chile.

33. See Beviglia-Zampetti and Sauvé (2006), as well as Fink and Nikomborirak (2008), for an analysis of rules of origin in services.

34. This requirement can potentially be an important consideration, because investors can launch cases themselves in investor-to-state arbitration, whereas they would need the support of their home government for state-to-state disputes.

35. As the recent example of the República Bolivariana de Venezuela shows, there are also political limits to the commitment value of trade agreements.

36. This inherent contradiction is also the subject of the current Doha Round of multilateral trade negotiations; however, as Marconini (2006, 42) notes, the emphasis on development there means that "the overriding objective is to preserve the space to make policy—development policy—and to avoid any possible further encroachment into the domestic regulatory realm."

37. For example, the ministry of finance led the negotiations process in the Chilean (Chile-U.S. FTA, Chile–EU Association Agreement) and Colombian (Colombia-U.S. FTA) cases, whereas the ministry of trade led negotiations for Costa Rica (CAFTA-DR-U.S.). In the case of the United States, the Office of the U.S. Trade Representative handles insurance negotiations, and the Treasury handles negotiations in other financial services.

38. Strictly speaking, a financial services chapter does not fully capture all domestic activities of the financial system, such as foreign investment in domestic nonfinancial securities; activities of nonregulated financial institutions (in NAFTA-type agreements); provisions on payments and capital movements; and elements of a country's financial infrastructure (for example, accounting services) and financial institution functions (for example, data processing, telecommunications, legal, and tax services).

39. For example, in the case of Chile, there were no financial services–specific consultations because of perceived lack of interest and the technical nature of the discussions, whereas in Costa Rica, they included public presentations following each negotiating round as well as a broad communications strategy.

40. Such lists correspond to a negative list of measures that, absent their inscription in reservation lists, would be found in breach of the key liberalizing provisions found in trade agreements—national treatment, market access (quantitative restrictions), local presence requirements, and MFN treatment.

41. NAFTA was the first FTA to which a country from the region was a party that included trade in financial services in its scope and devoted a specific self-contained chapter to such trade. Subsequently, Mexico has been a key player in incorporating financial services in its PTAs; of the 12 PTAs (all are FTAs) entered into by Mexico, 7 contain a financial services chapter.

42. However, it should be noted that domestic authorities retain the right to regulate such branches as they deem necessary for prudential purposes, including by establishing local capital requirements.

43. Provisions on denial of benefits—also known as *rules of origin*—allow parties to a PTA to deny the benefits of the agreement to a financial services supplier that is not owned or controlled by nationals of the other party. These provisions can be important because their restrictiveness helps determine the extent of preferential treatment entailed in market-opening commitments undertaken by the parties.

44. Roy, Marchetti, and Lim (2006) undertake this analysis for a broader set of PTAs and sectors (and compare PTA commitments to recent WTO offers) and reach the same conclusion.

45. These nuances include, for example, the definition and coverage of financial services supplier versus (regulated) financial institution in NAFTA-type agreements; the relationship between financial services and other chapters; the denial-of-benefits clause, which is the trade-in-services equivalent of rules of origin; restrictions on the imposition of capital controls or payments restrictions, which become particularly important in times of crisis; the existence of ratcheting or standstill clauses; and the use of a negative list approach, with its concomitant need to include all reservations in an appendix ("list it or lose it").

References and Other Resources

Arbeláez, María A., Andrés Flórez, and Natalia Salazar. 2006. "Financial Services in the Colombia-U.S. Free Trade Agreement." World Bank, Washington, DC.

Barth, James, Juan Marchetti, Daniel Nolle, and Wanvimol Sawangngoenyuang. 2006. "Foreign Banking: Do Countries' WTO Commitments Match Actual Practice?" Staff Working Paper ERSD-2006-11, Economic Research and Statistics Division, World Trade Organization, Geneva.

Beviglia-Zampetti, Americo, and Pierre Sauvé. 2006. "Rules of Origin for Services: Economic and Legal Considerations." In *The Origin of Goods: Rules of Origin in Regional Trade Agreements*, ed. Olivier Cadot, Antoni Estevadeordal, Akiko Suwa-Eisenmann, and Thierry Verdier, 114–46. London: Oxford University Press.

Bhagwati Jagdish, and Arvid Panagariya. 1996. *The Economics of Preferential Trade Agreements*. Washington, DC: AEI Press.

Bouzas, Roberto, and Hernán Soltz. 2005. "Argentina and the GATS: A Study of the Domestic Determinants of GATS Commitments." In *Managing the Challenges of WTO Participation: 45 Case Studies*, ed. Peter Gallagher, Peter Low, and Andrew Stoler, 38–52. New York: Cambridge University Press.

Claessens, Stijn. 2002. "Regulatory Reform and Trade Liberalization in Financial Services." Paper presented at the joint OECD–World Bank conference on Regulatory Reform and Trade Liberalization in Services, Paris, March 4–5.

Claessens, Stijn, and Tom Glaessner. 1998. "The Internationalization of Financial Services in Asia." Policy Research Working Paper 1911, World Bank, Washington, DC.

Claessens, Stijn, and Marion Jansen, eds. 2000. *The Internationalization of Financial Services: Issues and Lessons for Developing Countries*. The Hague: World Bank and World Trade Organization.

Clarke, George, Robert Cull, Maria Soledad Martinez Peria, and Susana Sánchez. 2003. "Foreign Bank Entry: Experience, Implications for Developing Economies, and Agenda for Further Research." *World Bank Research Observer* 18 (1): 25–60.

Contreras, Patricio. 2008. "Liberalization of Trade in Financial Services: New Trends in the Western Hemisphere." In *A Handbook of International Trade in Services*, ed. Aaditya Mattoo, Robert M. Stern, and Gianni Zanini, box 7.1, 316–26. Oxford, U.K.: Oxford University Press.

Contreras, Patricio, and Soonhwa Yi. 2004. *Internationalization of Financial Services in Asia-Pacific and the Western Hemisphere*. Singapore: Pacific Economic Cooperation Council.

Cornford, Andrew. 2004. "The WTO Negotiations on Financial Services: Current Issues and Future Directions." Discussion Paper 172, United Nations Conference on Trade and Development, Geneva.

Crawford, Jo-Ann, and Roberto Fiorentino. 2005. "The Changing Landscape of Regional Trade Agreements." Discussion Paper 8, World Trade Organization, Geneva.

de la Cruz, Javier, and Constantinos Stephanou. 2006. "Financial System Structure in Colombia: A Proposal for a Reform Agenda." Policy Research Working Paper 4006, World Bank, Washington, DC.

Demirgüç-Kunt, Asli, and Ross Levine. 2008. "Finance, Financial-Sector Policies, and Long-Run Growth." Policy Research Working Paper 4469, World Bank, Washington, DC.

Dobson, Wendy. 2002. "Further Financial Services Liberalization in the Doha Round?" International Economics Policy Brief PB02-8, Institute for International Economics, Washington, DC.

———. 2008. "Financial Services and International Trade Agreements: The Development Dimension," In *A Handbook of International Trade in Services*, ed. Aaditya Mattoo, Robert M. Stern, and Gianni Zanini, 289–38. Oxford, U.K.: Oxford University Press.

Dobson, Wendy, and Pierre Jacquet. 1998. *Financial Services Liberalization in the WTO*. Washington, DC: Institute for International Economics.

Echandi, Roberto. 2006. "The DR-CAFTA-US FTA Negotiations in Financial Services: The Experience of Costa Rica." World Bank, Washington, DC.

Fink, Carsten, and Martín Molinuevo. 2007. *East Asian Free Trade Agreements in Services: Roaring Tigers or Timid Pandas?* East Asia and Pacific Region Report 40175, World Bank, Washington, DC.

Fink, Carsten, and Deunden Nikomborirak. 2008. "Rules of Origin in Services: A Case Study of Five ASEAN Countries." In *GATS and the Regulation of International Trade in Services*, ed. Marion Panizzon, Nicole Pohl, and Pierre Sauvé, 111–38. Cambridge, U.K.: Cambridge University Press.

Gari, Gabriel. 2004. "Free Circulation of Services in Mercosur: A Pending Task." *Law and Business Review of the Americas* 10 (3): 545–76.

———. 2006. "In Search of a Strategy for the Liberalisation of Trade in Services in Mercosur." Presented at the Fourth Annual Conference of the Euro-Latin Study Network on Integration and Trade, Paris, October 20–21.

Goncalves, Marilyne Pereira, and Constantinos Stephanou. 2007. "Financial Services and Trade Agreements in Latin America and the Caribbean: An Overview." Policy Research Working Paper 4181, World Bank, Washington, DC.

Grosso, Massimo Geloso. 2003. "Managing Request-Offer Negotiations under the GATS: The Case of Insurance Services." OECD Trade Policy Working Paper 11, Working Party of the Trade Committee, Organisation for Economic Co-operation and Development, Paris.

Harms, Philipp, Aaditya Mattoo, and Ludger Schuknecht. 2003. "Explaining Liberalization Commitments in Financial Services Trade." Policy Research Working Paper 2999, World Bank, Washington, DC.

Hoekman, Bernard. 2006. "Liberalizing Trade in Services: A Survey." Policy Research Working Paper 4030, World Bank, Washington, DC.

Hoekman, Bernard, Aaditya Mattoo, and Philip English, eds. 2002. *Development, Trade, and the WTO: A Handbook*. Washington, DC: World Bank.

International Monetary Fund (IMF). 2005. *Balance of Payments Statistics: Yearbook 2005*. Washington, DC: IMF.

———. 2007. "Reaping the Benefits of Financial Globalization." Discussion paper, Research Department, International Monetary Fund, Washington, DC.

Johnston, R. Barry. 1998. "Sequencing Capital Account Liberalizations and Financial Sector Reform." Paper on Policy Analysis and Assessment 98/8, International Monetary Fund, Washington, DC.

Kaminsky, Graciela, and Sergio Schmukler. 2003. "Short-Run Pain, Long-Run Gain: The Effects of Financial Liberalization." NBER Working Paper 9787, National Bureau of Economic Research, Cambridge, MA.

Key, Sydney. 1997. *Financial Services in the Uruguay Round and the WTO*. Occasional Paper 54. Washington, DC: Group of Thirty.

———. 2003. *The Doha Round and Financial Services Negotiations*. Washington, DC: AEI Press. http://www.aei.org/book/456.

Kireyev, Alexei. 2002. "Liberalization of Trade in Financial Services and Financial Sector Stability (Analytical Approach)." IMF Working Paper 02/138, International Monetary Fund, Washington, DC.

Kono, Masamichi, Patrick Low, Mukela Luanga, Aaditya Mattoo, Maika Oshikawa, and Ludger Schuknecht. 1997. *Opening Markets in Financial Services and the Role of the GATS.* Geneva: WTO Special Studies.

Kono, Masamichi, and Ludger Schuknecht. 1998. "Financial Services Trade, Capital Flows, and Financial Stability." Staff Working Paper ERAD-98-12, Economic Research and Analysis Division, World Trade Organization, Geneva.

Kose, M. Ayhan, Eswar Prasad, Kenneth Rogoff, and Shang-Jin Wei. 2006. "Financial Globalization: A Reappraisal." IMF Working Paper 06/189, International Monetary Fund, Washington, DC.

Lane, Philip R., and Gian Maria Milesi-Ferretti. 2006. "The External Wealth of Nations Mark II: Revised and Extended Estimates of Foreign Assets and Liabilities, 1970–2004." IMF Working Paper 06/69, International Monetary Fund, Washington, DC.

Lehmann, Alexander, Natalia Tamirisa, and Jaroslaw Wieczorek. 2003. "International Trade in Services: Implications for the IMF." IMF Policy Discussion Paper 03/6, International Monetary Fund, Washington, DC.

Marchetti, Juan. 2004. "Developing Countries in the WTO Services Negotiations." Staff Working Paper ERSD-2004-06, Economic Research and Statistics Division, World Trade Organization, Geneva, Switzerland.

Marconini, Mario. 2006. *Services in Regional Agreements between Latin American and Developed Countries.* Santiago: United Nations.

Mattoo, Aaditya. 1999. "Financial Services and the World Trade Organization: Liberalization Commitments of the Developing and Transition Economies." Policy Research Working Paper 2184, World Bank, Washington, DC.

Mattoo, Aaditya, Randeep Rathindran, and Arvind Subramanian. 2001. "Measuring Services Trade Liberalization and Its Impact on Economic Growth: An Illustration." Policy Research Working Paper 2655, World Bank, Washington, DC.

Mattoo, Aaditya, and Pierre Sauvé, eds. 2003. *Domestic Regulation and Service Trade Liberalization.* Washington, DC: World Bank and Oxford University Press.

Norton, Joseph, and Mauricio Baquero-Herrera. 2006. "Financial Services in the FTAA Area: Sifting through the 'Spaghetti Bowl' of Existing and Divergent Treaty Arrangements and Approaches within the Western Hemisphere—The Need for a Viable Convergence Process." In *Derecho Económico,* vol. 5, 79–142. Bogotá: Universidad Externado de Colombia.

OECD (Organisation for Economic Co-operation and Development). 2000. "Cross-Border Trade in Financial Services: Economics and Regulation." *Financial Market Trends* 75: 23–60.

Roy, Martin, Juan Marchetti, and A. Hoe Lim. 2006. "Services Liberalization in the New Generation of Preferential Trade Agreements (PTAs): How Much Further Than the GATS?" Staff Working Paper ERSD-2006-07, Economic Research and Statistics Division, World Trade Organization, Geneva.

Sáez, Raúl. 2006. "Trade in Financial Services: The Case of Chile." World Bank, Washington, DC.

Sáez, Sebastián. 2005. "Trade Policy Making in Latin America: A Compared Analysis," Serie Comercio Internacional 55, Division of International Trade and Integration, United Nations Economic Commission for Latin America and the Caribbean, Santiago.

Salazar-Xirinachs, José M. 2002. "Proliferation of Sub-Regional Trade Agreements in the Americas: An Assessment of Key Analytical and Policy Issues." *Journal of Asian Studies* 13 (2): 181–212.

Sauvé, Pierre. 2007. "Adding Value at the Periphery: Aiming for GATS+ Advances in Regional Trade Agreements on Services." World Trade Institute, Berne, Switzerland.

Sauvé, Pierre, and Karsten Steinfatt. 2001. "Financial Services and the WTO: What Next?" In *Open Doors: Foreign Participation in Financial Systems in Developing Countries*, ed. Robert Litan, Paul Masson, and Michael Pomerleano, 351–86. Washington, DC: Brookings Institution Press.

Stephanou, Constantinos. 2009. "Including Financial Services in Preferential Trade Agreements: Lessons of International Experience for China." Policy Research Working Paper 4898, World Bank, Washington, DC.

Stephenson, Sherry. 2002. "Regional versus Multilateral Liberalization of Services." *World Trade Review* 1 (2): 187–209.

———. 2005. "Regionalism in Latin America." Presentation in World Bank course on "Regionalism in Developing Countries: Issues and Implications," Washington, DC, June 22–24.

Tamirisa, Natalia, Piritta Sorsa, Geoffrey Bannister, Bradley McDonald, and Jaroslaw Wieczorek. 2000. "Trade Policy in Financial Services." IMF Working Paper 00/31, International Monetary Fund, Washington, DC.

Valckx, Nico. 2002a. "WTO Financial Services Commitments: Determinants and Impact on Financial Stability." IMF Working Paper 02/214, International Monetary Fund, Washington, DC.

———. 2002b. "WTO Financial Services Liberalization: Measurement, Choice, and Impact on Financial Stability." Research Memorandum WO 705/0227, De Nederlandsche Bank, Research Department, Amsterdam.

Van Horen, Neeltje. 2006. "Foreign Banking in Developing Countries: Origin Matters." World Bank, Washington, DC.

Wagner, Constance. 1999. "The New WTO Agreement on Financial Services and Chapter 14 of NAFTA: Has Free Trade in Banking Finally Arrived?" *Law and Business Review of the Americas* 5 (5): 75–78.

World Bank. 2005. *Global Economic Prospects: Trade, Regionalism, and Development.* Washington, DC: World Bank.

WTO (World Trade Organization). 2006. "The General Agreement on Trade in Services: An Introduction." WTO, Geneva.

WTO (World Trade Organization) Secretariat. 1998. "Financial Services: Background Note by the Secretariat." Document S/C/W/72, WTO, Geneva.

PART I

Horizontal Issues

Architectural Approaches to the Treatment of Trade and Investment in Financial Services in Selected Preferential Trade Agreements

Pierre Sauvé and Martin Molinuevo

How are financial services best treated in preferential trade agreements (PTAs)? Do they warrant a special chapter in an agreement that takes account of their specific characteristics, or should they rather be incorporated into broader general disciplines on services and investment? Disciplines on trade in services typically follow the General Agreement on Trade in Services (GATS) approach of considering investment in services as a mode of supplying services alongside cross-border trade in services or the movement of services suppliers or consumers. Should investment in financial institutions be subject to disciplines on services trade or to general disciplines on investment, which typically cover investment in both goods and services? What specific provisions about financial services do PTAs commonly feature? Are these different architectural options reflected in the liberalization outcome of financial services? Is the choice of architecture relevant for shielding financial sector

The authors are grateful to Constantinos Stephanou for helpful comments and suggestions.

regulation (and dispute settlement procedures) from key provisions of investment chapters, notably those dealing with indirect expropriation and investor-state arbitration?

This chapter addresses some of these questions by reviewing a number of PTAs in East Asia and the Americas and analyzes how such agreements deal with the regulation of trade and investment in financial services. Special attention is devoted to the interface between services and investment chapters and, where relevant, their relationship to particular provisions about financial services.

Carving Out All Sectors

A first item to explore is the sectoral scope of PTAs. No trade agreement signed to date has established immediate free trade in all services sectors. For a variety of reasons, governments wish to exempt certain activities from the coverage of trade and investment disciplines or to maintain certain trade- and investment-restrictive measures in covered sectors. A key question is how specific agreements tackle such exemptions from the main disciplines of those agreements.

One way to limit the sectoral coverage of an agreement is simply to exclude an entire sector or subsector from the agreement's scope of coverage. Indeed, five agreements studied did not cover financial services at all. With the exception of the Trans-Pacific Economic Partnership Agreement (EPA), all of them followed the North American Free Trade Agreement (NAFTA) model. The exclusion of financial services from international disciplines can be explained by a number of factors, among which a country's preparedness to negotiate in light of the regulatory sensitivities and complexities of financial services is one of the most significant. Paradoxically, however, all agreements that have carved out financial services entirely involve countries that have agreed to liberalizing disciplines on financial services in other agreements. Seen in this light, the exclusion of financial services in certain agreements appears to stem from the inability of trading partners to agree on a common approach or liberalization outcome.

Sectoral carve-outs are the most radical form of exclusion from international disciplines. They entail that no provision of the agreement (unless otherwise explicitly provided for) applies to the excluded sector. Thus, the countries concerned retain full freedom to introduce or maintain any kind of restrictive measures vis-à-vis their trading partners. A less radical form of carve-out is found in the Japan-Mexico Free Trade Agreement (FTA), in which, despite the presence of a chapter dedicated to financial services (chapter 9), the parties agreed merely to be bound by their respective commitments under the Organisation for Economic Co-operation and Development (OECD) Codes of Liberalization and Capital Movements and GATS.[1]

How Are Financial Services Covered in PTAs?

Where financial services are included in PTAs, several models are possible. One follows GATS in covering investment in services under general disciplines on trade in services. Alternatively, investment in services can be governed entirely by disciplines on foreign investment that apply across the board to all economic sectors—primary (including agriculture), manufacturing, and services. Particular regulatory sensitivities of financial markets, however, raise the question of whether cross-border trade and investment in financial services should be addressed in a distinct chapter on financial services. Overall, five distinct architectural approaches can be distinguished, as follows.

No General Disciplines

China's Closer Economic Partnership Agreements (CEPAs) with the Special Administrative Regions (SARs) of Hong Kong, China, and Macao, China, feature a unique approach in the landscape of international trade agreements covering services. The text of these two agreements does not contain core provisions such as most-favored-nation (MFN) or national treatment, nor does it feature services-specific obligations such as that on market access. Indeed, both of the CEPAs lack the general disciplines that are listed in annex 3A of this chapter for selected PTAs. The obligations of the parties relating to either cross-border trade or investment in any services sector—including financial services—stem from the list of specific commitments adopted by China. This approach affords parties the freedom to undertake commitments solely in those areas where governments feel capable of doing so, rather than introducing disciplines that may be deemed burdensome on their regulatory capacity. Although the lack of general disciplines and of a rules-based dispute settlement mechanism raises doubts about actual enforceability, such agreements are not devoid of actual trade and investment preferences. Indeed, China has committed to significant liberalization undertakings in favor of services suppliers from its two SARs, effectively giving them a head start in its internal market prior to the full implementation of China's World Trade Organization (WTO) accession commitments.[2]

Nonetheless, the lack of general disciplines and the need to refer at all times to the schedules of commitments to assess the precise scope of what the package of market-opening elements precisely contains make this approach not particularly attractive to countries that wish to provide for broad commitments in a greater number of sectors. Moreover, it serves as a poor signal to foreign investors and services suppliers.

As for financial services, the lack of generally binding disciplines makes the introduction of a prudential carve-out or other regulatory provisions unnecessary. Rather, China's CEPAs allow the parties to undertake commitments exactly at the desired level of openness and to include in such schedules any financial services–specific regulatory consideration they may deem convenient. Whether such a high degree of regulatory discretion would prove attractive to other WTO members, particularly developed countries, is debatable.

Financial Services Covered by Services Chapters

Four agreements under review—the Lao People's Democratic Republic–U.S. Bilateral Trade Agreement, the Association of Southeast Asian Nations (ASEAN) Framework Agreement on Services, the ASEAN-China Agreement on Trade in Services, and the China–New Zealand FTA—provide for coverage of financial services under a general chapter on trade in services. Like GATS, these disciplines cover the supply of services not only through cross-border means (including consumption abroad), but also through the presence of natural persons and commercial entities. As such, foreign investment is covered by these agreements only insofar as it relates to services industries. The coverage of investment in financial services focuses primarily on foreign direct investment aimed at establishing a financial institution in the host market. Foreign participation that does not involve ownership or control over financial institutions, hence, falls outside the agreements' scope.

Some agreements go beyond this pattern. For instance, the ASEAN countries have additionally developed the ASEAN Investment Agreement, which also applies to investment in goods industries. Similarly, the China–New Zealand FTA features an investment chapter that covers investment in agricultural and manufacturing industries.

The substantive obligations governing services trade in the preceding agreements closely follow various GATS articles, in particular those on market access and national treatment. Financial services are covered by the general provisions that apply to all services, resembling the GATS Annex on Financial Services, or by a carve-out for prudential measures on financial regulation modeled after the GATS disciplines.

From this perspective, the treatment of financial services in the PTAs under review does not differ markedly from that found at the multilateral level. In principle, nothing prevents parties to the preceding agreements from expanding the financial services–specific disciplines of GATS by adopting common regulatory principles and other provisions on financial services while leaving the issue of liberalization commitments in financial services subject to the general obligations of the services chapter. The four PTAs under review, however, have not made use of such a possibility.

This approach offers the advantage of incorporating financial services into a familiar and well-accepted framework of international rules. However, such general disciplines offer only limited investment protection features, such as disciplines on expropriation, fair and equitable treatment, and investor-state arbitration, commonly found in investment chapters.

One of the agreements, the China–New Zealand FTA, has attempted to overcome this issue by extending the key protection disciplines featured in the investment-in-goods chapter (including fair and equitable treatment, guarantees against expropriation, and access to investor-state arbitration) to those sectors where commitments have been scheduled with regard to commercial presence under the agreement's chapter on trade in services.

Dual Coverage of Investment in Services

Most of the reviewed PTAs provide for dual coverage of investment in services. Financial services are covered by general GATS-like chapters on trade in services, encompassing all modes of supply. Furthermore, investment in services—including in financial services—is covered by the general disciplines on investment. Such dual coverage of investment in services can be complementary, but it may also lead to potentially conflicting overlaps.[3]

A horizontal investment chapter promotes equal treatment of investors regardless of the sector concerned and may thus promote a seamless investment regime, particularly for those firms engaged in both manufacturing and services-related activities. Meanwhile, a parallel services chapter may allow parties to establish disciplines specific to individual services sectors.

Overlapping coverage may arise when measures affecting foreign investment in services are subject to both sets of disciplines. Such overlaps might prove benign if the disciplines and levels of openness deriving from the services and investment chapters were identical. Conflict may arise, however, if a measure is allowed under one chapter but prohibited or not covered under the other. Inconsistencies of this type could undermine the transparency of the investment regime and potentially give rise to legal conflicts. To remedy such problems, most PTAs that provide for dual coverage of investment in services have established rules that define the relationship between the services chapter and the horizontal investment chapter. Drawing on recent work by Fink and Molinuevo (2007), box 3.1 offers an analysis of the agreements that provide for dual coverage on financial services, attempting to highlight the pros and cons that each approach entails.

Many agreements tackle the specifics of financial sector regulations by including an extra chapter or an annex specifically devoted to the sector. Countries in the Andean Community (Comunidad Andina) are seeking to develop such disciplines, and several negotiation rounds have been held. Because the liberalization obligations—national treatment or market access—are enshrined in the general chapters on services and investment, the specific chapter on financial services focuses on additional

---

Box 3.1

Links between Services and Investment Chapters

A brief review of the relationship between services and investment chapters in agreements that provide for dual coverage helps clarify how investment in financial services is covered.

Four agreements—the India-Singapore Economic Cooperation Agreement, the Japan-Malaysia EPA, the Jordan-Singapore FTA, and the U.S.-Vietnam BTA—have established a rule that gives precedence to the services chapter in case of inconsistencies.[a] Investment disciplines still apply insofar as they affect matters not covered by the services chapter. This rule again avoids inconsistencies between the two chapters and, at the same time, preserves some of the benefits of horizontal investment disciplines. However, a full understanding of such agreements would require joint reading of the two chapters and possible interpretation of what might be considered an inconsistency—a question that is not always straightforward.

The New Zealand–Singapore FTA and the European Free Trade Association (EFTA)–Republic of Korea FTA both provide that the national treatment and MFN obligations of their respective investment chapters do not apply to measures affecting commercial presence as governed by the services chapter. Because national treatment and MFN are the only two overlapping obligations in these FTAs, direct inconsistencies between the two chapters are avoided. This approach provides somewhat greater transparency, because the liberalization content related to commercial presence is solely determined by the services chapter.

Box 3.1 *(continued)*

However, a full understanding of the investment regime for services still requires joint reading of the services and investment chapters because the investment chapter's national treatment and MFN obligations still apply to those forms of investments not covered by the services chapter—notably investments with a minority equity stake and no effective foreign control.

The EFTA-Singapore FTA and the Japan-Philippines EPA feature a variation of the latter approach. These agreements entirely remove investment in services from the scope of the investment chapter's core liberalizing obligations. This rule offers a cleaner distinction of the roles of the services and investment chapters but implies a loss of discipline for minority investments in services. Curiously, in the case of the Japan-Philippines EPA, this rule applies only to measures adopted or maintained by the Philippines. For Japan, the relationship between services and investment disciplines remains undefined. This approach seems to offer the least transparent treatment of investment in services and may open the door to inconsistencies between services and investment disciplines.

A similar situation is encountered in the Japan-Singapore EPA. The agreement does not establish any rule defining the relationship between services and investment disciplines. However, Singapore has scheduled a reservation that stipulates (a) that the investment chapter's obligations on national treatment and performance requirements do not apply to sectors for which no specific commitments are undertaken and (b) that where sectors are subject to specific commitments, these commitments are effectively incorporated into the investment chapter. This reservation aims to eliminate potential inconsistencies regarding Singapore's disciplines and commitments in services and investment. No such reservation is found in the case of Japan, leaving the door open for potential inconsistencies.

The Australia-Singapore FTA and the Australia-Thailand FTA offer what appears to be the most transparent solution to avoiding inconsistencies. Liberalization undertakings in these two agreements are inscribed in a single schedule of commitments, which also covers investment in goods. This approach offers the benefit of consulting only one schedule of commitments to determine the level of openness of the investment regime, while taking full advantage of the complementary coverage of investment in services by two different sets of disciplines.

Source: Fink and Molinuevo 2007.

a. In the case of the Japan-Malaysia EPA, the precedence of services discipline applies only to inconsistencies with the investment chapter's obligations on national treatment, MFN, and performance requirements. The investment chapter takes precedence in the case of inconsistencies with all other investment disciplines. In the case of the U.S.-Vietnam BTA, precedence of services disciplines applies only to inconsistencies between "provisions set forth" in parties' schedule of specific services commitments and the BTA's investment disciplines (see article VII.6).

disciplines aimed at complementing the liberalization obligations. Such provisions on financial services include a prudential carve-out as well as language on recognition of regulatory measures by international bodies or third states in line with the GATS Annex on Financial Services.

Some agreements introduce further financial services–specific disciplines, such as those dealing with access to payment and clearing services for locally established foreign financial institutions (European Free Trade Association [EFTA]–Singapore FTA), commitments on new financial services (Japan-Philippines EPA), or cooperation in the development of capital markets (Japan-Singapore EPA). These agreements seek to reap the benefits of having financial services subject to GATS-like disciplines under a common framework for commitments on all services activities, while also addressing the particularities of financial services by introducing specific provisions in this regard.

Finally, dual coverage ensures that the treatment of foreign investors in financial institutions does not fall short of that afforded to foreign investors in other sectors. In particular, investors in services benefit from the investment protection provisions featured in the general investment chapters, such as fair and equitable treatment, guarantees against direct and indirect expropriation, and access to investor-state arbitration. However, governments pursuing such an approach need to ensure that the relationship between services and investment disciplines is clearly defined in a way that avoids potential inconsistencies that may give rise to legal conflicts.

Financial Services Covered Separately by Services and Investment Chapters

The only exceptions are the Australia-Singapore FTA and the EPA between the Caribbean Forum of the African, Caribbean, and Pacific Group of States (CARIFORUM) and the European Commission (EC). These two agreements split disciplines on financial services into two separate chapters, one on cross-border trade in services and one on foreign investment. All agreements that feature a chapter on cross-border trade in services (which does not cover commercial presence) and a separate chapter on foreign investment (which applies to both goods and services) have carved out financial services from their scope and confined the sector to a special, dedicated chapter.

The main liberalization obligations, including national treatment and market access (the latter only in the case of the CARIFORUM-EC EPA), are enshrined in the respective chapters on cross-border trade in services and investment. Although the investment chapter in the Australia-Singapore FTA adopts a broad definition of *investment* and features standard investment protection disciplines (guarantees against expropriation, access to investor-state arbitration), the CARIFORUM-EC EPA focuses exclusively on establishment and foreign direct investment. Hence, the latter agreement can be seen as extending GATS-like disciplines to investment in goods sectors, but without incorporating traditional investment protection disciplines. These disciplines are left to bilateral investment treaties between the individual member countries of CARIFORUM and the European Union.

In addition to the general disciplines on services and investment, both agreements feature a chapter on financial services that does not contain liberalization obligations. Instead, this chapter, like those found in agreements that provide for dual coverage, features only additional provisions specific to financial services, such as the prudential carve-out and new financial services.

As in the case of dual-coverage agreements, this approach provides common liberalization disciplines for all services or investment transactions, regardless of the sector, while avoiding interpretational conflicts that may arise from overlapping disciplines. In contrast to agreements with a specific chapter on financial services, keeping the liberalization undertakings under the general services and investment disciplines adds transparency to the agreement, because it avoids unnecessary reiterations and possible discrepancies in the scope of the provisions and in their application. Furthermore, the additional regulatory disciplines on financial services found in the financial services chapters serve to complement the liberalization undertakings, allowing the parties to address the regulatory specifics of the sector.

Financial Services Covered by a Dedicated Chapter

A number of agreements have opted for carving out financial services from the general disciplines on services and investment. Such agreements dedicate an individual chapter to the liberalization obligations and all other provisions on financial services.

NAFTA pioneered such an approach, and not surprisingly, the majority of agreements that follow the NAFTA model for services and investment also follow this approach toward financial services[4]—with the notable exception of four agreements that have excluded financial services outright from their scope. Three other agreements that do not directly follow the NAFTA model also have confined rules on financial services to a single chapter of the agreement; they are the Chile–EC Association Agreement, the EFTA–Republic of Korea FTA, and the Republic of Korea–Singapore FTA. Those three agreements all feature disciplines on national treatment and market access, in line with GATS articles XVI (Market Access) and XVII (National Treatment), as well as a carve-out for regulatory measures taken for prudential reasons. They further provide some financial sector–specific disciplines with respect to, for example, transparency and data processing in financial services. In essence, the content of the dedicated chapter on financial services found in those agreements does not differ much from the disciplines found under other models described so far, especially those with dual coverage. General disciplines on national treatment, market access, and domestic regulation, which are common to both types of agreements, are closely aligned, as are a number of financial services–specific provisions.

The structure of the financial services chapter of agreements based on the NAFTA model features two particular characteristics. First, the main liberalization disciplines do not apply equally to cross-border trade in financial services and to investment in financial services. Rather, such disciplines flow from the interplay of different provisions on cross-border trade or investment in financial services. Only the MFN obligation in these agreements covers evenly both means of financial services supply. The market-access obligation (similar to GATS article XVI) applies instead only to established services suppliers, whereas cross-border trade and investment in financial services are subject to two separate national treatment provisions.

Second, although reservations under NAFTA are scheduled using a negative list approach, the financial services chapters of the Free Trade Agreement between Central America, the Dominican Republic, and the United States, the Chile-U.S. FTA, and the Singapore-U.S. FTA feature a combination of a positive list of sectors and a negative list of trade-restrictive measures when it comes to reservations on cross-border trade in services (see annex 3A). The parties provide a list of financial services allowed to be supplied on a cross-border basis; no obligations are undertaken with regard to cross-border financial operations not explicitly included in that list. The parties may further list restrictive measures on the cross-border provision of those services on a negative-list basis—partially reverting to the original NAFTA approach. Furthermore, the Nicaragua–Taiwan, China, FTA and the Panama-Singapore FTA rely entirely on a GATS-like positive list for the scheduling of commitments on financial services, leaving the Panama–Taiwan, China, FTA as the only agreement in the sample that adheres to the original NAFTA approach by relying on negative listing for financial services.

The NAFTA-like model on financial services is tailored to the particularities and regulatory sensitivities of financial services. As such, it allows the parties to provide for liberalization disciplines and specific provisions on financial services that would not necessarily suit other services sectors. Nonetheless, the reiteration of the main obligations and the fact that not all disciplines apply equally to all means of services supply add an element of complexity to these agreements. Furthermore, the observation that most agreements have deviated from the NAFTA negative list for financial services suggests the all-encompassing nature of negative listing may not be entirely suitable for the services sector. Indeed, one could argue that the four modes of supply featured in agreements following the GATS model provide a simpler and more transparent solution, while the accompanying positive listing ensures the parties the needed degree of comfort to undertake commitments in a regulatory-sensitive sector.

One characteristic is common to all agreements that have confined financial services to a dedicated chapter. In addition to several financial services–specific provisions (transparency, data processing in financial services, access to payments, and clearing services), disciplines regarding investment in financial services in these agreements fall short of those provided for investment in general.[5] In particular, financial services chapters typically do not guarantee an obligation for fair and equitable treatment and may limit access to investor-state arbitration.[6]

Furthermore, such agreements limit access to arbitration claims to the review of a joint committee on financial services, which may decide whether the prudential carve-out applies to a particular measure. In sum, although investors in financial services are better protected under agreements that provide dual coverage, the financial chapters of the latter agreements seem to better acknowledge the regulatory sensitivities of financial markets. However, nothing prevents countries engaged in dual-coverage agreements from including such limitations on investor-state arbitration in their financial services chapters if they deem them desirable on policy grounds.

Concluding Remarks

The architectural approach toward liberalization and regulatory disciplines in financial services is closely linked to the overall architecture found in particular PTAs—specifically their services and investment chapters. Countries that have followed the GATS approach may thus find it natural—and more familiar—to adopt such an approach toward financial services or to introduce a special chapter expanding on the GATS Annex on Financial Services. Similarly, countries that have relied on a NAFTA-like approach may feel more at ease with a financial services chapter modeled after that agreement's separate disciplines on financial services. That some countries have experimented with differing architectures across various agreements can be seen both as a manifestation of the "learning-by-doing" properties of services negotiations and as a result of the need of some countries to adopt a differing approach when negotiating with some partners, particularly with large OECD countries with a tradition of more comprehensive investment disciplines and greater offensive interests in trade and investment in financial services.

All competing architectural approaches can ultimately generate the same level of market opening, even if they do not afford the same degree of regulatory transparency and protection to investors. Equally, the ability of parties to maintain or introduce restrictive measures on financial services on regulatory grounds can be preserved under any approach by introducing specific provisions—such as by using a prudential carve-out, creating limitations on market access or national treatment, or qualifying recourse to investor-state dispute settlement.

However, this chapter's depiction of differing approaches to the treatment of trade and investment in financial services in PTAs yields a number of general observations. They can be summarized as follows:

- Not all agreements cover financial services. However, all countries that are parties to the agreements under review have entered into at least one preferential agreement that provides for the liberalization of financial services.
- Some countries have chosen to entirely reproduce GATS disciplines and the GATS Annex on Financial Services in their preferential agreements. This approach offers the advantage of negotiating commitments on financial services under a known set of international rules, while allowing additional provisions to be established in dedicated chapters or in an annex on financial services.
- A number of agreements have complemented the GATS approach with investment chapters. Although this approach establishes a level playing field for all foreign investors, regardless of the sector in which investment occurs, clear rules are needed to avoid overlaps between services and investment disciplines that may give rise to legal conflicts. Furthermore, the fact that a number of countries have restricted access to investor-state arbitration by financial investors suggests that international arbitration is not always seen as desirable in sensitive sectors such as financial services.

- Although liberalization disciplines are typically left to the concerned services and investment chapters, a number of provisions have been added in dedicated chapters or annexes that take account of the specifics of the financial sector. Such an option provides parties with the ability to address regulatory concerns and to agree on relevant additional disciplines.
- The coverage of financial services by a single dedicated chapter seems to capture the common interests of the parties in providing for substantial liberalization disciplines and allows them to tailor such disciplines to the particularities of financial services. However, approaches to such dedicated financial services chapters vary. NAFTA-like agreements tend to resort to complex provisions to take account of the different means of supplying financial services (by cross-border trade or local establishment) and the regulatory sensitivities that such different modes can entail.
- Dedicated chapters on financial services are also used for circumscribing the extent to which investors and investments in financial services are subject to various investment provisions. This approach is most notable in the case of investment protection disciplines, particularly investor-state arbitration.
- The scheduling of commitments on financial services often shies away from pure negative listing. Most agreements have followed GATS-style hybrid lists in scheduling commitments on financial services or have introduced a positive listing of sectors for cross-border services, even as they resort to negative lists under services or investment chapters. Only one agreement (Panama–Taiwan, China, FTA) under review has relied exclusively on negative lists for financial services, in line with the original NAFTA approach.
- Finally, this review suggests that bilateral PTAs—particularly North-South FTAs—are more likely to result in departures from the GATS architecture than are South-South agreements or regional groupings (with the notable exception of NAFTA). Moreover, deviations from WTO practice that address new issues in trade and investment rule make market opening appear to be more frequent under FTAs than under customs unions.

Annex 3A: Substantive Obligations and Scheduling Approaches in PTAs

Table 3A.1 shows the main substantive obligations of PTAs studied in this chapter. The various scheduling approaches adopted in PTAs are shown in table 3A.2.

Table 3A.1 Main Substantive Obligations in Selected PTAs

Agreement	Trade in services (including commercial presence)	Investment	Trade in financial services
China–Hong Kong, China, CEPA; China–Macao, China, CEPA	"Progressive reduction of barriers"; obligation entirely subject to specific commitments		
ASEAN-China Trade in Services Agreement	NT, MA Domestic regulation	No investment chapter; investment in services covered by services chapter	GATS AFS incorporated in agreement
Lao PDR–U.S. BTA	NT, MA	No investment chapter; investment in services covered by services chapter	No financial services chapter; financial services covered by services or investment chapters or both
India-Singapore ECA	NT, MA	NT, PR, limitations on senior managers and boards of directors	No financial services chapter; financial services covered by services or investment chapters or both
Andean Community	Domestic regulation MFN, NT	FET, expropriation, ISDS NT[a]	No financial services chapter; financial services covered by services or investment chapters or both
Mercosur	MFN, NT, MA Domestic regulation	MFN, NT, PR FET, expropriation, ISDS	No financial services chapter; financial services covered by services or investment chapters or both
U.S.-Vietnam BTA	MFN, NT, MA	MFN, NT, PR, limitations on senior managers and boards of directors	No financial services chapter; financial services covered by services or investment chapters or both
New Zealand–Singapore FTA	Domestic regulation NT, MA Domestic regulation	FET, expropriation, ISDS MFN, NT ISDS	No financial services chapter; financial services covered by services or investment chapters or both

Japan-Singapore EPA	NT, MA Domestic regulation	MFN, NT, PR FET, expropriation, ISDS	Liberalization disciplines on financial services governed by services or investment chapters. Financial services chapters or annexes incorporate or largely follow GATS AFS. Some agreements introduce additional disciplines, such as provisions on new financial services or access to domestic payment and clearing services
Japan-Philippines EPA	NT, MA Domestic regulation	MFN, NT, PR FET, expropriation	Liberalization disciplines on financial services governed by services or investment chapters. Financial services chapters or annexes incorporate or largely follow GATS AFS. Some agreements introduce additional disciplines, such as provisions on new financial services or access to domestic payment and clearing services
Japan-Malaysia EPA	MFN, NT, MA	MFN, NT, PR FET, expropriation, ISDS	Liberalization disciplines on financial services governed by services or investment chapters. Financial services chapters or annexes incorporate or largely follow GATS AFS. Some agreements introduce additional disciplines, such as provisions on new financial services or access to domestic payment and clearing services
Jordan-Singapore ETA	NT, MA Domestic regulation	NT, PR, limitations on senior managers and boards of directors FET, expropriation, ISDS	Liberalization disciplines on financial services governed by services or investment chapters. Financial services chapters or annexes incorporate or largely follow GATS AFS. Some agreements introduce additional disciplines, such as provisions on new financial services or access to domestic payment and clearing services

(continued)

Table 3A.1 *(continued)*

Agreement	Trade in services (including commercial presence)	Investment	Trade in financial services
ASEAN Framework Agreement on Services, Australia-Thailand FTA	NT, MA Domestic regulation	MFN, NT FET, expropriation, ISDS	Liberalization disciplines on financial services governed by services or investment chapters. Financial services chapters or annexes incorporate or largely follow GATS AFS. Some agreements introduce additional disciplines, such as provisions on new financial services or access to domestic payment and clearing services
EFTA-Singapore FTA	MFN, NT, MA Domestic regulation	MFN, NT, limitations on senior managers and board of directors FET, expropriation, ISDS	Liberalization disciplines on financial services governed by services or investment chapters. Financial services chapters or annexes incorporate or largely follow GATS AFS. Some agreements introduce additional disciplines, such as provisions on new financial services or access to domestic payment and clearing services
EFTA–Rep. of Korea FTA	MFN, NT, MA Domestic regulation	MFN, NT, limitations on senior managers and board of directors FET, expropriation, ISDS	MFN, MA, NT Transparency, domestic regulation, ISDS (from investment chapter)
EC–Chile Association Agreement	NT, MA Domestic regulation	NT (preestablishment only)	NT, MA Transparency, data processing

Agreement	Services	Investment	Financial services
CARIFORUM-EC EPA	MFN, NT, MA	MFN, NT, MA	Liberalization disciplines on financial services governed by services and investment chapters; no liberalization disciplines in financial services chapter
Australia-Singapore FTA	NT, MA Domestic regulation	NT Expropriation, ISDS	Liberalization disciplines on financial services governed by services and investment chapters; no liberalization disciplines in financial services chapter
Rep. of Korea–Singapore FTA	NT, MA, local presence requirements	NT, PR, limitations on senior managers and boards of directors	NT, MA
Panama–Taiwan, China, FTA	Domestic regulation NT, MFN, local presence requirements Quantitative restrictions (notifications only)	FET, expropriation, ISDS NT, MFN, PR, limitations on senior managers and boards of directors FET, expropriation, ISDS	Transparency, domestic regulation, expropriation, ISDS Cross-border trade: NT, MFN, limitations on cross-border purchases of financial services Investment: right of establishment, NT, MFN, limitations on senior managers and boards of directors Expropriation, transparency, ISDS
CAFTA-DR-U.S.; U.S.–Chile FTA; Nicaragua–Taiwan, China, FTA; Panama-Singapore FTA; Singapore-U.S. FTA	NT, MA, MFN, local presence requirements Domestic regulation	NT, MA, MFN, PR, limitations on senior managers and boards of directors FET, domestic regulation, expropriation, ISDS	Cross-border trade: NT, MFN, limitations on cross-border purchases of services Investment: NT, MA, MFN, limitations on senior managers and boards of directors Expropriation, transparency, payments and clearing services, ISDS

Source: Authors' compilation.

Note: AFS = Annex on Financial Services; ASEAN = Association of Southeast Asian Nations; BTA= Bilateral Trade Agreement; CAFTA-DR-U.S. = Free Trade Agreement between Central America, the Dominican Republic, and the United States; CARIFORUM = Caribbean Forum of the African, Caribbean, and Pacific Group of States; CEPA = Closer Economic Partnership Agreement; EC = European Commission; ECA = Economic Cooperation Agreement; EPA = Economic Partnership Agreement; EFTA = European Free Trade Association; FET = fair and equitable treatment; FTA = Free Trade Agreement; GATS = General Agreement on Trade in Services; ISDS = investor-state dispute settlement; MA = market access; Mercosur = Southern Cone Common Market; MFN = most-favored-nation treatment; NT = national treatment; PR = performance requirements.

a. A network of bilateral investment treaties between the Andean countries complements the nonbinding national treatment disciplines enshrined in the Andean Community's Decision No. 439.

Table 3A.2 Scheduling Approaches in Selected PTAs

Agreement	Chapter on services	Chapter on investment	Chapter on financial services
ASEAN-China Trade in Services Agreement; China–Hong Kong, China, CEPA; China–Macao, China, CEPA; Lao PDR–U.S. BTA	Positive	No investment chapter	No financial services chapter
Australia-Thailand FTA	Positive	Positive	No financial services chapter
Andean Community	Negative	No reservation lists	No financial services chapter
India-Singapore ECA	Positive	Positive (for India) Negative (for Singapore)	No financial services chapter
ASEAN Framework Agreement on Services, EFTA-Singapore FTA, Japan-Malaysia EPA, Japan-Philippines EPA, Jordan-Singapore FTA, Mercosur, New Zealand–Singapore FTA, U.S.-Vietnam BTA	Positive	Negative	No financial services chapter
Japan-Singapore EPA	Positive	Negative	Commitments on financial services undertaken under services and investment chapters; no liberalization disciplines in financial services chapter

CARIFORUM-EC EPA	Positive	Positive	Commitments on financial services undertaken under services and investment chapters; no liberalization disciplines in financial services chapter
Australia-Singapore FTA	Negative	Negative	Commitments on financial services undertaken under services and investment chapters; no liberalization disciplines in financial services chapter
Chile-EC Association Agreement	Positive	Positive	
EFTA–Rep. of Korea FTA	Positive	Negative	
Rep. of Korea–Singapore FTA; Nicaragua–Taiwan, China, FTA; Panama–Singapore FTA	Negative	Negative	
CAFTA-DR-U.S., Chile-U.S. FTA, Singapore-U.S. FTA	Negative	Negative	Negative (positive list of sectors allowed for cross-border financial services)
Panama–Taiwan, China, FTA	Negative	Negative	Negative

Source: Authors' compilation.

Note: ASEAN = Association of Southeast Asian Nations; BTA= Bilateral Trade Agreement; CAFTA-DR-U.S. = Free Trade Agreement between Central America, the Dominican Republic, and the United States; CARIFORUM = Caribbean Forum of the African, Caribbean, and Pacific Group of States; CEPA = Closer Economic Partnership Agreement; EC = European Commission; ECA = Economic Cooperation Agreement; EPA = Economic Partnership Agreement; EFTA = European Free Trade Association; FTA = Free Trade Agreement; Mercosur = Southern Cone Common Market.

Notes

1. Moreover, articles 109 and 111 of the chapter on financial services state, respectively, that "the dispute settlement procedure provided for in Chapter 15 shall not apply to this Chapter" and that "the provisions of Chapters 7 (Cross-Border Trade in Services) and 8 (Investment) shall not apply to measures referred to in paragraph 1 of Article 107 (Scope and Coverage)."

2. Less than 18 months after the entry into force of China's CEPA with Hong Kong, China (January 1, 2004), almost 800 Hong Kong, China, services suppliers had been awarded certificates to benefit from the preferences of the agreement. However, despite the highly developed financial sector in Hong Kong, China, only nine of those certificates were awarded to financial services suppliers (see Fink 2005, 165–66; Gao 2004).

3. Complementary coverage occurs whenever an investment transaction is covered by one set of disciplines but not by the other. It can emanate either from the different definitions of *investment* or from the different obligations established by the two sets of disciplines.

4. This group consists of the Free Trade Agreement between Central America, the Dominican Republic, and the United States; the Chile-U.S. FTA; the Nicaragua–Taiwan, China, FTA; the Panama-Singapore FTA; the Panama–Taiwan, China, FTA; and the Singapore-U.S. FTA.

5. See chapter 2 in the present volume for a detailed review of the rules and disciplines typically featured in financial services chapters in PTAs.

6. Although such agreements may reduce guarantees against investment in financial services, it grants host countries greater regulatory space in the case of a financial crisis and affords them the right to introduce measures to safeguard only certain banks (likely, national banks), rather than all banks established in their territory.

References and Other Resources

Adlung, Rudolf, and Martin Molinuevo. 2008. "Bilateralism in Services Trade: Is There Fire behind the (BIT) Smoke?" WTO Staff Working Paper ERSD 2008-01, Economic Research and Statistics Division, World Trade Organization, Geneva. http://www.wto.org/english/res_e/reser_e/wpaps_e.htm.

Fink, Carsten. 2005. "A Macroeconomic Perspective on China's Liberalization of Trade in Services." In *China's Participation in the WTO*, ed. Henry Gao and Donald Lewis, 161–80. London: Cameron May.

Fink, Carsten, and Martín Molinuevo. 2007. *East Asian Free Trade Agreements in Services: Roaring Tigers or Timid Pandas?* East Asia and Pacific Region Report 40175, World Bank, Washington, DC.

Gao, Henry S. 2004. "The Closer Economic Partnership Arrangement (CEPA) between Mainland China and Hong Kong: Legal and Economic Analyses." In *Trading Arrangements in the Pacific Rim: ASEAN and APEC*, ed. Paul J. Davidson (looseleaf). New York: Oceana. http://ssrn.com/abstract=752785.

Goncalves, Marilyne Pereira, and Constantinos Stephanou. 2007. "Financial Services and Trade Agreements in Latin America and the Caribbean: An Overview." Policy Research Working Paper 4181, World Bank, Washington, DC.

Key, Sydney. 2003. *The Doha Round and Financial Services Negotiations*. Washington, DC: AEI Press. http://www.aei.org/book/456.

Sauvé, Pierre, and Karsten Steinfatt. 2001. "Financial Services and the WTO: What Next?" In *Open Doors: Foreign Participation in Financial Systems in Developing Countries*, ed. Robert Litan, Paul Masson, and Michael Pomerleano, 351–86. Washington, DC: Brookings Institution Press.

Skipper, Harold D. Jr. 2001. *Insurance in the General Agreement on Trade in Services*. Washington, DC: AEI Press.

CHAPTER 4

Conducting a Trade-Related Regulatory Audit in Financial Services

Pierre Sauvé

International awareness of the advantages of open services markets and their contribution to overall economic development has grown in tandem with recognition that opening services markets to foreign competition is no easy task. Doing so involves a broad and complex set of policies, regulatory instruments, institutions, and constituencies—domestic and foreign, public and private. Experience has shown that considerable care must be given to assessing the nature, pace, and sequencing of regulatory reform and liberalization undertakings if they are to meaningfully sustain a country's growth and development prospects. These considerations are of particular salience in the financial sector, given the sector's complexity, regulatory intensity, and systemic importance. Moreover, further problems may arise from noneconomic considerations, such as the access to credit by poor households or by small corporate borrowers.

The author is grateful to Panagiotis Delimatsis, senior research fellow at the World Trade Institute, for his assistance in preparing the nonconforming measures in financial services listed in annex 4A. Annex 4B draws on work by Pierre Sauvé that appeared in OECD (2002).

This chapter highlights a number of considerations during the preparations and the conduct of negotiations on trade in services, including financial services, especially by developing countries and emerging economies. Particular emphasis is placed on the relationship between market opening and domestic regulation in services markets by offering a rationale and methodology for approaching multilateral or preferential services negotiations. Trade negotiations should be seen as an opportunity to conduct an audit of domestic regulatory regimes, practices, and institutions, which helps assess current practices and the potential for further reform efforts.

Preparing for Services Negotiations

The complexity of services sector reform and the critical need for sound regulation can present formidable challenges, especially to developing countries, which often have weak regulatory regimes and enforcement capacities.[1] Such countries need gradual liberalization and investment in trade-capacity building.

Aside from weaker implementation capacities, developing countries are also likely to face difficulties in identifying where their negotiating interests—both offensive and defensive—ultimately lie in the services field. Thus, strengthening negotiating capacities is crucial for these countries.

To share the gains arising from the reciprocal opening of services markets, developing countries must overcome what for many of them are acute informational deficits regarding the nature and importance of impediments to their own services exports in foreign markets. Strengthening domestic processes of policy dialogue and consultations with key stakeholders in the private sector and civil society and, just as importantly, within government, can help address such an informational deficit.

Putting together targeted negotiating requests also requires detailed information about the full range of measures preventing effective access to the markets of key trading partners. The breadth of services trade and the diversity of sectors render information gathering a large and complex task—one that many developing countries, even larger ones, find difficult.

Similarly, to make meaningful negotiating offers, a country needs to feel confident of its own ability to manage the regulatory, sectoral, and economywide consequences of such offers. Developing a healthy culture of two-way consultations with key domestic stakeholders in both the public and private spheres is thus a likely precondition for harnessing the development potential of trade agreements and for securing a progressively higher level of liberalization commitments.

Although all members of the World Trade Organization (WTO) suffer an information deficit in services negotiations, many developing countries can be at a particular disadvantage, lacking the large network of embassies, organized industry associations, foreign affiliates, chambers of commerce, and even individual company presence in foreign markets from which governments in many developed countries can source information. Such uneven access to information means the negotiating requests emanating from some developed partners tend to be more specific in nature, focusing on previously identified and rank-ordered, sector-specific, or horizontal measures whose progressive elimination or liberalization is being sought. Many developing countries are unlikely to be in a position to make similar types of requests, particularly in the early stages of the request-offer process.

Making the most of engagement in services negotiations also implies being clear on the nature and implications of the negotiating proposals being tabled. The Uruguay Round's General Agreement on Trade in Services (GATS) negotiations saw a number of instances in which WTO members scheduled full commitments with no remaining limitations on national treatment and market access whose ultimate commercial value to their trading partners was greatly diminished by their incomplete implementation and enforcement.

More, therefore, needs to be done to assist services negotiators from developing countries in achieving successful services negotiations. Two important starting points should be mentioned in this regard. First, negotiators need to take a broad view of trade and investment in services and the multiplicity of measures whose combined effects ultimately determine the quality of scheduled commitments. This task is not easy given the great sectoral diversity of services markets and the tendency to treat sectors and various policy instruments in isolation from one another. This difficulty is magnified by the lack of sectoral expertise that many developing countries have in trade-related regulatory matters.

Second, negotiators need to be in a position to connect all the dots that make up development-enhancing commitments. That is, they must be able to formulate a series of pertinent policy questions (and ultimately an effective negotiating strategy) that will help ensure effective access—and not only access in theory—at the end of the negotiations.

To make the latter point more specific, note that opening services markets typically involves a considerable number of policy parameters and various layers of impediments, some of which may overlap. First, many of these impediments are narrowly sectoral in character and relate to a host of regulatory measures that may potentially affect the quality and certainty of access to, and presence in, services markets. Second, many other policy parameters may not be sector specific, relating to more generic or horizontal policy measures. And third, still other policy measures may lie outside the parameters of what is traditionally considered the central focus of services negotiations (for example, standards-related issues, competition policy, and government procurement).

An important question confronting governments, then, concerns the practical implications of legally binding commitments under services agreements and what commitments to make. Clearly, the answer depends to some extent on the offers made by the country's trading partner, both within and outside the services negotiations. At the same time, however, choosing what to bind and at what level is likely to have important implications for domestic economic performance and regulatory conduct. In particular, the differences between de novo liberalization and mere commitments to bind the status quo are substantial.

Governments thus need to be clear on the broad policy objectives they would like to achieve through their services agreements. Such clarity implies determining the extent to which countries may wish to use such agreements as an anchor of ongoing policy reforms or as a precursor of future reforms (notably through a precommitment to future market opening). The idea here is to gain a greater ex ante sense of the likely opportunity costs flowing from various approaches to liberalization and policy bindings under services agreements (including the choice *not* to make new or improved binding commitments).

Governments also need to gain greater clarity over the desirable length of transition periods toward greater market openness. Liberalization cannot be achieved or decreed overnight, particularly in services markets, but is typically best pursued in a progressive, orderly, and transparent manner, so as both to allow incumbents to prepare for greater competition and to allow the government to anticipate and mitigate possible distributional downsides and put in place a proper regulatory framework.

Weaknesses in regulatory regimes and regulatory enforcement capacity often are a main cause of the reluctance of developing countries to schedule bound commitments, because implementing those commitments and reaping their expected benefits requires a sound underlying regulatory framework. Providing technical assistance to developing countries for building regulatory capacity and strengthening institutions should thus be an important dimension of any aid-for-trade package in services negotiations.

Trade and investment liberalization is hardly ever without distributional consequences. The gains and losses arising from a change in domestic conditions of competition can affect different groups in society, and a careful assessment needs to be made of the effect of liberalization on vulnerable groups, including (workers in) state-owned enterprises, geographically remote households or firms, and low-income communities, all of which may have more limited access to finance.

Addressing the Challenge of Domestic Regulation in Services Trade

Many services sectors are highly regulated. Such regulation is intended to achieve a range of policy objectives, such as consumer protection, equitable or universal access to health and educational services, environmental protection, and—in the case of financial services—enhancement of a country's financial system stability. Such regulation is an essential part of both good governance and a well-functioning market economy. Accordingly, both GATS and the preferential services agreements recognize the right of countries to regulate the supply of services. Furthermore, given asymmetries with respect to the degree of development of regulations in different countries, trade agreements covering services typically also recognize the particular need of developing countries to exercise this right by introducing new regulation in the future. This right is usually recognized through the inclusion of a *prudential carve-out*.

Liberalization of trade in services can intersect with domestic regulation in two main ways. First, in making regulations, governments need to take into account a wide range of factors. One consideration may be the economic outcome of such regulation, which may also affect trade and investment. Information on the potential economic and trade costs may assist governments in seeking the most efficient regulatory means of achieving their policy objectives. Indeed, positive effects in terms of overall democratic governance are likely to include the more efficient and transparent design, implementation, and enforcement of regulations.

Second, the process of liberalizing services markets can require new or different types of regulatory intervention. For example, ensuring that the expected benefits of liberalization are realized or that important policy objectives continue to be achieved within the new market structure may be important. Thus, liberalization of services markets, far from entailing deregulation, often necessitates regulatory reform or reregulation.

This process of regulatory review and development involves the consideration of a number of factors, including, but not limited to, the following:

- What is the purpose of the regulation? What policy objective is to be achieved?
- Will the proposed regulation be effective in achieving that objective? If so, is it the most efficient way to achieve the objective?
- How will the regulation be implemented?

These questions are merely indicative and are certainly not exhaustive. Countries may not view all of these points as being important, or they may assign different degrees of importance to different factors. Considering and weighing these different factors, while essential for effective liberalization that serves national objectives, including development or equity objectives, can be a challenging process, in particular for developing countries with limited administrative capacity.

Because the financial sector ranks among the most heavily regulated of all major services sectors, the relationship between domestic regulation and financial market opening is a crucial element of trade policy discussions in the sector. Financial market opening is often viewed as involving a significant qualitative shift in the *nature* of financial market regulation rather than a far-reaching reduction in its incidence. Simply stated, pro-competitive regulatory reform aimed at promoting new market entry and the greater contestability of domestic financial markets need not be regarded as an exercise in regulatory disarmament. Precisely because financial liberalization often requires significant amounts of new regulation, countries—particularly those with weak regulatory capacities—may be loath to undertake far-reaching liberalization commitments in the context of trade agreements.

More often than not, given the complexity and slow pace of domestic regulatory reform efforts, countries will prefer to adopt a sequenced approach to market opening. Proper sequencing can help overcome the legitimate concerns (a) of host countries over the readiness of domestic financial institutions to face greater competitive challenges and (b) of financial authorities over the risks of more open financial markets. Trade agreements are particularly well suited to the pursuit of a sequenced approach to market opening, promoting orderly adjustment over time and allowing countries to bolster their regulatory and supervisory capacities prior to or in the context of market opening.

An important aspect of prudential regulations is that they may be set at a level that could still be perceived as a de facto violation of national treatment—if, for instance, such requirements fall more heavily on new (foreign) entrants than on (domestic) incumbents, thereby conferring an edge to the latter. This aspect illustrates the difficulty of compiling a full assessment of trade-inconsistent regulatory measures in the financial sector. Thus, performing a trade-related regulatory audit whose aim is to identify all measures that could be deemed to violate the concept of equal competitive opportunities is not as straightforward as it may at first appear.

A Trade-Related Regulatory Audit in Services: Means and Ends

The process of negotiations in services trade is both time and information intensive. This aspect may place a particularly heavy burden on negotiators from developing countries, which are likely to be handicapped by significant human resource constraints and limited sectoral expertise, both in Geneva and in national capitals.

The two-way interaction afforded by request-offer negotiations in services can nonetheless be put to good use if it can underpin attempts to benchmark a country's domestic approach to services regulation with that of its main trading partners, thereby helping to identify means of achieving greater policy convergence or to move in the direction of best (often pro-competitive) regulatory practices. Such benchmarking—and the related need (in response to potential requests from trading partners) to identify more precisely what policies and measures can (and cannot) be addressed in the negotiations—may also spur a useful policy dialogue among trade officials, sectoral regulators, and officials in other government agencies and departments, as well as among key stakeholders in business and civil society. This dialogue may further clarify the policy objectives pursued in the negotiations.

Performing an audit of a country's regulatory regime in the context of negotiations on services trade and investment liberalization may generate positive policy spillovers in terms of domestic regulatory conduct and design and contribute to a strengthening of consultations within and outside government in the services field. Among the main reasons governments might be interested in engaging in a trade-related regulatory audit are the following:

- Ensuring that key regulatory objectives are met in the most efficient manner (that is, in the manner that is least wasteful of scarce public resources), including prudential or social policy objectives.

- Identifying antiquated or inefficient regulations and adopting international best practices. In the field of financial services, such an effort may allow a benchmarking of the degree to which domestic regulations approximate agreed-on international standards.
- Encouraging, where feasible, the adoption of (pro-competitive) regulation that is market-access friendly.
- Building trust within the government (by encouraging a unified approach to domestic regulation) through closer dialogue among trade negotiators, line ministries, and sectoral regulators.
- Deepening the dialogue with key stakeholders in government (including regional and local governments), as well as with producers and consumers.
- Anticipating—and preparing for—the negotiating (market-opening) requests of key trading partners.

A useful starting point for such an audit is to prepare a list of nonconforming measures—that is, the equivalent of a negative list of measures that would be in breach of the key liberalizing provisions found in trade agreements, including national treatment, market access (quantitative restrictions), local presence requirements, and most-favored-nation (MFN) treatment. The following should be described comprehensively:

- The sectoral nature of the listed non-conforming measures (for definitional purposes)
- The level of government at which they are applied (that is, national, subnational, or municipal)
- Their legal anchoring (that is, the full citation of the law or regulation in question)
- The precise nature of their nonconformity.

Annex 4A provides examples of the negative listing of nonconforming measures in financial services found in a number of preferential trade agreements concluded by countries in Asia.

The use of such an audit was pioneered in the context of preparing the negative lists of nonconforming measures defining the parties' legally binding commitments under the North American Free Trade Agreement (NAFTA). In Canada, over the course of four months, a small group of interns, chosen for their expertise in law, compiled such a list of federal measures under the supervision of a member of the services negotiating team. When a draft of the inventory was completed, the

Canadian trade-negotiating team was able to sit down with representatives from the line ministries and sectoral regulatory agencies and ask them to verify the accuracy of the information. The team was able to engage in a policy dialogue with the representatives on the rationale behind restrictive measures, the means available to achieve such objectives through other measures, and the scope for removing such nonconforming measures.

The negative listing exercise described here focuses on measures that either are overtly discriminatory (in the case of measures violating the national treatment and MFN provisions) or are overtly limiting to the degree of competition allowed in market (in the case of market-access or nondiscriminatory quantitative restrictions).

As noted earlier, such an audit may not always provide a full reading of all nondiscriminatory measures, especially prudential measures that may still be unduly burdensome or possible disguised restrictions to trade. Identifying such measures is inherently more difficult and requires considerably more dialogue among trade negotiators, line ministries, and sectoral regulators, as well as substantial technical competence on the part of trade ministries. The last point is further complicated by the tendency, which is prevalent in most countries, for financial officials (rather than trade officials) to lead negotiations on trade and investment in financial services.[2]

Despite those caveats, experience shows that a trade-related regulatory audit that maps the universe of explicitly restrictive governmental measures affecting trade and investment in financial services (and trade in services more broadly) can still yield important gains in transparency. In turn, such transparency can help promote a culture of pro-competitive regulatory reform. Conducting an audit is indeed a useful means of preparing for services negotiations: it allows the individuals involved to master the sectoral intricacies and the technical details that are the very currency of services negotiations, it provides services suppliers with a one-stop inventory of restrictive measures maintained at home and in the markets of key trading partners, and it delineates a roadmap of measures to target and rank order in future negotiations. None of this is readily possible without precise information on the regulatory status quo. Conducting an audit and, better still, agreeing to list nonconforming measures (whether in a legally binding manner as under NAFTA-type negative-list agreements or merely for transparency purposes, as is the case in the GATS approach of hybrid commitments) is useful both for negotiation purposes and for domestic reforms. In the area of financial services, a regulatory audit centered on restrictive measures may also be

of use to the extent that it focuses attention on the economywide incidence of various types of discriminatory measures or measures that
inhibit market access, such as provisions governing capital transactions
(for example, capital controls) that may be negotiated in other chapters
of a trade agreement.

Key Questions Involving Services Negotiations and Domestic Regulations

The reader is referred to annex 4B for the key questions that arise in connection with the trade- and investment-related incidence of domestic regulation. These questions related to the following:

- Measures affecting market access, including cross-border supply
- Measures governing ownership and commercial presence
- Regulatory measures (including of a prudential nature)
- Measures relating to licensing
- Measures governing the movement of natural persons
- Preferential liberalization measures
- Universal services obligations.

Annex 4A: Examples of Nonconforming Measures in Financial Services

This annex lists some examples of nonconforming measures found in
existing free trade agreements (FTAs).

China–Association of Southeast Asian Nations (ASEAN) FTA: Singapore's Schedule of Commitments

Sector: Financial services.

Subsector: Acceptance of deposits and other repayable funds from the
public.

Industry classification: Not applicable.

Type of reservation: Market access and national treatment.

Level of government: National.

Description: Only institutions licensed or approved as banks, merchant
banks, and finance companies can accept deposits. If a foreign financial

institution is subject to legislation in its home country that requires the institution to confer lower priority to depositors of its foreign offices vis-à-vis the home-country depositors in receivership or winding-up proceedings, the Monetary Authority of Singapore (MAS) may exercise appropriate differentiated measures against that foreign financial institution in Singapore to safeguard the interest of the Singapore office's depositors. MAS may require foreign banks to incorporate under Singapore law.

Phase-out: None.

China-ASEAN FTA: Singapore's Schedule of Commitments

Sector: Financial services.

Subsector: Life insurance services, including annuity, disability income, accident, and health insurance services.

Industry classification: Not applicable.

Type of reservation: Market access and national treatment.

Level of government: National.

Description: None, except (a) foreign parties can acquire equity stakes of only up to 49 percent in aggregate in locally owned insurance companies, provided that the acquisition does not result in any foreign party being the largest shareholder; (b) insurance companies must be established as branches or subsidiaries; and (c) for activities related to the use, including via investment, of monies from any social security, public retirement, or statutory savings scheme, special provisions apply.

Phase-out: None.

Japan-Thailand FTA: Thailand's Schedule of Commitments

Sector: Financial services.

Subsector: Life insurance services.

Industry classification: CPC 81211.

Type of reservation: Market access.

Level of government: National.

Description: Foreign equity participation is limited to 25 percent of registered share capital. New establishment is subject to license approved by the Minister of Finance with the consent of the cabinet.

Phase-out: None.

Japan-Thailand FTA: Japan's Schedule of Commitments

Sector: Financial services.

Subsector: Insurance and insurance-related services.

Industry classification: Not applicable.

Type of reservation: Market access.

Level of government: National.

Description: Commercial presence is in principle required for insurance contracts on the following items and any liability arising from them: (a) goods being transported within Japan and (b) ships with Japanese registration that are not used for international maritime transport. Commercial presence is required for insurance intermediation services in Japan.

Phase-out: None.

Japan-Philippines Economic Partnership Agreement (EPA): Philippine's Schedule of Commitments

Sector: Financial services.

Subsector: Commercial banking.

Industry classification: Not applicable.

Type of reservation: Market access and national treatment.

Level of government: National.

Description: Foreign capital participation in commercial banks is limited as follows: (a) acquisition of up to 60 percent of the voting stock of an existing bank and (b) investment in up to 60 percent of the voting stock of a new banking subsidiary incorporated under the laws of the Philippines. Non-Filipino citizens may become members of the board of directors of a bank to the extent of the foreign participation in the equity of that bank.

Phase-out: None.

Japan-Philippines EPA: Japan's Schedule of Commitments

Sector: Financial services.

Subsector: Banking services.

Industry classification: JSIC 612 (banks, except the central bank); JSIC 621 (financial institutions for small businesses).

Type of reservation: Market access and national treatment.

Level of government: Central government.

Measures: Deposit Insurance Law (Law No. 34 of 1971), article 2.

Description: The deposit insurance system covers only financial institutions that have their head offices within the jurisdiction of Japan.

Phase-out: None.

Singapore-U.S. FTA: U.S. Schedule of Commitments

Sector: Financial services.

Subsector: Insurance services.

Industry classification: Not applicable.

Type of reservation: National treatment.

Level of government: Federal.

Measures: 46 Code of Federal Regulation, section 249.9.

Description: When more than 50 percent of the value of a maritime vessel whose hull was built under federally guaranteed mortgage funds is insured by a non-U.S. insurer, the insurer must demonstrate that the risk was substantially first offered in the U.S. market.

Phase-out: None.

Singapore-U.S. FTA: Singapore's Schedule of Commitments

Sector: Financial services.

Subsector: Banking services.

Industry Classification: Not applicable.

Type of reservation: National treatment.

Level of government: National.

Measures: Banking Act, Chapter 19; Central Provided Fund Act, Chapter 36.

Description: Only foreign banks with qualifying full bank privileges may apply to provide Supplementary Retirement Scheme accounts and Central Provident Fund Investment Scheme accounts. Only foreign banks with qualifying full bank privileges will be permitted to apply to accept fixed deposits under the Central Provident Fund Investment Scheme and Minimum Sum Scheme.

Phase-out: None.

Singapore-U.S. Free Trade Agreement: Singapore's Schedule of Commitments

Sector: Financial services.

Subsector: Banking services.

Industry classification: Not applicable.

Type of reservation: Market access and national treatment.

Level of government: National.

Measures: Banking Act, Chapter 19; MAS Notice 619.

Description: Only a maximum of 20 new wholesale bank licenses will be granted by the MAS between June 30, 2001, and June 30, 2003. Quantitative limits on the number of wholesale bank licenses will be removed for U.S. banks three years after the date of entry into force of this agreement. Wholesale banks are not permitted to (a) accept Singapore-dollar fixed deposits of less than S$250,000; (b) offer savings accounts; (c) operate interest-bearing Singapore-dollar current accounts for natural persons who are Singapore residents; (d) issue Singapore-dollar bonds and negotiable certificates of deposit, unless requirements pertaining to minimum maturity period, minimum denomination, or class of investors contained in the *Guidelines for Operation of Wholesale Banks* issued by the MAS are complied with.

Phase-out: None.

Annex 4B: Services Negotiations and Domestic Regulation—Key Questions

Measures Affecting Market Access, Including Cross-Border Supply

1. Are there policy restrictions on new entry? If so, do such restrictions affect all new entrants or specifically entry by foreign services suppliers? Is there a limit on the number of firms (foreign firms) allowed in the market?
2. If entry is restricted, what are the reasons provided by the government? Where and how clearly are such limits spelled out?
3. Are there services that locally established foreign firms are not allowed to supply?
4. Can foreign firms or services suppliers access the market on a cross-border basis (that is, without an established presence)?
5. Are there any services that nonestablished foreign firms are prevented from offering in the importing market?

6. If cross-border supply is restricted, what are the reasons provided by the government? Where and how clearly are such limits spelled out?
7. Are there restrictions on cross-border purchases of certain categories of services by consumers (firms or individuals) in the importing country?
8. Can nonestablished foreign services providers solicit business from foreign customers on a cross-border basis?
9. Are there any restrictions on the electronic transmission of services by nonestablished foreign services providers?
10. Can the policy rationale for restricting cross-border supply be addressed through other less trade- or investment-restricting means (for example, bonding requirements)?
11. Are foreign suppliers required to establish a local presence as a precondition for serving the importing market?
12. Does the state or a designated provider hold exclusive or monopoly rights in particular market segments?
13. Is entry in the sector subject to economic needs tests? What is the policy rationale for maintaining quantitative limits to competition in the sector? Where and how are such tests spelled out?
14. Are there restrictions on the purchase of land by nationals or foreigners?

Measures Governing Ownership or Commercial Presence

1. Is private ownership in the provision of services allowed?
2. Is foreign ownership in the provision of services allowed? If so, what is the maximum foreign equity permitted?
3. Are foreign suppliers required to establish locally through a particular legal form of establishment (that is, subsidiary, branch, representative office)?
4. Are such establishments subject to investment screening on the part of the host country? Is there a value threshold above which mergers and acquisitions in the sector are subject to investment screening or vetting by the host country's competition authority?
5. Are foreign-established operators subject to particular performance requirements (for example, local hiring and training, local sourcing)?
6. Does the host country restrict payments or transfers by locally established foreign operators to their parent companies in the home country?
7. Are foreign firms required to form joint ventures with domestic firms to provide services in the domestic market?
8. Are there restrictions regarding the joint ventures, partnerships, or associations that locally established foreign firms can form with domestic firms?

9. Are there restrictions on the use of the international or foreign name of a firm?

Regulatory Measures

1. Who regulates the sector in the importing country? Are regulatory agencies independent from the relevant sectoral ministries?
2. Is the sector subject to potentially trade- or investment-restricting regulation maintained at the subnational level? Where can information on the nature of such policy measures be obtained?
3. How transparent is the regulatory regime in the importing country? How are laws and regulatory decisions made public?
4. Are stakeholders consulted or allowed prior comment in advance of regulatory decisions?
5. In what sectors do foreign services providers require prior authorization before entering or serving the market? Where and how clearly are such authorization procedures spelled out? Are authorization procedures maintained at the subnational level?
6. Do foreign firms enjoy equal standing before regulatory bodies in commenting on proposed legislative or regulatory changes?
7. What recourses exist in the importing country for foreign services providers to appeal administrative decisions? Are such appeal procedures available at both the federal and subnational levels? Do foreign services suppliers enjoy standing before such bodies? Must foreign services providers have a local presence to enjoy standing?
8. Does the government or a relevant regulatory agency regulate prices or tariffs?
9. Do foreign suppliers face particular restrictions in becoming members of professional bodies or industry associations in the importing country?
10. Which of the following government programs are available to locally established foreign services providers: (a) tax breaks, (b) preferential access to credit, (c) below-market interest rates, (d) export financing, (e) government-provided risk insurance, (f) underwriting of feasibility studies, and (g) subsidies for research and development activities?
11. Are any specific services standards enforced? If so, by whom? Do such standards comply with international standards? Are standards-related matters also subject to subnational regulation? Where can foreign services suppliers find information on standards-related issues in the importing country?

Measures Relating to Licensing

1. If the number of providers is not restricted by policy, what are the main types of licenses that providers must obtain to operate in the market?
2. What regulatory agencies are responsible for issuing licenses? Where and how clear are conditions governing the granting of licenses spelled out?
3. Are licenses required of domestic or foreign companies (or both)?
4. Are foreign services suppliers subject to different or additional licensing conditions from domestic suppliers?
5. Is the validity of a license and the right to supply the market restricted temporally or geographically? Do licenses grant exclusivity periods or market segments?
6. Where services markets are regulated at both the national and subnational levels, are separate licenses required to supply services in each jurisdiction? Is a local presence required in each jurisdiction for licensing purposes?
7. In sectors in which the number of services providers is limited by policy, through what mechanisms and according to what criteria are licenses allocated?
8. Once licenses have been allocated, are there restrictions on the ability of foreign-established services suppliers to sell or dispose of their licenses?

Measures Governing the Movement of Natural Persons

1. Are there residency, permanent residency, or nationality requirements for any of the following categories of personnel employed by locally established foreign services suppliers: (a) members of the board of directors, (b) executives, (c) managers, (d) key personnel or experts, (e) unskilled workers, and (f) other staff categories?
2. Are there particular categories of intracorporate transferees or professionals whose entry and stay is subject to labor certification tests in the importing country?
3. Does the importing country provide scope for allowing nonprofessional essential personnel to enjoy temporary entry privileges (that is, no labor certification tests) during the execution of a services contract by a foreign services provider?
4. What scope exists for the importing country to grant temporary entry privileges (no labor certification tests) to spouses of intracompany transferees granted temporary entry rights?

Preferential Liberalization Measures

1. Are there any preferential agreements affecting the supply of services in the importing country? What services-related measures are subject to preferential treatment? Are preferential measures maintained at the subnational level? Do preferential measures also apply to the movement of natural persons? If so, what categories are covered?
2. What conditions must foreign services suppliers fulfill to meet the requirements of existing mutual recognition agreements to which home-country services suppliers are parties? Do foreign services providers need to be locally established (that is, have a local presence) to be eligible for participation in such agreements?
3. Does the importing country maintain preferential access arrangements for services providers from developing countries?

Universal Services Obligations

1. Does the government maintain universal services or access obligations?
2. How are these obligations defined?
3. Are smaller firms exempt from such obligations?

Notes

1. This section draws on Sauvé (2006).
2. The advantages of such a split of competencies are depicted, for instance, in the case study on Colombia in chapter 6 of this volume.

References and Other Resources

Delimatsis, Panagiotis. 2007. "Due Process and 'Good' Regulation Embedded in the GATS: Disciplining Regulatory Behaviour in Services through Article VI of the GATS." *Journal of International Economic Law* 10 (1): 13–50.

Krajewski, Markus. 2006. "Services Liberalization in Regional Trade Agreements: Lessons for GATS 'Unfinished Business.'" In *Regional Trade Agreements and the WTO Legal System*, ed. Lorand Bartels and Federico Ortino, 175–200. London: Oxford University Press.

Mattoo, Aaditya, and Pierre Sauvé, eds. 2003. *Domestic Regulation and Services Trade Liberalization*. Washington, DC: World Bank and Oxford University Press.

OECD (Organisation for Economic Co-operation and Development). 2002. *Managing Request-Offer Negotiations under GATS*. Paris: OECD.

Sauvé, Pierre. 2002. "Completing the GATS Framework: Addressing Uruguay Round Leftovers." *Aussenwirtschaft* 57 (3): 310–41.

———. 2006. "Toward an Aid for Trade Regime for Services." *BRIDGES* 10 (7): 15–17.

PART II

Country Case Studies

CHAPTER 5

Trade in Financial Services

The Case of Chile

Raúl E. Sáez

The purpose of this chapter is to describe and analyze Chile's experience with the liberalization of trade in financial services, starting from the unilateral measures taken in the 1970s to the commitments in the negotiations with the European Union (EU) and the United States in the early years of the 21st century. In addition, this chapter argues that these past experiences helped Chile's government, its supervisory agencies, and its private sector better address current negotiations on trade in financial services.

The chapter is organized as follows. The first section provides a general overview of Chile's economic and regulatory policies on financial trade in services that evolved to the point when the negotiations with the EU and the United States began. The next section addresses the international commitments undertaken by Chile during this period, and the third section analyzes what issues were involved in bilateral negotiations on financial services and how Chile prepared to address them.

The views presented in this chapter are those of the author and do not represent those of the government of Chile; neither do they constitute a legal interpretation of the agreements and legal texts cited. Constantinos Stephanou, Luis Oscar Herrera, Christian Larraín, Sebastián Sáez, and Pierre Sauvé provided comments and suggestions. None of them is responsible for remaining errors.

The fourth section then considers how the negotiations were organized, including the relationship with stakeholders in both the public (Central Bank and regulatory agencies) and the private (financial services organizations) sectors. The next section examines in detail the negotiations with the EU and the United States, including the major features of the texts negotiated and the commitments undertaken by Chile. The consequences of these commitments and the negotiations are the subject of the sixth section, followed by a seventh section that draws some policy lessons from Chile's experience. The chapter ends with some final thoughts on preparing for a bilateral negotiation in financial services.

Chile's Financial System

This section first describes the liberalization of financial services in Chile from the 1970s onward, the financial crisis of the early 1980s, the policy responses to the crisis, and the consolidation during the 1990s, leading to full convertibility in 2001. Second, it presents the situation of the financial system, including the degree of openness to foreign providers, on the eve of negotiations with the EU and the United States.

Unilateral Financial Services Liberalization in Chile

Chile was an early reformer in the Latin American context.[1] In the mid-1970s, the Chilean capital market was considered a textbook case of financial repression (Reinstein and Rosende 2001). Thus, the first measures adopted by the military regime that took power in 1973 aimed at liberalizing and privatizing the financial system.

All state-owned banks were privatized, with only the BancoEstado remaining as a state-owned bank. Specialized banks were phased out, ending the existing segmentation and promoting banks that would provide a full range of deposit-taking and lending services. Other measures adopted from 1974 onward included the freeing of interest rates, the elimination of credit controls, and the reduction of reserve requirements on deposits. Regarding cross-border liberalization, direct access to foreign credit was authorized, and banks were allowed to borrow overseas and to lend those funds domestically. Moreover, foreign banks were authorized to open branches or subsidiaries (Marshall 1991). These reforms led to much innovation in services, and new products emerged in all major segments of the market: consumption, enterprises, and mortgages. Nonetheless, the share of foreign banks in the domestic market remained quite small: in 1981, they held less than 7 percent of deposits and provided 6.5 percent of outstanding loans (Marshall 1991).

Similar measures were taken in the insurance industry: insurance premiums were freed; foreign companies were allowed to enter the Chilean market, either by setting up subsidiaries or by buying shares of domestically owned companies; and the purchase of insurance abroad was permitted.

One of the most fundamental reforms was introduced in 1981. The existing pay-as-you-go pension system was replaced by a new system of pension funds, based on individual and compulsory retirement savings accounts.[2] The pension funds are managed by private pension fund managers (*administradoras de fondos de pensiones*, or AFPs) that have only certain financial instruments at their disposal. The range of eligible instruments and the limits on them have varied over time. Initially, the funds could be invested only in fixed-income instruments: bonds issued by the Central Bank and the government, time deposits, and bonds issued by private enterprises. Stocks from corporations became eligible in 1989, and investment in collective investment schemes and derivatives was authorized in 1998. Investment in foreign-issued securities was allowed at the end of 1990, with an upper limit of 10 percent of the fund. This limit was gradually increased over the decade, reaching 16 percent for overall investment abroad with a sublimit of 10 percent for variable-income securities in 1999 (Cowan and De Gregorio 2005).

In parallel, the health care industry was reformed, enabling employees to contract with a private health care plan using the compulsory 7 percent payroll tax for health coverage. An alternative option allowed them to remain with the government-managed National Health Fund (Fondo Nacional de Salud, or FONASA).

However, no reforms regarding bank supervision were adopted, despite a growing "moral hazard" problem after the Central Bank established a guarantee on deposits in 1977 (Reinstein and Rosende 2001). Only when some of the problems related to insufficient supervision became evident as the financial crisis of the early 1980s broke out were minimum principles of supervision established.

The financial crisis started in the second half of 1981 and reached its climax in January 1983, when the two major private banks, two other banks, and four financial companies had to be taken over, and two other banks and one financial company were closed down.[3] As a result, 50 percent of outstanding loans ended up under state control (Reinstein and Rosende 2001). One of the key factors that accounted for the severity of the financial crisis was insufficient banking regulation despite the increased liberalization of the financial sector. Some authors argue that this situation was the result of efforts not to weaken the market's role through a heavy regulatory framework (see Ffrench-Davis 2003; Meller 1996; Reinstein and Rosende 2001).

In 1986, after the crisis, a new banking act was passed. The new law explicitly established the financial services that a bank can provide. These services are, among others, to take deposits, issue bonds, provide loans, perform foreign exchange operations, and issue credit cards. The law allows banks to provide other services, but only through completely separate subsidiaries with their own capital and management. Such subsidiaries are divided into two categories: (a) those that are complementary to the banking business and (b) those that support the banking business. The former include securities agencies, stock brokerages, mutual funds managers, leasing companies, credit card administrators, and financial advisory agencies. The latter comprise companies that provide collection services and electronic transfer networks. New regulations were introduced for lending: loans to a single debtor, including parties related to the bank (a major cause of the collapse of banks in 1982–83), are limited to a percentage of the bank's net worth.

The 1986 banking act required banks to maintain a technical reserve in cash or in Central Bank bonds. In addition, a full guarantee was established for sight deposits. In the case of time deposits, a partial guarantee was introduced, covering 90 percent of the deposit per person up to a maximum amount. The Superintendencia de Bancos e Instituciones Financieras (Superintendency of Banks and Financial Institutions, or SBIF) has to publish, at least three times a year, information and updates of the institutions, and the institutions have to hire at least two private risk-rating agencies. One of the major innovations of the 1986 act is the requirement for banks to make provisions regarding risky loans. Finally, the new law sets a debt-to-capital ratio of 20. If the actual ratio surpasses this limit, the bank is presumed to be at risk, and therefore corrective actions must be taken. Moreover, the 1986 law maintained the separation between banking, insurance, and pension fund management. Banks could not—and still cannot—participate in the business of managing pension funds or insurance.

The new law did not change the operation of foreign banks in Chile. It allows them to operate as subsidiaries (that is, Chilean stock corporations) or branches of foreign corporations.[4] Under both legal forms, foreign-owned banks can provide the same financial services as domestically owned banks, and they undertake the same separation of activities. For regulatory purposes, both subsidiaries and branches of foreign banks receive the same treatment. That is, they have the same minimum capital requirement, and they are considered to be entities separate from their parent companies. In other words, what Chile's banking act defines as a *branch* is not a direct branch. The only difference between a subsidiary and a branch is that the latter has no board of directors in Chile.

The reforms adopted in the years following the crisis were aimed at the market failures and risks involved in financial intermediation, particularly banking. They were not intended to reestablish strict controls, state-owned financial institutions, credit controls, fixed interest rates, and other related measures. In other words, no backtracking occurred in financial liberalization. Indeed, and quite to the contrary, plans were made for the reprivatization of the financial institutions that were taken over by the government.[5]

In this postcrisis period, the participation of foreign-owned banks started to become substantial. At the end of 1984, their share in deposits was already 16 percent and further increased to 18 percent in 1989. In the case of loans, their share rose from 9 percent in 1984 to 15 percent in 1989 (Marshall 1991).

In the 1990s, the banking industry was again fully private (with the exception of the BancoEstado) and showed significant growth. Loans as a percentage of GDP grew from 59 percent in 1990 to 68 percent in 1998, the number of branches increased from 1,121 to 1,527, and the number of employees rose from 36,000 to 44,000. The spread between loans and deposits fell from 9 percent in the early 1990s to 4 percent in 1997.[6] Through their subsidiaries, banks diversified their activities into leasing, mutual fund management, financial advisory services, and stock brokerage.

In 1997, a new reform of the General Banking Act was adopted; it aimed at creating a globally integrated banking system through a mix of deregulation and modernization. This act represented the most significant changes to the regulation of banks since 1986, as follows.

First, the criteria for capital requirements of the 1988 Basel Capital Accord (Basel I) were adopted. Accordingly, minimum capital as a percentage of risk-weighted assets was set at 8 percent. Second, the powers of the SBIF were revised to make them closer to the recommendations of the Basel Committee and, at the same time, to promote a self-regulatory approach. The SBIF was authorized to rate banks according to their management practices and solvency. Third, the scope of activities that banks can perform was expanded. Banks were authorized, through subsidiaries, to provide services such as securitization, factoring, insurance brokerage (excluding insurance related to the pension system), and underwriting. Fourth, the internationalization of banks was encouraged. Banks were allowed to provide cross-border services from Chile to domestic and foreign enterprises operating abroad, and they were authorized to open subsidiaries abroad that provided the same financial services as those provided in Chile.

Finally, objective criteria were established for granting (or rejecting) a banking license. These criteria meant lifting the existing de facto limit on the number of banking licenses and eliminating an economic needs test in bank licensing. The new law also removed the requirement that all investments in the banking sector had to go through the investment regime of Decree Law 600.[7]

The liberalizing measures described previously proved very helpful during bilateral negotiations on trade in financial services a few years later.

Foreign Exchange Controls in Chile

Although not directly related to financial services, the issue of foreign capital controls is important because emerging economies may face different conditions for their application in the context of comprehensive trade agreements.

An understanding of Chile's position regarding capital account controls requires a brief explanation of the legal basis and practice of capital controls in the 1990s, in particular the well-known unremunerated reserve requirement (URR), or *encaje*, on foreign loans. The Central Bank Act, which has constitutional legal standing,[8] states that the Central Bank (Banco Central de Chile) has as its purpose to look after the stability of the currency and the normal functioning of the internal and *external* payments services.[9] For this purpose, the Central Bank can regulate the amount of currency and credit in circulation, the *performance of credit transactions and foreign exchange*, as well as the issuance of regulatory provisions regarding monetary, credit financing, and *foreign exchange matters*.[10] Regarding the foreign exchange transactions, the Central Bank Act specifies the measures that can be adopted, including the following:[11]

- Repatriation payments accrued abroad by individuals and entities resident in Chile[12]
- Reserve requirements on credits, deposits, or investments in foreign currency *originating or sent abroad* with a limit of 40 percent
- Authorization requirements on payment or remittance obligations related to imports of goods and services, royalties, other payments

made in foreign currency abroad or to persons not having residence in Chile and on the remittance of foreign currency for purposes of investments, capital contributions, loans, or deposits abroad

- Restrictions on transactions performed in the "formal exchange market," which was mostly made up of banking institutions
- Limits on holdings in foreign currency or investments denominated in foreign currency that banking entities or persons may maintain within the country or abroad.

As can be seen, the legal power of the Central Bank to adopt measures restricting payments and transfers is quite broad and covers both the current and the capital accounts, which mainly reflects the experience of and lessons learned from the 1982–83 economic and financial crisis.

Extensive exchange controls were reintroduced during the 1982–83 crisis. The controls on outflows were gradually removed during the 1990s and were completely eliminated in April 2001. However, starting in June 1991, the URR on short-term capital inflows was introduced. It required that a certain percentage of foreign capital inflow be deposited in a non-interest-bearing account in the Central Bank. The rate was initially set at 20 percent for a period ranging from 90 days to one year. It was raised to 30 percent in January 1992 and then reduced to 10 percent for foreign loans, capital contributions, and investment. Several reasons were given for the use of the URR (Cowan and De Gregorio 2005): (a) to prevent an appreciation of the peso by reducing capital inflows, (b) to allow for some degree of independence of monetary policy in the context of a managed crawling-peg foreign exchange policy, and (c) to reduce the vulnerability of the economy to "hot money" flows by making short-term inflows relatively more costly.

After the introduction of a freely floating exchange rate in September 1999, a series of measures was adopted that led to the full opening of the capital account. The URR in place during most of the 1990s was reduced to 0 percent in September 1998 and completely eliminated in April 2001, together with all remaining restrictions on foreign exchange operations. However, the Central Bank board retained the power to impose future capital and foreign exchange controls.

Macroeconomic Conditions and the Financial System at the Beginning of the 21st Century

When the time came to negotiate financial services bilaterally with the EU and the United States, Chile had a privatized and liberalized financial market that was open to foreign competition and a financial system that was supervised by strong institutions. The financial system was well capitalized, and foreign-owned institutions and institutional investors provided depth to the market. Similarly, Chile's macroeconomy was characterized by stable economic conditions and prudent fiscal management. Because they are important in determining the consequences of liberalizing financial services, each of these aspects is discussed in turn.

In 2000 and 2001, the Chilean economy grew by 4.5 and 3.4 percent, respectively. Although the economy recovered fast from the effect of the Asian crisis in 1998, in 2002 it was hit by deteriorating external conditions, and GDP growth fell to 2.2 percent (see table 5.1). Inflation was low and fell toward the lower bound of the Central Bank's target range of 2 to 4 percent, while the public sector's net debt reached 11 percent of GDP.[13] In the three years from 2000 to 2002, Chile ran small current account deficits, amounting to 1.2 percent, 1.6 percent, and 0.9 percent of GDP, respectively.

The financial sector was equally stable. In 2000, the solvency indicators were strong, and the share of nonperforming loans in the banking sector was relatively low (see table 5.2). Commercial bank assets exceeded 90 percent of GDP, insurance company assets and net assets of mutual funds were growing, and pension funds represented just under 60 percent of GDP. The state's participation in bank assets and securities trading through its single bank was 13 percent and 2 percent, respectively. An important feature of Chile's domestic financial market is the high participation of foreign-owned financial institutions. In the early years of this decade, it was just under 50 percent in terms of banking assets and above 50 percent in securities trading, insurance premiums, and pension fund management. The country of origin of foreign investment in financial

Table 5.1   Basic Macroeconomic Indicators of the Chilean Economy, 2000–05

Macroeconomic variables	2000	2001	2002	2003	2004	2005
GDP per capita (purchasing power parity, current US$)	9,268	9,696	9,967	10,461	11,290	12,173
Nominal GDP (US$ billion)	75.8	68.6	67.3	73.7	95.0	115.3
Real GDP growth (% annually)	4.5	3.4	2.2	3.9	6.2	6.3
Inflation rate (end of period)	4.5	2.6	2.8	1.1	2.4	3.7
Current account balance (% of GDP)	−1.2	−1.6	−0.9	−1.3	1.7	0.6
Public sector net debt (% of GDP)	10.8	10.9	11.0	13.1	10.8	7.7
Central government balance (% of GDP)	−0.6	−0.5	−1.2	−0.5	2.2	4.7

Sources: Data from the World Bank and International Monetary Fund.

Table 5.2   Basic Characteristics of Chile's Financial System, 2000–05

Characteristic	2000	2001	2002	2003	2004	2005
Size and depth						
Contribution of financial services to GDP (%)[a]	13.6	13.9	13.8	13.2	12.5	12.6
Total commercial bank assets (% of GDP)[a]	93.1	94.8	92.8	88.7	88.5	—
Stock market capitalization (% of GDP)	80.0	82.0	71.0	118.0	124.0	—
Stock market turnover (% of GDP)	8.0	6.0	5.0	9.0	12.0	—
Domestic outstanding government debt (% of GDP)	28.0	27.6	27.8	28.2	21.3	—
Domestic outstanding private sector debt (% of GDP)	18.1	23.0	23.6	27.4	23.2	—
Domestic credit to the private sector (% of GDP)	63.5	63.1	64.9	62.4	63.1	—
Total insurance company assets (% of GDP)	16.4	19.5	20.3	24.9	—	—
Total net assets of mutual funds (% of GDP)	6.1	7.4	10.0	11.7	13.4	—
Total pension fund assets (% of GDP)	59.8	55.0	55.8	64.5	59.1	—
Concentration						
Concentration ratio of top 3 commercial banks (% of total assets)	39	40	56	55	—	—
Concentration ratio of top 3 securities firms (% of total securities trading)	42	36	35	37	—	—
Concentration ratio of top 3 insurance companies (% of total premiums)	22	25	20	22	—	—
Concentration ratio of top 3 pension funds, if applicable (% of total assets)	70	71	71	72	—	—
Bank performance						
Return on assets	1.0	1.3	1.1	1.3	1.2	—
Return on equity	12.7	17.7	14.4	16.6	16.7	16.4
Cost-to-income ratio (operating expenses/gross income)	57.9	56.1	55.2	53.6	57.1	—
Operating expenses/total assets	3.0	2.9	2.9	2.7	2.5	—
Bank solvency and asset quality						
Bank capital to assets	7.5	7.2	7.2	7.3	7.0	—
Bank capital adequacy ratio	13.3	12.7	14.0	14.1	13.6	13.0
Bank nonperforming loans/total loans	1.7	1.6	1.8	1.6	1.2	0.9
Bank provisions/nonperforming loans	145.7	146.4	129.5	133.2	165.5	176.9

Sources: Data from Central Bank of Chile, World Bank; International Monetary Fund; Standard and Poor's; Bank for International Settlements; Asociación de Supervisores de Seguros de América Latina (Association of Latin American Insurance Supervisors); Investment Company Institute; Asociación Internacional de Organismos Supervisores de Fondos de Pensiones (International Association of Pension Fund Supervisory Agencies); Superintendencia de Bancos e Instituciones Financieras (Superintendency of Banks and Financial Institutions of Chile); Superintendencia de Valores y Seguros de Chile (Superintendency of Securities and Insurance of Chile); Superintendencia de Pensiones (Superintendency of Pensions).

Note: — = not available.

a. Includes "financial services and business services," according to Chile's national accounts.

institutions included Canada, the EU (mostly Spain), and the United States. Thus, for domestic financial institutions, potential foreign competition was nothing new (see table 5.3).

In April 2001, a number of reforms liberalized international trade in financial services, including the following:

- The tax paid by foreign institutional investors on fixed-income debt was reduced from 35 percent to 4 percent.
- A system of voluntary retirement savings plans managed by all financial institutions (banks, insurance companies, collective investment funds, and pension fund managers) was created.[14]
- The investment limits for insurance companies were raised and made more flexible, but in turn, self-regulation was promoted and transparency standards were increased.
- Managers of multiple investment funds were created.[15]
- The number of available pension funds in the mandatory system was expanded to five, with differences in their composition between fixed- and variable-income financial instruments.

Table 5.3   Internationalization and Privatization of Chile's Financial System, 2000–03

Characteristic	2000	2001	2002	2003
State ownership				
State ownership of commercial banks (% of total assets)	13	13	15	16
State ownership of securities firms (% of total securities trading)	2	3	5	7
State ownership of insurance companies (% of total premiums)	0	0	0	0
State ownership of pension funds, if applicable (% of total assets)	0	0	0	0
Foreign ownership				
Foreign ownership of banks (% of total assets)	46	47	45	41
Foreign ownership of securities firms (% of total securities trading)	56	52	50	47
Foreign ownership of insurance companies (% of total premiums)	60	53	54	59
Foreign ownership of pension funds (% of total assets)	56	56	55	56

Sources: Superintendencia de Bancos e Instituciones Financieras (Superintendency of Banks and Financial Institutions of Chile); Superintendencia de Valores y Seguros de Chile (Superintendency of Securities and Insurance of Chile); Superintendencia de Pensiones (Superintendency of Pensions); Stephanou 2005.

- Agricultural commodities stock exchanges were created.
- A 4 percent tax was imposed on the interest on foreign-contracted loans.
- The government sent legislation to the National Congress to gradually raise the foreign investment limit of pension funds to 30 percent.

Chile's Trade Commitments in Financial Services before the Negotiations with the EU and the United States

After almost two decades of unilateral trade liberalization, Chile began to actively negotiate free trade agreements (FTAs) in 1990. This new policy was aimed at complementing the unilateral reduction of tariffs with improved and more secure access to export markets; removing nontariff barriers faced by Chilean exports; and, in the case of Latin America, restoring Chile's political relationship with the region after its return to democracy. Table 5A.1 shows how active Chile has been in negotiating trade agreements.

The first agreements were negotiated with countries in Latin America within the framework of the Asociación Latinoamericana de Integración (Latin American Integration Association, or ALADI), created in 1980.[16] ALADI was created in the context of trade in goods, so these agreements, called *economic complementation agreements*, were limited in scope. In this first wave of trade agreements, Chile did not negotiate disciplines in trade in services, including financial services, and in investment. Chile and its Latin American partners did not see negotiating services as a priority; the Uruguay Round negotiations, which for the first time included services at the multilateral level, had not yet reached a successful conclusion.

The negotiation of an FTA with Canada represented a turning point in Chile's model for negotiating bilaterally. In 1994, Chile was invited to join the North American Free Trade Agreement (NAFTA), but after the U.S. Congress passed NAFTA, the negotiations with Chile were indefinitely postponed. However, Canada offered Chile the possibility of negotiating an agreement modeled after NAFTA as an interim agreement until political conditions in the United States became more favorable.

This negotiation gave Chile the opportunity to strengthen its negotiating teams and gain expertise in new areas, such as investment, services, intellectual property rights, and government procurement. However, Canada and Chile did not negotiate a chapter on financial services. The two countries committed to negotiate such a chapter, based on NAFTA chapter XIV, no later than April 1999, two years after the initial FTA negotiations were concluded. Again, when Chile and Mexico agreed in April 1998 to replace their ALADI-style goods-only agreement with an agreement based on the NAFTA model, the financial services chapter was left for future negotiation. These negotiations were to start no later than June 1999. In both cases, the deadlines were not respected.[17]

Financial services were not negotiated with Canada and Mexico because Chile's negotiating team felt that in an accession to NAFTA the country would need financial services as a negotiating chip with the United States. Thus, Chile's only significant commitments in financial services before the negotiations with the EU and the United States were made in the context of the Uruguay Round. Financial services were not fully excluded, however. Both FTAs contain, in their respective investment chapters, a provision on the protection of investors in financial institutions regarding transfers, expropriation, and compensation.

At the time of the negotiations, Chile still had capital controls in place—in particular, the URR. Thus, that issue had to be addressed. Canada, following the NAFTA model, expected strong commitments by Chile with regard to capital transfers, whereas the Chilean negotiators wanted to protect the Central Bank's right to adopt restrictions on capital flows in the future. The solution reached at the time was that of an annex, granting exemptions from the obligations on transfers and investment.

In annex G-09.1 of the Canada-Chile FTA, which is reproduced in annex 5D of this chapter, Chile reserves the right to apply a reserve requirement with a maximum rate of 30 percent for not more than two years. Chile also reserves the right to require that certain transactions be carried out in the formal exchange market (defined in annex G-09.1), but authorization to access that market must be granted without delay. The same annex was soon afterward introduced in the new Chile-Mexico FTA.

Chile followed a very conservative and cautious approach in negotiating its financial services schedule in the Uruguay Round and did not even consolidate the status quo.[18] Chile left unbound cross-border trade and consumption abroad (modes 1 and 2) for all financial services except (a) reinsurance and retrocession and (b) brokerage of reinsurance. Its commitments in mode 4, movement of natural persons, were limited to its general commitments in services regarding intracompany transferees. Chile also maintained an economic needs test for commercial presence in all scheduled financial services.[19]

Almost all of Chile's commitments were in commercial presence (mode 3). In insurance services, both life and general insurance are included, as well as insurance brokerage. However, Chile's list does not include any of the services auxiliary to insurance, such as consulting, actuarial, risk, and claim settlement services. Foreign-owned providers have to establish commercial presence in Chile according to the domestic insurance legislation (that is, as stock corporations and through separate companies for life and nonlife insurance). Chile excluded from its insurance commitments all insurance related to the mandatory social security system, including health insurance provided by the social security health providers (*instituciones de salud previsional*, or Isapres) and FONASA.

In banking services, Chile consolidated establishment through subsidiaries and branches as allowed by the banking act. However, not all services permitted to be provided directly or indirectly by banks were listed. The commitments in securities services include the trading of publicly offered securities and stock of corporations, risk rating, custodial services by securities brokers, financial advisory services, portfolio management by securities brokers, and warrants (see table 5A.1). Other important areas of services, such as pension fund management, were left out. Clearly, in 1997, Chile did not consolidate its level of external liberalization in the General Agreement on Trade in Services (GATS).

This conservative approach was not motivated by Chile's bargaining strategy. It had more to do with the fact that domestic legislative and regulatory changes, especially in banking, were still pending. The reform of the banking act and the conclusion of the negotiations on financial services in GATS coincided. Thus, the uncertainty related to the outcome of the legislative process did not allow for larger commitments in banking services.

In GATS, Chile also addressed the issue of the Central Bank's powers to restrict market access for all modes of supply. The text can be found in annex 5C. As can be seen there, the text reproduces the relevant text of the Central Bank Act, specifically mentions the URR, and generally reserves all existing rights of the Central Bank. This text became a model for some of the bilateral negotiations that came later.

Preparing the Negotiations: The Issues Involved

For the bilateral negotiations with the EU and the United States, a number of key issues had to be defined. Initially, the decision making involved only the public sector: the Ministry of Finance, the Central Bank, and the financial regulators. Only when the negotiations started was the private sector involved through periodic consultations.

The first key issue addressed was how financial services would relate to other aspects of a bilateral negotiation—in particular, whether they would be used as a bargaining chip. Clearly, any FTA with the EU or the United States would have to include financial services. For both partners, the sector was an important one in which they expected Chile to make commitments. Thus, Chile agreed to negotiate financial services as a sign of goodwill and expected, in turn, that both the EU and the United States would agree to address areas of special interest to Chile.[20] However, the parties also decided that the level of commitments in financial services would be independent of the negotiations on other issues. In other words, Chile would not, for example, exchange market access in agriculture for concessions in financial services. This negotiating stance was possible because the counterparts understood that the Ministry of Finance had sole and full responsibility in the conduct of negotiations in financial services.

The second key issue was that of precedents. By coincidence, the negotiations with the EU and the United States were being conducted at the same time. In addition, Chile was still negotiating an FTA with the Republic of Korea. The problem was how to manage the three negotiations without setting precedents in one that could weaken Chile's negotiating position in another. In the case of Korea, Chile was able to commit only to future negotiations on financial services. Given that the United States did not have congressional authority to negotiate trade agreements when the negotiations with Chile began, those with the EU advanced much faster. By early 2002, it was clear that Chile was going to have to wrap up the financial services negotiations with the EU by April. The fact that the EU was not prepared to follow a NAFTA-style approach in investment and services helped conceptually in distinguishing the two negotiations. However, undoubtedly what was going to be agreed on with the EU in April 2002 was seen by the United States as Chile's limits in negotiating financial services: in particular, no commitments regarding the social security system and no substantial regulatory changes.

The third negotiating issue was how financial services would be included in an FTA: as a separate chapter as in NAFTA or as an annex of specific commitments as in GATS. Chile's negotiating team decided that financial services should be in a separate, self-contained chapter that would not contain provisions on services in general. A chapter on financial services was felt to give more comfort to the Ministry of Finance, the regulators, and even the industry because it would underscore the independent character of the negotiations on financial services. This strategy was in accordance with the U.S. approach, but not with that of the EU.

The latter followed the GATS model, which meant that financial services would be just an additional sector within services. In the end, the EU accepted negotiation of a separate financial services chapter, but still following a GATS approach regarding key provisions and the listing of commitments.

Fourth, Chile had to review its financial services legislation for an assessment of where it stood with respect to obligations such as national treatment; market access (economic needs tests, quantitative restrictions, requirements regarding juridical forms of establishment, and so on); modes of supply; residency requirements for senior management; and board of directors composition. In-house lawyers and economists, in collaboration with the regulatory agencies, conducted the review. The goal was to define a NAFTA-like negative list of nonconforming measures.

The most-favored-nation (MFN) clause was not seen as an important issue because Chile is not a member of any customs union or common market. The violations of national treatment were few and mostly related to residency requirements. In the case of market access, the potential non-conformities were almost exclusively related to the obligation of a specific juridical form for establishment or commercial presence. In most cases, financial institutions in Chile have to be local stock corporations. Also, foreign financial institutions have to be subsidiaries and cannot be direct branches.[21] Finally, no quantitative restrictions existed, such as limits on share ownership, market shares, or types of operations that foreign institutions could perform.

Fifth, and finally, Chile had to decide how far it would go in its commitments and whether liberalization beyond the status quo was possible or desirable. Although the negotiating team was aware that some flexibility would have to exist, at least a preliminary decision had to be made.

The first issue that arose regarding commitments was the treatment of the privatized social security system, both for pension funds and health care. Foreign ownership was not restricted; in fact, as shown in table 5.3, foreign-owned institutions manage a majority of pension fund assets. However, neither the United States nor the EU has a similar compulsory privatized system. This fact appeared as an important asymmetry, and the negotiators decided that as in Chile's commitments in GATS and in the agreements with Canada and Mexico, all financial services related to the compulsory social security system would be carved out.[22]

The second issue was whether Chile would be asked to modify certain aspects of its financial legislation or the structure of its financial system. The latter was discarded because bilateral FTAs do not require the harmonization of the participants' financial regulation. Changes in Chile's financial regulation would occur only if the EU or the United States considered the existing measures to be important limitations to market access. Chile's negotiators decided their stance would be that the negotiations should not lead to reforms of Chile's financial legislation or to additional liberalization. In other words, at most Chile would agree to lock in the status quo.

There were several reasons for this decision. First, the Ministry of Finance saw bilateral trade agreements in general as only a third-best option for trade liberalization, after unilateral liberalization and multilateral negotiations. This conclusion simply followed from the theory of trade policy: unilateral opening is the first-best policy. In addition, the view that unilateral reforms provided more flexibility and that the requests from the EU and the United States would be more "mercantilistic" than really liberalizing prevailed within the administration. Second, the Ministry of Finance was concomitantly introducing a package of reforms of the capital market. Third, the ministry and the regulators were comfortable with the level of openness already reached in Chile.

A final issue related to capital controls and balance-of-payments measures. These measures were treated separately from the financial services negotiations because the former was related to the investment chapter and the latter constituted a general exception. A separate negotiating team, including only Ministry of Finance and Central Bank officials, worked on these issues. When the negotiations with the EU and the United States started, the URR had already been reduced to zero, and the Central Bank was dismantling the remaining exchange controls. However, the Central Bank was still allowed to impose exchange controls and restrictions on capital outflows and inflows. Thus, Chile's negotiating position was that (a) the powers of the Central Bank to reinstate the URR, as well as other exchange controls, had to be preserved, and (b) a general balance-of-payments exception such as the one contained in GATS was necessary in case of balance-of-payments difficulties.

Even though the URR had been eliminated, it was still considered in government circles and among members of the National Congress as an important policy tool that should not be given up. In all previous negotiations involving commitments on capital flows, the ability to reinstate the URR was protected, and the same was expected in the negotiations with the EU and the United States. In addition, if the result of the negotiations implied a change in the Central Bank Act, a special quorum would be required when it came to a vote in the National Congress because of the law's constitutional standing. It was feared that this requirement would make the agreement more difficult to pass.

Therefore, Chile's negotiating position was not only to prevent further liberalization beyond the status quo, but also to introduce exceptions regarding transfers and balance of payments.

Preparing for and Conducting the Negotiations: Informing the Private and Public Sectors

In preparing for negotiations, the negotiation team's coordination with other domestic actors was organized on two parallel tracks. The first track involved the allocation of responsibilities among agencies and the structure of the negotiating team. The second track was the establishment of a permanent dialogue with both the financial services supervisors and the private sector. In the first phase, this dialogue provided mainly general information on the content and the concepts in the negotiations. In the second phase, the emphasis focused on keeping the regulators and the private sector informed of the progress of the negotiations.

This section describes how the preparatory work was organized, what the responsibilities of the different agencies were, and how the negotiating team was structured. The relationship with the stakeholders not present at the negotiating table—in particular, the private sector—is also presented. Finally, the relationship between the financial services negotiator and the lead negotiators is described.

The Central Bank and separate superintendencies are responsible for regulating financial services in Chile, with the Ministry of Finance playing a policy-making role. The superintendencies are autonomous institutions that relate to the government through a ministry. The SBIF regulates banks and financial companies and the Superintendencia de Valores y Seguros (Superintendency of Securities and Insurance, or SVS) regulates, among others, stock corporations, securities issuers, securities brokers, stock brokers, stock and commodity markets, collective investment fund managers (except for pension funds), risk-rating agencies, insurance and reinsurance companies, insurance brokers, and claim settlement services providers. Their relationship with the government is through the Ministry of Finance. The Superintendencia de Pensiones (Superintendency of Pensions, or SP)[23] regulates pension funds and is related to government through the Ministry of Labor. However, in the period from 2000 to 2006, the minister of finance headed the capital markets committee with the participation of all three superintendents: banks, securities and insurance, and pension funds.[24]

In 2000, the minister of finance created the Committee for International Negotiations in Financial Services, which the Ministry of Finance's international affairs coordinator heads. Its members are representatives of the three regulatory agencies (SBIF, SVS, and SP); the Central Bank; and the head of the Services, Investment, and Air Transport Department of the Ministry of Foreign Affairs, which is the government's trade-negotiating agency.

The Organization of Negotiations with the United States

Although negotiations with the EU started much earlier than those with the United States,[25] the discussions on financial services began first with the United States. Not much discussion occurred within the government of who would lead the financial services negotiations: the Ministry of Finance was the clear choice because it bears the legal responsibility for the proper functioning of the financial markets, because the supervisory agencies work closely with the ministry, and because it has access to adequate technical expertise. The ministry's core team was made up of four persons: a lead negotiator, a senior legal adviser (with expertise in financial services) hired from outside the ministry, a junior economist from the ministry's Capital Markets Division, and a junior lawyer from the ministry's International Affairs Department. The rest of the team was brought in from other agencies. The Central Bank appointed two representatives: a specialist on financial markets and an expert on capital account management. The other members came from the SBIF and the SVS. From the start, the decision had been that no commitments would be made in financial services related to the privatized social security system, and hence no representatives from the respective regulatory agencies were present at the negotiations.[26]

The first rounds with the United States served mostly to exchange information regarding the country's respective regulatory regimes. These meetings were important because issues that were to be discussed were raised early on. The level of transparency that was achieved with such an extensive and deep exchange of information created an atmosphere of trust between both sides that would prove to be helpful toward the end of the negotiations, when the difficult issues had to be resolved. As the negotiations progressed, the rounds focused more on the text itself. Generally, the U.S. side tabled proposals, and Chile reacted to those proposals and in some cases, presented alternatives to the U.S. text in the following round.

Because it was the first bilateral negotiation in financial services for Chile, several sessions were necessary to familiarize the regulators with the terms and concepts used. With that information, they were able to review all of Chile's financial legislation for possible nonconforming measures when the text advanced. This stage was certainly one of the most crucial because the "list it or lose it" approach of the negative list system made the design of the reservations the key aspect of the negotiations. In addition, poorly drafted reservations could have weakened Chile's negotiating position.

In the final stages of the negotiations, only the core team from the Ministry of Finance was at the table, but it was in close contact with the supervisory agencies and the Central Bank, in particular when issues regarding the agencies' regulatory powers were under negotiation. The core team reported on the progress of the negotiations directly to the minister of finance, who was present at the final round of the negotiations in Washington, D.C.

The negotiation of the financial services chapter was, despite the initial efforts, not conducted in complete isolation. Of particular concern for the financial services team was what was going to be negotiated in investment, services, electronic commerce, and government procurement. From the NAFTA model, the team knew that certain obligations undertaken in the investment chapter would apply to financial services. Therefore, the lead negotiator of investment was jointly appointed by the Ministry of Foreign Affairs and the Ministry of Finance to ensure permanent contact between the two teams. Moreover, given that the lead negotiator in services was a negotiator from the Office of the United States Trade Representative who was also in the financial services group, certain issues were clearly going to be raised in both groups. Thus, a representative for the financial services team was part of the overall services team. This strategy would allow the Chilean services team to raise red flags in the services group when a specific issue was perceived as possibly setting an undesirable precedent for financial services and, conversely, the Chilean financial services team would be fully aware when an issue was also being discussed in the services group.

Direct contact also took place between the financial services team and the leaders of the negotiations, because the international affairs coordinator of the Ministry of Finance sat in a small executive committee with the lead negotiator and his deputy, both from the General Directorate of International Economic Relations of the Ministry of Foreign Affairs. So the lead negotiator of financial services was informed of what was going on in the rest of the negotiating groups in the Chile-U.S. rounds and could influence negotiating positions in other groups.

The concern regarding electronic commerce was that obligations in electronic commerce could be invoked as a means to bypass restrictions to cross-border trade agreed on in the financial services negotiations. Thus, a representative of the Ministry of Finance and the financial services team also sat at the electronic commerce table. In the end, such fears proved unfounded. Since the agreement followed the NAFTA model, the presence of special provisions for dispute settlement on financial services was guaranteed, and therefore the team on financial services did not need to actively participate in the negotiation on the general dispute settlement chapter.

The government of Chile also buys financial services: it buys insurance for its buildings, its agencies hold checking accounts, its temporary cash surpluses are invested in financial instruments, and so on. Would these services be included in government procurement? One important issue is that by law certain ministries and government agencies are obligated to use only the checking account that the government holds in the state-owned bank, BancoEstado. In the end, financial services were excluded from the commitments in government procurement and a reservation regarding the exclusive right of BancoEstado to hold certain government accounts was scheduled in the financial services chapter.

From the start, the issue of capital controls was of great concern to Chile. However, the U.S. financial services team made it clear from the beginning that the issue was not going to be addressed in the financial services negotiations. The Chilean view was that in general there was a connection between the negotiations on investment, services, and financial services, on one hand, and the issue of capital controls, on the other. Thus, the Chilean negotiating teams for the three chapters participated in the discussions regarding the application of capital controls, in particular the URR. In the end, as will be explained later, the issue was resolved at a separate table in the last negotiating round at the highest political level.

The Organization of Negotiations with the EU

The financial services chapter was negotiated much faster with the EU. In only three rounds, the final text was agreed on. The EU presented its GATS schedule with no bilateral improvements. Even so, Chile agreed to expand its positive list of GATS commitments in response to specific EU requests because otherwise closing the overall negotiations would have been impossible. In addition, Chile's lead financial services negotiator in the Uruguay Round was brought into the negotiating team, and the regulatory agencies provided information and were consulted as required when new financial services were gradually added to Chile's schedule.

Negotiations on the text of the services chapter were well advanced when those on financial services started. Thus, less coordination occurred in the negotiations with the EU than in those with the United States. This is understandable, however, given that the services chapter in the Chile-EU agreement is the (already accepted) GATS text and that of financial services is an application of the same text to financial services. The financial services team also led the negotiation of the special chapter on current payments and capital transfers, not because of any particular relationship to the financial services negotiations, but because the expertise on the issues was in the Ministry of Finance. Given the model of the negotiations, unlike the Chile-U.S. agreement, no provisions on the resolution of investment disputes between an investor and the state would exist. Thus, the financial services team did not coordinate its work with the team negotiating the general dispute settlement chapter.

The lead negotiator in financial services reported to the head negotiator, as did all the other group leaders. No one from the Ministry of Finance participated at the highest level of decision making. Thus, less direct contact took place among the interested parties than in the case of the U.S. negotiations, and the various negotiators had less knowledge of what was going on in the rest of the negotiations with the EU.

The Dialogue with the Private Sector

The relationship with the private sector was constructed directly and indirectly. Direct dialogue occurred through meetings of the heads of the main financial industry associations, of which the most active were the bankers' and insurers' associations.[27] The lead negotiators met separately with each association before and after each round. They reported, to the extent possible, on the progress made, on what was expected of the following round, and on the specific requests of the EU and the United States. Contrary to negotiations in goods, no "side room" existed where the private sector was waiting for news of what was happening or was being periodically consulted on issues that appeared at the table. Representatives of the financial private sector never attended the rounds, except for general informational meetings after each round in Santiago (but not in the United States or in Brussels).

In parallel, the Ministry of Finance hired a consulting firm to conduct a two-stage study to develop an independent opinion on the effect of the financial services negotiations with the United States. In the first stage, the consultants collected information on the views of the private sector regarding the negotiations, with an emphasis on their reaction to the U.S. requests and what, if anything, they expected Chile to obtain as concessions. To obtain more precise views from the private sector, the consultants had to explain what was involved in the negotiations and the implications that concepts such as national treatment, market access or establishment, and cross-border trade would have on the private sector. In the second stage, the consultants analyzed the potential effect of the FTA on the financial services industry.

The study examined four subsectors: banks, pension fund management, mutual fund management, and stockbrokerage firms. More specifically, it analyzed the effect on efficiency and stability of obligations regarding national treatment, MFN treatment, right of establishment, cross-border trade, new financial services, and regulatory changes, as well as the interaction between the taxation of financial services and cross-border trade. The negotiating team used the results of the study to confirm, or contradict, the views expressed by the industry's associations and as a guide for assessing the potential effect of the requests of the negotiating counterpart.

As the negotiations progressed and the United States started to place market-opening demands on the table, the critical issues for the private sector became readily apparent. The issue that raised immediate concern was the request for direct branching of banks and insurance companies, and it remained so until the conclusion of the negotiations. Opposition to that request was quite strong and vocal, so the negotiating team had to assume the issue was going to be one of the red lines in the negotiations. The United States tabled this request before the EU did, and the Chilean negotiating team was prepared to say no to both. In contrast, there was no opposition, in particular from the insurance industry, to some of the cross-border requests of the EU and the United States.

The Outcome of the Negotiations with the United States and the EU

Privileging unilateral liberalization, Chile had made commitments in financial services only in the context of the Uruguay Round, but not in bilateral negotiations. Starting in 2001, financial services chapters were negotiated in the EU Association Agreement and in the U.S. FTA.

Given the significant commercial interests of both the EU and the United States, financial services could hardly be excluded or left for future negotiations. In the case of the EU, the main pressure stemmed from the large presence of Spanish financial institutions in the Chilean market. Although they had a much smaller presence in Chile, financial services were also an area of interest for the United States. The Chilean negotiating team was aware that these negotiations would become the template for Chile's future commitments in financial services, and therefore it had to proceed with negotiations carefully.

Although both negotiations advanced in parallel, the approach and the results differ.

The Chile-EU Agreement

The European Commission had a mandate that required it to follow the GATS model. Regarding investment, the commission could take up only those provisions for which a specific mandate had been granted. In what follows, two dimensions of the agreement are examined: (a) the provisions on financial services and (b) the provisions on transfers and capital movements.

The chapter on financial services. Following Chilean policy regarding financial services negotiations, a separate self-contained chapter was constructed using the GATS definitions of modes of supply and disciplines. No changes were made to the GATS texts incorporated in the chapter to minimize any uncertainties regarding the legal interpretation. Thus, the market-access and national treatment provisions and the structure of commitments (positive listing) are the same as in GATS.

However, because of the heavy regulation of financial services (which is necessary for prudential reasons, in particular for addressing market failures and information asymmetries), not all disciplines of GATS were adopted in the financial services chapter, and others were taken from the Annex on Financial Services and from the Understanding on Commitments in Financial Services. Table 5B.1 summarizes the main disciplines of the Chile-EU financial services chapter and their corresponding legal text.

Because the specific commitments were being made on the basis of a positive list, and to maintain their integrity and prevent an expansion through automatic and artificial "innovation," the Chile-EU text specifies that any new financial service must be within the scope of the subsectors and financial services already scheduled. Also, to prevent cases where the adoption of an innovation could require a legal change outside the jurisdiction of the executive branch, the text includes a provision establishing that the introduction of the new financial service must not require a new law or the modification of an existing law. Likewise, the right to regulate new financial services was confirmed, with the power to decide on the juridical form under which the new financial service could be supplied and to require an authorization prior to the supply of the financial service. It should be pointed out, though, that the rejection of a new financial service can be made only on prudential grounds.

Regarding data processing, the financial services chapter authorizes the transfer of information, both into and out of the country, by electronic or other means in the ordinary course of business. Additionally, when the data contain personal information, the transfer and processing of such data have to conform with domestic laws on privacy protection of the country in which the information originates.

A standard different from GATS was established regarding prudential regulation. The agreement grants the right to adopt or maintain "reasonable" measures for the purposes of (a) protecting investors, depositors, financial market participants, policy holders, or persons to whom a fiduciary duty is owed by a financial services supplier; (b) maintaining the safety, soundness, integrity, or financial responsibility of financial services suppliers; and (c) ensuring the integrity and stability of a party's financial system. This text comes from NAFTA article 1410 on exceptions. However, as in GATS, where such measures do not conform to the provisions of the chapter, they may not be used to avoid commitments or obligations. Thus, the GATS text was made more precise by incorporating provisions from NAFTA.

Finally, the financial services chapter contains specific provisions on the information that could be exchanged and on the panelists in a dispute settlement. In particular, the president of the tribunal must have expertise in financial services.

By following the GATS negotiating model, the negotiation was centered on the specific commitments to which the agreed disciplines would apply. As mentioned, Chile aimed at locking in the unilateral reforms already taken and avoiding any further liberalization. This conservative approach was a consequence of past and still ongoing changes in domestic legislation.

By the time the negotiations started (end-2001), the Ministry of Finance consolidated and confirmed the direction of the reforms adopted during the 1990s. This confirmation allowed an expansion of the commitments compared to those existing in GATS. In other words, a larger number of financial services was included, reflecting the greater level of openness.[28]

The approach followed by Chile in the negotiations favored commitments under the modality of "commercial presence" (mode 3 in GATS); it made more limited commitments under the other modes, "cross-border trade" and "consumption abroad." Regarding commercial presence, Chile did make a significant concession to the EU in comparison with all other World Trade Organization (WTO) members: the economic needs test was eliminated for all subsectors listed in Chile's schedule in the EU Association Agreement. Regarding the "movement of natural persons" (mode 4), Chile did not make more commitments than those already made with the WTO.

Another important difference with Chile's GATS commitments concerns the sale of insurance for international maritime transport and international commercial aviation; insurance for goods in international transit (marine, aviation, and transport, or MAT, insurance); and the brokerage of such insurance. In the agreement with the EU, Chile committed to allowing the cross-border supply of such insurance and its direct purchase outside the country (consumption abroad).[29]

Regarding social security, Chile stressed the need to level the commitments in some sectors, given the differences between the systems in the EU and Chile. In the EU, social security services are provided by the government in the majority of the member states. Thus, they are a priori carved out of the scope of GATS and therefore not subject to commitments. In contrast, in Chile, these services are provided by the private and public sectors and therefore would be covered by the agreement with the EU. The situation created a significant asymmetry in market-access negotiations. Chile followed its WTO commitments and did not incorporate those services related to the mandatory social security system in its commitments, but it agreed to list the management of voluntary retirement pension funds.

This decision implies that the administration of compulsory pension fund accounts by AFPs is not listed in Chile's commitments. However, given that Chile has bilateral investment treaties with almost all EU member states, investors in pension fund management obtain protection through those treaties.

The chapter on current payments and capital movements. The chapter on current payments and capital movements applies to "all current payments and capital movements between the Parties."[30] Regarding the current account, the provisions oblige a state to allow payments and transfers in freely convertible currency and in accordance with the International Monetary Fund's Articles of Agreement. With respect to the capital account, the free movement of capital relating to investments made in accordance with the laws of the host country and with the relevant provisions of the agreement is established as an obligation. The liquidation or repatriation of such capital and of any profit earned is to be allowed.

The chapter contains an additional article allowing exceptions and safeguards when under "exceptional circumstances, payments and capital movements between the Parties cause or threaten to cause serious difficulties for the operation of monetary policy or exchange rate policy of either Party." In such case, a party may apply measures for not more than one year, which can be extended.[31]

In addition, Chile reserved in an annex[32] the powers of the Foreign Investment Committee and the government to establish special investment regimes in the future. The language follows to a certain extent the annex to the transfers article of the Canada-Chile FTA. In the same annex, the powers of the Central Bank to introduce measures that affect current payments and capital movements are also reserved, following Chile's schedule in GATS (see annex 5C of this chapter).[33]

The Chile-U.S. Agreement

In the case of the United States, although the authority to negotiate under the Trade Promotion Authority granted by the U.S. Congress did not make an explicit reference to financial services, it did state that the principal U.S. negotiating objectives were (a) to reduce or eliminate barriers to international trade in services, including regulatory and other barriers that deny national treatment and market access or unreasonably restrict the establishment or operations of services suppliers, and (b) to free the transfer of funds relating to investments. For the latter objective, the negotiating position of the United States was heavily influenced by the lobby of the asset management industry and the insurance industry, particularly through the Office of the United States Trade Representative.

The financial services negotiation with the United States was based on NAFTA, which was already eight years old when the negotiations with Chile began. Thus, during the negotiations, NAFTA was updated and improved; the Chile-U.S. FTA now incorporates areas from GATS not covered in NAFTA. These areas include provisions from both the Annex on Financial Services and the Understanding on Commitments in Financial Services. Table 5B.2 summarizes the provisions of the chapter as well as the origin of the text negotiated by Chile and the United States.

The financial services chapter is very much self-contained. It includes most of the disciplines on measures that affect financial services, and the relationship to other chapters is clarified through the explicit incorporation of disciplines, notably from the investment chapter.[34] The chapter applies to *financial services*, as defined in the GATS annex, and two modes of supply are distinguished: (a) the establishment of financial institutions of the other party and investments of the other party in financial institutions (mode 3 in GATS) and (b) cross-border trade in financial services (modes 1, 2, and 4 in GATS). An important qualification is that financial institutions, as in NAFTA, are defined as only those institutions that are regulated as such. The only significant difference from NAFTA is the treatment of activities or services forming part of a public retirement plan or a statutory social security system or those conducted with a guarantee of public financial resources. In the Chile-U.S. FTA, the language of the GATS annex is used. That is, if such activities are conducted in competition between private financial institutions or between public and private entities, then they are covered by the disciplines of the chapter; otherwise, they are carved out. This approach is one way in which the chapter moves in the direction of a hybrid model, comprising elements of both GATS and NAFTA.[35]

The principles of nondiscrimination are established in separate national treatment and MFN articles. In the case of national treatment, some differences with NAFTA were introduced. First, unlike in NAFTA, no special provisions limit national treatment to the specific circumstances of a state or province.[36] However, in scheduling its reservations, the United States specified that national treatment is applied on the basis of the "home-state rule." That is, foreign (Chilean) banks or insurance companies, when seeking establishment in a specific U.S. state, will receive the treatment that the state gives to its banks or insurance companies.

Another important departure from NAFTA is the inclusion of a "Market Access for Financial Institutions" article. It follows paragraph 2 of GATS article XVI on market access. However, the limitations on the participation of foreign capital in financial institutions were not included as a restriction to market access. Also, unlike GATS article XVI, the article does not regulate the cross-border modes of supply of financial services.

In terms of scheduling, Chile was not comfortable with the idea of following a negative list approach. Chile first raised the issue of the "zero quota." That is, prohibiting a specific financial service on a national treatment basis in the future should be legitimate. But as soon as the market-access article is combined with a negative list, such a prohibition would be impossible because it would be a direct violation of the article.[37] In addition, commitments on commercial presence in both NAFTA and the Understanding on Commitments in Financial Services are based on an article on the right of establishment. Finally, under a negative list approach any nonconforming measure not listed is supposed to be understood as eliminated.

Therefore, this article applies only to commitments in insurance and insurance-related services, following a positive list approach. In the case of banking and other financial services (excluding insurance), a provision on the "Right of Establishment with Respect to Certain Financial Services" was drafted as a modified version of NAFTA article 1403. Compared to the NAFTA article, the text is more streamlined and clearer on the conditions under which right of establishment is granted. Commitments for these financial services are therefore based on a distinct provision, not on the market-access article, and the scheduling followed a negative list approach. Thus, for banking and other financial services, the approach taken was that of NAFTA, whereas insurance and insurance-related services followed the GATS model.

There are two types of specific commitments on cross-border trade. With respect to cross-border supply, the parties established that a positive and limited list of services would be allowed.[38] This is another important difference from NAFTA. And unlike NAFTA, there is no standstill of the level of openness to cross-border supply, except for the listed services. The rest of the article is as in NAFTA. Both parties agree to allow consumption abroad, but the host country is not required to permit cross-border suppliers to do business or solicit in its territory. Registration of cross-border financial services suppliers may also be required, which implies that no automatic authorization exists for cross-border financial services, including those provided through the Internet.

An important rule of origin for financial institutions and financial services suppliers is that they must not be branches of noncountry institutions. For example, the branch of a European-owned bank in Chile or the United States is not covered by the provisions of the agreement. Thus, as in NAFTA, only subsidiaries from third countries can benefit from the agreement.

As in NAFTA, an article on new financial services allows for their introduction, but some of the innovations negotiated with the EU that relate to protection of legislative and supervision powers were incorporated. As in the Chile-EU agreement, the introduction of a new financial service is permitted, provided that its introduction does not require the party to adopt a new law or modify an existing law. However, the regulatory authority can refuse the authorization only for prudential reasons.

Specific provisions regarding the treatment of confidential information and its protection were incorporated in terms similar to those in GATS. With respect to "senior management and boards of directors," the commitments resemble the standard set by NAFTA, ensuring that the host country cannot require that financial institutions hire persons of a specific nationality or that more than a minority of the boards of directors of a financial institution be composed of nationals or residents of the country.

The provisions on nonconforming measures follow NAFTA. Reservations can be scheduled only for national treatment, MFN, market access, senior management and boards of directors, and establishment. As in NAFTA, the concept of *ratcheting* to nonconforming measures is included. That is, if such a measure is unilaterally modified in the direction of making it more conforming, presumably liberalizing it, then that change automatically becomes the new level of commitment with no possibility of backtracking. Chile felt some discomfort with ratcheting for requiring a specific juridical form.[39] Experience in the regulation of financial services shows that requiring a specific juridical form (generally incorporation) is needed to ensure appropriate public disclosure. In the future, cases may exist in which the removal of such a requirement may have to be reinstated. Therefore, a note in Chile's nonconforming measures states that ratcheting does not apply to market access for financial institutions or for right of establishment of certain financial services.

An article on exceptions was negotiated with the purpose of preventing limits on the application of measures for prudential reasons. The text comes from the GATS Annex on Financial Services and contains the same caveat that when those measures do not conform to the obligations taken in the agreement, they should not be used to avoid those obligations or commitments.[40] A footnote was added to include the possibility that prudential measures regarding financial services could be adopted by agencies not normally considered to be financial services regulators, such as the Ministry of Labor. This provision was important for Chile because the pension fund regulator, the Superintendencia de Pensiones (SP), is formally related to the Ministry of Labor. The exceptions, as in NAFTA, extend to measures of general application for reasons of monetary, credit, and exchange rate policies.[41] Unlike in NAFTA, an additional paragraph based on GATS introduces the possibility of adopting or enforcing measures to prevent deceptive or fraudulent practices or to deal with default on financial services contracts.

Transparency of regulatory changes has become a key issue in a globalized financial services industry: there is a general recognition that financial services must be subject to regulation and good supervision, but standards differ across jurisdictions. The transparency article in the Chile-U.S. FTA builds on NAFTA article 1411 but goes further in imposing transparency and dialogue on the regulators. These provisions partly reflect the position of the U.S. financial services industry in the WTO negotiations. The goal of these provisions is to ensure that regulatory practices do not limit or negatively affect the rights of financial services providers. An important obligation for Chile is to respond in writing to the "substantive comments" received from interested persons in the process of developing new regulations or modifying existing ones. Chile was easily able to accept these strong obligations because domestic policy was already moving in that direction. However, some concern existed about how soon Chile's agencies and Central Bank would be able to fully comply; the obligations required setting up special offices and training personnel, so a two-year grace period after the entry into force of the trade agreement was included.

To operate in the host-country market, foreign-owned financial institutions must have access to the payments and clearing system and be allowed to participate in self-regulatory organizations in which membership is required for providing financial services. Both issues are taken into account in the agreement, based on NAFTA and the Understanding on Commitments in Financial Services.

The chapter also contains an article on expedited availability of insurance products. The article has only a declaratory purpose, but it reflects the offensive interest of the U.S. insurance industry in the negotiations. Chile's insurance law requires that insurance companies register new models of insurance policies in the Deposit of Policies of the SVS. If no objections are made, the companies can contract insurance six days after registration. However, for all MAT insurance policies and nonlife insurance policies contracted with juridical persons with annual premiums greater than approximately US$6,700, the registration requirement does not apply. The United States wanted this provision established as a precedent on how insurance regulators should expedite the approval of new products.[42]

One final aspect of the chapter is worth noting: the dispute settlement mechanism for financial services. The procedures for consultations and the dispute itself, as well as the provisions on investor-state disputes, are similar to those in NAFTA, which means they are quite different from those of the Chile-EU chapter. For instance, in state-to-state disputes, all members of the tribunal have to be experts on financial services, not just the president, as laid down in the Chile-EU agreement.[43] The most important differences are found in disputes between a state and private investors.

In the Chile-U.S. chapter, if an investor makes a claim that is based on the obligations of the investment chapter and the host country argues that the measure is of a prudential nature, the case is taken to the Financial Services Committee. There, bilateral discussions between government experts will determine if a defense is valid. If they agree that the measure taken falls within the prudential carve-out, that decision will be binding.

In negotiating its specific commitments with the United States, Chile followed an approach similar to the one adopted in the Uruguay Round and in the negotiations with the EU. Commitments related to the social security system would, if possible, be excluded, and no substantive changes should be made to the regulatory structure of the financial system. A particular negotiating goal was to maintain the existing separation between subsectors and not to introduce changes to the juridical form under which financial services were provided.

As noted previously, commitments in cross-border trade cover consumption abroad and cross-border supply. For the former, the current level of openness was consolidated. That is, Chilean consumers would be allowed to purchase financial products from U.S. financial services providers abroad. The services excluded from this commitment are all those insurance products whose purchase is compulsory under Chilean law.[44] Thus, none of the existing restrictions were removed. In the case of cross-border supply, the United States requested that those financial services contained in the Understanding on Commitments in Financial Services be covered. Most of them were included in Chile's list.[45] Credit reference and analysis were excluded because Chile's legislation requires commercial presence for providing credit-rating services. Moreover, the commitments on cross-border advisory services cannot, in and of themselves, be construed to require the party to permit the public offering of securities *as defined under its relevant law* in its territory by cross-border suppliers of the other party.

The commitments in commercial presence are regulated by two different provisions: (a) commitments in insurance and insurance-related services are made under the market-access article, and (b) commitments on banking and other financial services are made under the right-of-establishment provision.[46] Thus, Chile's scheduling is a hybrid between the positive list and negative list approaches.

In addition, a number of specific commitments were listed in an annex. As with the EU, Chile accepted a commitment on voluntary pension plans and on nondiscrimination in the compulsory system.

In the same annex is a commitment regarding portfolio management: financial institutions organized outside Chile would be allowed to provide investment advice and portfolio management services. The annex also contains a "best endeavors" commitment of not requiring product approval for insurance services, which implies that new products are allowed unless they are disapproved within a reasonable time. In addition, limitations on the number or frequency of product introductions are not allowed. Interestingly, Chile's legislation had already met this commitment at the time of the negotiation, but that of the United States had not.

Finally, perhaps the most controversial commitment regarding insurance services was the opening of establishment of U.S. insurance companies as branches in Chile. However, the commitment does not cover *direct* branching. Chile can choose how to regulate branches, including their characteristics, structure, relationship to their parent company, capital requirements, technical reserves, and obligations regarding risk patrimony and their investments. The capital of these branches will be separate from that of the parent, as is currently the case of foreign bank branches established in Chile.

One major outstanding issue was still unresolved when the financial services chapter was closed: capital controls and the balance-of-payments exceptions. Throughout the negotiations, the United States refused to accept such measures, even after the Asian crisis.[47] Undoubtedly, this stance caused grave concern on the Chilean side, particularly because the negotiators felt the United States was not recognizing Chile's rights to adopt certain measures on the capital account, even those that followed GATS and the Articles of Agreements of the International Monetary Fund. The sensitivity of the issue is underscored by the fact that it had to be resolved at the highest political level.[48]

As a solution, Chile and the United States agreed on an annex applicable to measures adopted by Chile that could be subject to dispute settlement by U.S. investors. The annex, reproduced in annex 5D of this chapter, establishes rules for the submission of a claim by a U.S. investor in case Chile applies a future measure that breaches an obligation when applying a restriction on payments and transfers. The claim can be submitted only within one year after the measure is adopted and can refer only to a reduction in the value of transfers, not subsequent effects on profits. However, claims can be immediately submitted when restrictions affect (a) transfers related to foreign direct investment and (b) payments pursuant to a loan or bond issued in a foreign market, provided that such payments are made in accordance with the maturity date agreed on in the loan or bond agreement. The spirit of the text is to distinguish between volatile and nonvolatile capital flows, reflecting Chile's application of the URR to address the former in the 1990s.[49] This annex would become a template that was later used in the U.S agreements with Colombia, Peru, and Singapore. In addition, the Chile-U.S. FTA does not contain safeguard provisions as in GATS in case of (a threat of) a balance-of-payments crisis—an important difference with the Chile-EU agreement.

The Aftermath of the Negotiations

The financial services negotiations with the EU and the United States did not raise much interest among members of the press, the public, or the National Congress of Chile. This lack of interest can be explained by the lack of offensive or defensive interests in Chile's financial sector, the highly technical nature of the issues, and the already very open financial services industry in Chile. Naturally, the industry associations (which include both domestic and foreign-owned companies) followed the negotiations closely, as did the regulators and the Central Bank.

The agreement with the EU was sent to the National Congress in the second half of 2002. Because Chile's commitments in financial services were, in the end, an expanded version of its WTO commitments, no issues were controversial. The social security system had been left out of the agreement, with the exception of voluntary savings plans for pensions, and all the powers for controlling capital flows contained in the Central Bank Act had been included in an annex and in Chile's schedules. Allowing the cross-border provision of MAT insurance was not controversial because it was already the practice. Accordingly, no major effect was expected on the domestic financial industry or on its regulation and supervision.

The U.S. agreement was more controversial and involved two requests on the part of the United States. The first was to allow *direct* branching for U.S. banks and insurance companies. The United States considered the prohibition of direct branching a restriction on trade in financial services through commercial presence. The local industry, both banks and insurance companies, immediately opposed the request because they feared the enormous size of U.S. banks and insurance companies might drive local companies out of the market. Chile did not agree to this concession, and thus foreign banks cannot operate as direct branches.

The second request was to lift the limits on investment abroad of pension funds. This request proved politically very difficult because, at the same time, the government was trying to gradually lift that limit through domestic legislation. At the time, the main Chilean trade unions generally had a critical or skeptical view of the management of pension funds by private companies. Allowing the investment overseas of such funds added to this view. The United States requested the lifting of the limit on investment in foreign financial instruments, arguing that the limitation was something similar to a performance requirement and a trade barrier for U.S. asset management firms willing to supply Chilean pension funds. At the time, no pressure was coming from the domestic pension fund industry to lift the limit on foreign investment because the government was already pushing corresponding legislation. Pointing to certain U.S. pension funds with similar limitations, the Chilean negotiation team refused to accede to U.S. requests.

Because commitments on those two sensitive issues were avoided, the legislative passage of the financial services commitments was largely uneventful. Some discussion came up about the annex on capital controls, but in the end, the National Congress accepted the provisions, given that Chile would still be allowed to take measures in the face of volatile short-term capital flows.

To date, no significant effects on the domestic financial services industry have occurred. Of course, the time since the agreements entered into force has not been long enough to see any substantial consequences, particularly without additional liberalization. The only reform necessary was a modification of Chile's domestic insurance law, allowing establishment through "branches."[50] No other legal changes were required as a result of the financial services negotiations with the EU and the United States. The most important change is the introduction by the regulatory agencies of a process for receiving and responding to comments on new regulations on their Web sites. The Central Bank and the superintendencies have already begun to request comments by publishing proposals for new regulations on their Web sites. This outcome was what the technical team expected—that is, little effect in the short term and a potential beneficial effect in the longer term from the greater certainty of market access and investor protection provided by the trade agreements. Whether the agreements will attract more U.S. and European financial institutions remains to be seen.

Lessons from the Chilean Experience

No two trade negotiations are alike. The circumstances, initial conditions, and goals vary from country to country. Aspects of the Chilean experience will not be reproduced in the future: in particular, Chile had 10 years between the first contacts to negotiate an FTA with the United States and the actual negotiations. Although the decision was exogenous, in some ways Chile was able to choose when to start negotiating. For the United States, negotiating with Chile (and, similarly, Singapore) constituted an opportunity to establish new precedents that were based on the experiences of NAFTA and GATS. At least in Chile's case, this opportunity permitted some very fruitful discussion regarding the chapter's text. The Singapore-U.S. and Chile-U.S. financial services texts have been used by the United States as its template in other FTA negotiations. The EU represents a different experience. The EU approach is one of extending GATS to the bilateral level, with minor changes in provisions and the same approach of listing commitments. However, this approach does not mean that there is no room for other economies negotiating with the United States or the EU to accommodate their specific circumstances and objectives.

When Chile began negotiating with the EU and the United States, the macroeconomic environment was stable, with small and manageable fiscal and current account deficits, low inflation, and a freely floating exchange rate, all in a context of fully liberalized international capital flows. Thus, unlike Mexico (which faced the Tequila crisis shortly after NAFTA entered into force), Chile's economy has continued to grow, and no signs of instability in its financial system have arisen since the agreements entered into force.

Chile's financial system showed healthy indicators and had an already significant participation of foreign-owned financial institutions in its domestic market. As in the case of tariff liberalization, where the pain suffered from trade liberalization of a specific industry depends on the initial level of market-access restrictions, the effect of a bilateral (or multilateral) agreement in financial services will depend on how open domestic financial institutions are to international competition. The jury is still out on the consequences for Chile's financial industry, but in the short term, dramatic effects have certainly not occurred.

If the agreements with the EU and the United States did not really lead to substantive new liberalization, the question naturally arises whether, and why, they were important. One explanation is that both the EU and the United States showed a systemic interest in including financial services as part of trade commitments in general, whether at the multilateral or the bilateral level. Both the EU and the United States pushed for the adoption of the same commitments in cross-border trade as in the GATS Understanding on Commitments in Financial Services. For the EU, an additional motivation can be found in the investments by Spanish banks in Chilean financial institutions. For the United States, the FTA with Chile served as a precedent for other negotiations.

In addition are the usual benefits associated with any trade agreement: predictable rules for market access, nondiscrimination guaranteed through a foreign treaty (and not only by domestic law), a dispute settlement mechanism, and limitations and rules for the application of restrictions on capital flows.

Having previously moved unilaterally in the direction of opening the financial sector to foreign competition facilitated the negotiations. These actions included the lifting of barriers particularly disturbing to foreign financial services providers, such as the use of an economic needs test; limitations on the number of licenses, and on the share of foreign ownership; and the prohibition, for foreign-owned institutions, on providing certain services. In addition to enhancing the competitiveness and the role of the financial sector as an instrument for allocating resources, the removal of such barriers reduces the opposition to negotiating financial services. However, such liberalization requires strengthening and modernizing supervisory agencies. The Chilean financial crisis of 1982–83 clearly shows that liberalization and deregulation without proper strengthening (not weakening) of the powers and role of regulatory entities can have disastrous consequences. Having in place strong, professional, competent regulators that use international standards to the extent practicable contributes greatly to the success of financial services liberalization. In addition, having already adopted national treatment as a basic standard in the development and application of financial regulation is an important element in successful negotiations.

Chile's experience provides several lessons for other countries:

- Both the United States and the EU have templates for the text in financial services. The United States uses an updated version of NAFTA chapter XIV, and the EU uses GATS. Both are already well-known texts and can be considered the two world standards for liberalizing trade in financial services. Certain provisions are not negotiable, especially national treatment and market access. However, other parts of the text can be adapted to the specific circumstances of a country, providing more flexibility for the needs and interests of the negotiation partner.

- Careful drafting of reservations (in the U.S. approach) or of limitations to market access and national treatment (in the EU approach) is a crucial aspect of constructing a negotiating position. Poorly drafted or excessively broad reservations or limitations weaken a country's negotiating position. Poorly drafted text can easily be rebutted, forcing the negotiating team back to the drafting table and weakening its negotiating position. Overly broad, unclear, and vague reservations or limitations may appear to be a way of avoiding commitments. Of course, perfectly legitimate reasons exist for reservations or limitations: preserving the financial system's regulatory structure, ensuring transparency, including prudential measures,[51] or simply limiting the degree of commitment. The negotiators should clearly identify and communicate these objectives. Reservations for future measures— for example, "Country X reserves the right to maintain or adopt any measure regarding financial service Y"—are particularly strong and are the equivalent of an unbound commitment in GATS. Thus, their use should respond to very clearly specified circumstances that may strengthen their justification.

- It is difficult to conclude whether following the GATS or the NAFTA model is more liberalizing. The obligations established by the text and by the level of commitments made are more influential.

- Exchange of information and coordination with the teams negotiating other chapters is very important—in particular those on investment, trade in other services, e-commerce, government procurement, and dispute settlement. The specific organization may vary from country to country, but timely participation in other groups and information on the progress at other negotiating tables can save financial services negotiators a lot of trouble, because their objectives and negotiating positions can be weakened by commitments or contradictory provisions in other areas (and vice versa).

- The content and nature of financial services negotiations were a novelty for the regulators and the private sector in Chile. Therefore, having good channels of communication and consultation with all stakeholders, both in the public and the private sectors, is important. In particular, the consequences of the negotiations for the policies and actions of the supervisory agencies should be made transparent. These agencies must be made comfortable that their regulatory prerogatives are not being undermined. The private sector must also constantly be kept informed because opposition may arise against certain demands from the negotiators' counterparts. It is better to have a dialogue with the private sector than to ignore their concerns completely. A delicate balance and a careful distinction between legitimate concerns and outright protectionist stances are required.

- Finally, assessing whether Chile accomplished the objective of avoiding cross-sector links is difficult, if not impossible. Certainly, the fact that Chile agreed to negotiate financial services immediately and not to leave it for future negotiation made the negotiations with the EU and the United States viable to begin with. However, in both cases, the financial services negotiations were closed before the overall package was completed. Thus, concluding one way or another whether Chile's level of commitments in financial services influenced the market-access commitments made by the EU and the United States in their areas of interest is difficult.

Final Thoughts on Preparing for a Bilateral Negotiation in Financial Services

The inclusion of a financial services chapter has become the standard not only for North-North and North-South preferential trade agreements, but also increasingly in South-South agreements. Emerging economies have to be prepared to negotiate commitments on financial services, including the possibility of having to adopt measures that liberalize trade in financial services. This section addresses some of the issues that should be raised and debated to take advantage of the opportunity for bilateral negotiation of a financial services chapter.

In general, negotiations should be approached in a pragmatic way. First and foremost, one should avoid grand illusions such as converting the domestic financial market into a major global financial services center. Instead, such negotiations rather are mercantilist in character. Market-access and national treatment commitments are requested in exchange for often limited commitments on the part of trading partners (especially if these partners are substantially large economies). In particular, in a negotiation with a country that is an exporter of financial services, that exporter's request for commitments will not be based on a truly trade-liberalizing strategy. Rather, market-access requests will be based on the specific petitions of the domestic exporting financial services industry and will focus on reduced entry and supervision burdens.[52] Thus, carefully assessing and anticipating the direction and form of these requests is a crucial element in the preparation of bilateral negotiations.

Of course, if a small country has offensive interests, they should be identified from the start, and a strategy for pursuing them in the negotiations should be designed. This aspect relates, for instance, to countries such as Colombia, El Salvador, and Guatemala, which may be interested in providing financial services to migrant workers in the United States.

Such interests should also be identified early to assess any political costs that might outweigh the economic benefits of trade liberalization (which mainly accrue to consumers of financial services). Defensive positions will likely emanate from the domestic industry, but financial regulators should also be consulted because they are important stakeholders in the negotiation. Moreover, clarifying the defensive priorities will help when concessions become necessary for closing the negotiations.

Another important reminder is that the purpose of these negotiations is enhanced market-access opportunities, not financial integration in terms of mutual recognition or harmonization of prudential standards. That is, the EU or the United States will not be looking to integrate financially with negotiation parties in the same sense as has been done in the EU single market. The basic and fundamental commitment the EU and the United States seek is an environment based on national treatment. Thus, after the negotiations, the financial services providers of the small economy will not necessarily be granted the right to open branches in the foreign market on the basis of their home-country supervision.

A good starting point for assessing the likely scope of negotiations and the nature of likely requests emanating from key partners is to perform a thorough review of all domestic legislation on the basis of what are considered barriers to trade in services.[53] Despite the differences in the GATS and NAFTA templates used by the EU and the United States, respectively, in practice no substantive differences really exist in the preparation needed for one or the other approach.

The list of existing nonconforming measures (or its GATS equivalent, limitations on market access and national treatment) must be carefully drafted. Poorly drafted measures or limitations weaken the negotiating position, and the defensive priorities may be inadequately protected. Furthermore, they reflect poor preparation and weak technical expertise from the negotiating team. Similarly, future nonconforming measures should be strategically drafted, which is the equivalent of not listing particular subsectors under the GATS approach. This aspect is crucial to constructing the negotiating position. In the end, such measures are going to be the core of the negotiation, and the team has to be prepared for this critical stage well ahead of time.

Not only will this exercise be useful in developing a host country's negotiating strategy; it will also be very important when the time comes to draft the nonconforming measures (if the negotiating approach is like that of NAFTA) or the limitations to market access and national treatment (if the GATS approach is taken).

Once trade restrictions have been mapped and the priorities of the counterpart have been analyzed, the negotiating team should develop a forward-looking strategy or "roadmap." This strategy includes defining the negotiating priorities, both offensive and defensive, and particularly determining what are going to be the red lines. As Echandi has stated clearly in his Costa Rica case study (see chapter 7), the goal is to minimize surprises. Another goal should be to avoid picking secondary fights. For example, maintaining limitations on national treatment (that is, discrimination between domestic- and foreign-established providers) or certain market-access restrictions such as equity limitations has little justification today. Much more important is the issue of the form of establishment (subsidiaries versus branches) because it directly affects the ability of the domestic regulators to supervise a global bank. That is, the U.S. Federal Reserve can exert pressure on Germany's regulator to address problems at the local branch and the parent bank, but Chilean or Salvadoran regulators perhaps cannot do the same when they see problems in the local branch of a U.S. bank in their market. The counterpart has to clearly know the political and technical limits and understand that going beyond them will put at risk the outcome of the negotiation. This discussion has to be credible, and exaggerations should be carefully avoided.

As already mentioned, in a negotiation with a major economy, such as the EU, Japan, or the United States, the major economy's commitments in financial services are unlikely to go beyond those they have already consolidated under GATS. Furthermore, such economies will tend to have certain templates for their negotiations. However, this does not mean that there will be no negotiation. Room always exists for making changes to the template. The team has to be creative at the margins. That is, windows of opportunity need to be used to modify the text to accommodate specific domestic concerns, without changing the substance of underlying obligations. For example, although very similar, the texts negotiated by Chile, Colombia, Singapore, and the Central American countries with the United States are not identical. Normally, the major economies have bound their level of openness in GATS, and therefore their lists reflect their limitations. Such limitations can be used to obtain accommodation to a small country's sensitivities. Certain minimum obligations will always be nonnegotiable, but room may exist for phasing out nonconforming measures over time.

However, in all of this, selectivity is necessary. Very early in the negotiations, the negotiating team must identify those key issues on which it needs breathing space or differentiation. Identifying those issues will entail tough choices: trade-offs will be necessary, and demands will have to be accepted without changes in some areas.

Good coordination with other negotiating teams is also essential. Under NAFTA-type agreements, certain obligations and definitions of the investment chapter need to be included in the chapter on financial services. Hence, close coordination between the financial services and investment teams is very important. In NAFTA-type agreements, the chapter on cross-border trade in services may also contain provisions applicable to financial services. If the financial services team feels that in the dispute resolution mechanism, disputes in financial services panels should be entirely or partially composed of experts, then coordination with that team will also be required.

In approaching the negotiations in financial services, one must define how such services relate to the broader context of a preferential trade agreement. This point is quite clear when negotiating with a developed economy, given that the inclusion of financial services is generally a major offensive interest of developed economies. Thus, when negotiating with a major country, the smaller country should make every effort to insist that the fact of having accepted a financial services chapter should be considered a major commitment, worth concessions outside the financial services chapter.

Scheduling commitments in financial services in exchange for commitments in other areas is a matter of dispute. Finance ministries and financial regulators dislike the idea of liberalizing financial services in exchange for a bigger quota, say, in apples or bovine meat. In the experience of Chile, the financial services chapter, including the commitments (an offensive interest for the EU and the United States), was closed before the overall negotiation was concluded. Although it helped reach an agreement, the fact that Chile for the first time engaged in bilateral commitments in financial services did not lead to greater opening in agriculture or temporary entry of persons (offensive interests of Chile) with the EU or the United States.

Trade-offs and links will also be influenced by the institutional setup (that is, which agency leads negotiations in financial services). In some countries, the Ministry of Finance or the Treasury leads negotiations; in others, the Ministry of Trade or its equivalent takes the lead; and in some cases, negotiations are conducted by the financial services regulator (Japan in the World Trade Organization) or the monetary authority (Singapore). Chile and Colombia managed to isolate the financial services negotiations by concentrating the negotiations in the Ministry of Finance, but this arrangement is not feasible in all institutional settings.

What matters is that, irrespective of who leads the negotiating team, all relevant agencies should be incorporated in the decision-making process at the highest possible level. This strategy not only allows a wider range of views to be expressed, thereby enriching the debate on the negotiating strategy, but also provides a sense of government ownership once consensus has been reached. Two levels of collective decision making can be suggested: the ministerial level (for political responsibility and endorsement) and the technical level (that is, senior ministerial advisers).

Consensus among the different stakeholders both in and out of the government about the goals of the negotiations, the strategy, and its benefits and potential downsides for the country is essential. Without consensus, the negotiating strategy will be less effective. The negotiating team will have to constantly revisit the issues, uncertain about the scope of its mandate. This uncertainty, in turn, drastically weakens the negotiating ability of the team, and the team's positions will not be seen as credible.

Such consensus existed in the case of Chile. Since the early 1990s, the country adopted as one of its goals negotiation of an FTA with the United States. This objective was ratified by every Chilean government from

1991 onward. When the time came to negotiate financial services, no one within the government or the industry questioned the Ministry of Finance's decision to engage. This consensus among the various stakeholders facilitated the establishment of a common negotiating position supported by the regulators and the industry. In Costa Rica, some dissent occurred within government agencies (see chapter 7). For the private sector, what arises in negotiations tends to be rather novel; therefore, there is an aspect of educating the stakeholders about what is being done and what implications are involved.

Consulting civil society on issues linked to financial services liberalization should also be considered in the broader negotiation strategy. In Chile, no consultations with civil society regarding financial services took place, because for most people and nongovernmental organizations, financial services liberalization is an extremely technical subject, and they do not see its direct relationship to their daily life. Opposition to negotiating financial services will arise from groups opposed to preferential trade agreements in general, focused on trade in goods in most cases. In this situation, government negotiators may well be responsible for considering the effects that the negotiations may have on consumers of financial services. Nonetheless, an effort should be made whenever possible to reach out to civil society representatives to impart greater political legitimacy to negotiating outcomes.

One final point should be made about capital flows. Negotiations and commitments regarding capital flows (or the elimination of capital controls) do not fall under the financial services chapter. Their scope is broader, so they are part of the investment chapter in the U.S.-NAFTA template (and apply through an explicit reference to financial services) and are a whole separate section on the current and capital accounts in the EU template. The issue is seen—and should be seen—as separate from the specific commitments in financial services. The reason is that the issue of capital controls affects all commitments involving the capital account, regarding investment in all sectors of the economy. A team made up of finance and central bank officials should take up this crucial aspect in the negotiation of a preferential trade agreement.

Annex 5A: Summary of Chilean Trade Agreements

In recent years, Chile has negotiated a number of trade agreements. Table 5A.1 shows the status of the treaties negotiated between 1991 and 2006, the model on which the treaties are based, and the main areas covered.

Table 5A.1 Chilean Trade Agreements, 1990–2006

Agreement	Status	Model	Main areas covered
Economic complementation agreement with Mexico	Replaced by free trade agreement in 1999	ALADI	Trade in goods
Economic complementation agreement with R.B. de Venezuela	In force since July 1993	ALADI	Trade in goods
Economic complementation agreement with Bolivia	In force since July 1993	ALADI	Trade in goods
Economic complementation agreement with Colombia	In force since January 1994	ALADI	Trade in goods
Economic complementation agreement with Ecuador	In force since January 1995	ALADI	Trade in goods
Economic complementation agreement with Mercosur	In force since October 1996	ALADI	Trade in goods
Free trade agreement with Canada	In force since July 1997	NAFTA	Trade in goods, trade in services, investment, telecommunications; government procurement and financial services under negotiation
Economic complementation agreement with Peru	In force since July 1998	ALADI	Trade in goods
Trade preferences agreement with Cuba	Negotiations concluded in August 1998; not yet in force	ALADI	Trade in goods
Free trade agreement with Mexico	In force since August 1999	NAFTA	Trade in goods, trade in services, investment, air transportation services, telecommunications, intellectual property; government procurement and financial services under negotiation
Free trade agreement with Central America	Signed in October 1999; partially in force[a]	NAFTA	Trade in goods, trade in services, air transportation services, telecommunications, government procurement; investment and financial services not covered

Agreement	Status	Model	Coverage
Association agreement with the European Union	In force since February 2003	GATT and GATS	Trade in goods, trade in services, trade in financial services, establishment of investors, government procurement, intellectual property
Free trade agreement with the United States	In force since January 2004	NAFTA	Trade in goods, trade in services, trade in financial services, investment, government procurement, telecommunications, e-commerce, intellectual property
Free trade agreement with the Republic of Korea	In force since April 2004	NAFTA	Trade in goods, trade in services, investment, government procurement, intellectual property; financial services to be included no later than 4 years after the entry into force
Free trade agreement with EFTA	In force since December 2004	Based on EU-Chile agreement	Trade in goods, trade in services, establishment of investors, government procurement, intellectual property; financial services to be negotiated 2 years after entry into force
Free trade agreement with China	In force since October 2006		Trade in goods
Trans-Pacific economic association agreement (Brunei Darussalam, Chile, New Zealand, and Singapore)	In force since November 2006	NAFTA	Trade in goods, trade in services, government procurement, intellectual property; investment and financial services to be negotiated 2 years after entry into force
Free trade agreement with Panama	Signed in 2006	NAFTA	Trade in goods, trade in services; financial services may be incorporated 2 years after entry into force
Tariff preferences agreement with India	Signed in March 2006; under legislative ratification		Trade in goods

Source: Data from Dirección General de Relaciones Económicas Internacionales de Chile (Directorate for International Economic Relations).

Note: ALADI = Asociación Latinoamericana de Integración (Latin American Integration Association); EFTA = European Free Trade Association (Iceland, Liechtenstein, Norway, and Switzerland); GATT = General Agreement on Tariffs and Trade; GATS = General Agreement on Trade in Services; Mercosur = Mercado Común del Sur (Southern Cone Common Market); NAFTA = North American Free Trade Agreement.

a. The free trade agreement enters into force bilaterally with each country of Central America and the Dominican Republic when the negotiation of a bilateral protocol of tariff preferences for goods is concluded.

Annex 5B: Origin of the Texts of the Chile-EU and Chile-U.S. Financial Services Chapters

Tables 5B.1 and 5B.2 summarize the contents of the Chile-EU and Chile-U.S. financial services chapters, respectively. The tables also show the origin of the text of the various articles.

Table 5B.1   Origin of the Texts of the Chile-EU Financial Services Chapter

Chile-EU text	Source	Other provisions
Article 116, Scope	GATS, article I GATS, Annex on Financial Services	Text excludes government procurement. Text excludes subsidies granted by the parties.
Article 117, Definitions	GATS, article I GATS, article XXVIII GATS, Annex on Financial Services Understanding on Commitments in Financial Services	
Article 118, Market access	GATS, article XVI	
Article 119, National treatment	GATS, article XVII	
Article 120, Schedule of specific commitments	GATS, article XX	
Article 121, New financial services	Understanding on Commitments in Financial Services	
Article 122, Data processing in the financial services sector	Understanding on Commitments in Financial Services	The domestic law regulating the protection of individuals of the territory of origin of the data prevails.
Article 123, Effective and transparent regulation in the financial services sector	NAFTA, article 1411	Applies agreed international standards for regulation and supervision and fight against money laundering.
Article 124, Confidential information	GATS, article III bis GATS, Annex on Financial Services	
Article 125, Prudential carve-out	NAFTA, article 1410.1 GATS, Annex on Financial Services	
Article 126, Recognition	GATS, Annex on Financial Services	

Table 5B.1   *(continued)*

Chile-EU text	Source	Other provisions
Article 127, Special Committee on Financial Services	NAFTA, article 1412	
Article 128, Consultations	NAFTA, article 1413	
Article 129, Special provisions on dispute settlement	Drafted by Chile and the European Union	Consultations take place in the Special Committee on Financial Services. Chair of tribunal must be an expert in financial services.

Source: Author's compilation based on GATS and NAFTA documents.
Note: GATS = General Agreement on Trade in Services; NAFTA = North American Free Trade Agreement.

Table 5B.2   Origin of the Texts of the Chile-U.S. Financial Services Chapter

Chile-U.S. text	Source	Comments
Article 12.1, Scope and coverage	NAFTA, article 1401 GATS, Annex on Financial Services	Paragraph regarding whether certain activities, such as public retirement plans, statutory systems of social security, or those conducted with the guarantee of the party, are covered is based on the Annex on Financial Services.
Article 12.2, National treatment	NAFTA, article 1405	Text contains no provisions on subnational treatment and no concept of equal competitive opportunities.
Article 12.3, Most-favored-nation treatment	NAFTA, article 1406	
Article 12.4, Market access for financial institutions	GATS, article XVI	Text excludes the provision on limits to foreign ownership, which was considered a violation of national treatment.
Article, 12.5 Cross-border trade	NAFTA, article 1404	Text contains an important modification to NAFTA's approach. It includes no standstill, as in NAFTA, and, in the case of cross-border supply, it applies only to a limited positive list of financial services, similar to the approach in the Understanding on Commitments in Financial Services.
Article 12.6, New financial services	NAFTA, article 1407	Text is modified.

(continued)

Table 5B.2   *(continued)*

Chile-U.S. text	Source	Comments
Article 12.7, Treatment of certain information	GATS, article III bis GATS, Annex on Financial Services	
Article 12.8, Senior management and board of directors	NAFTA, article 1408	Text is modified.
Article 12.9, Nonconforming measures	NAFTA, article 1409	
Article 12.10, Exceptions	GATS, Annex on Financial Services NAFTA, article 1410 GATS, article XIV	New text was added regarding measures to prevent fraudulent and deceptive practices.
Article 12.11, Transparency	NAFTA, article 1411	Text significantly expands the obligations of NAFTA.
Article 12.12, Self-regulatory organizations	NAFTA, article 1402	
Article 12.13, Payment and clearing systems	Understanding on Commitments in Financial Services	
Article 12.14, Expedited availability of insurance services	New	
Article 12.15, Financial Services Committee	NAFTA, article 1412	
Article 12.16, Consultations	NAFTA, article 1413	
Article 12.17, Dispute settlement	NAFTA, article 1414	
Article 12.18, Investment disputes in financial services	NAFTA, article 1415	
Article 12.19, Definitions	Based on chapter text NAFTA, chapter 14 GATS, where relevant	
Annex 12.5, Cross-border trade	Understanding on Commitments in Financial Services	
Annex 12.9, Specific commitments and right of establishment provision	NAFTA, article 1403	

Source: Author's compilation based on GATS and NAFTA documents.
Note: GATS = General Agreement on Trade in Services; NAFTA = North American Free Trade Agreement.

Annex 5C: Chile's Commitments in Financial Services in the Uruguay Round

This annex describes Chile's Schedule of Specific Commitments negotiated in the Uruguay Round and contained in WTO document GATS/SC/18/Suppl.3.[54] Chile's schedule is presented, first with the horizontal limitations, then the general market-access or national treatment limitations, and finally the subsectors in which commitments were made, organized by mode of supply. The horizontal, market-access, and national treatment limitations in services that also apply to financial services are not included here and can be found in WTO document GATS/SC/18.

Horizontal Notes

In addition to the horizontal limitations mentioned previously for all financial services, a specific horizontal entry in the schedule describes the partial segmentation of financial activities reflected in the structure of Chile's financial system. Banks cannot directly provide insurance and securities dealing services. They must do so through separate subsidiaries.

For insurance and reinsurance services, the horizontal note also specifies how such services may be supplied through establishment in Chile's market. The same company cannot provide both life insurance services and general insurance services. Credit insurance companies must be incorporated and can provide that type of insurance only. An important exclusion to Chile's commitments in insurance is that they exclude all insurance products related to the social security system.

A number of horizontal notes concerning securities services describe the terms under which services such as the trading of publicly offered securities, financial portfolio management, risk rating, custodial services, and advisory services can be supplied in Chile.

General Market-Access or National Treatment Limitations

The schedule specifies that Chile did not bind all financial services and all modes of supplies, the measures that the Central Bank can adopt according to its act, for reasons of maintaining macroeconomic stability and the normal functioning of the payments system. Those measures include limitations on payments and transfers in and out of Chile, such as a reserve requirement on loans.

In the case of commercial presence, establishment in financial services requires the passing of an economic needs test and, furthermore, the type of commercial presence may be restricted or set down in a nondiscriminatory fashion. Finally, repatriation of capital is allowed only after two years of presence.

Commitments on Cross-Border Supply

For mode 1 (cross-border supply), Chile made binding commitments only for reinsurance and retrocession services, including brokerage of reinsurance. A registration requirement acts as a market-access limitation, and a tax on ceded insurance premiums as a national treatment violation.

Commitments on Consumption Abroad

Chile did not make any commitments in this mode of supply in the Uruguay Round negotiations.

Commitments on Commercial Presence

This is the mode of supply in which Chile made the most commitments in the 1990s. Chile's schedule lists financial services related to banking services, insurance and reinsurance services, and securities services.

The banking services listed include some that are considered to be the main business of banks (taking deposits and granting loans) and some that Chilean law defines as complementary to a bank's main business. All limitations are related to specific requirements of juridical form in market access, but there are no limitations on national treatment.

In addition to the horizontal exclusion of insurance related to the social security system, in insurance services, Chile's list excludes health insurance provided by private companies in the context of the social security system.[55] Both life and nonlife insurance are included as well as insurance brokerage, but none of the services auxiliary to insurance, such as consulting, actuarial, risk assessment, and claim settlement services.

The securities services listed include the trading of publicly offered securities and stock of corporations, risk rating, custodial services by securities brokers, financial advisory services, portfolio management by securities brokers, and warrants.

Commitments on Presence of Natural Persons

Chile did not make commitments on mode 4, presence of natural persons, specific to financial services. In all subsectors listed, mode 4 is "Unbound, except as indicated in the horizontal section." However, in its services commitments, which also apply to financial services, Chile did make a commitment regarding transfers of natural persons within a foreign enterprise established in Chile and of senior and specialized personnel employed for at least two years prior to application to admission into Chile who are performing the same types of duties as in the parent company.

Annex 5D: Transfer and Payment Regulatory Provisions in Chile's Trade Agreements

This annex provides the text of provisions in Chile's trade agreement that regulate transfers and payments.

GATS (1997): GATS/SC/18/Suppl.3

[For all modes of supply] Unbound in respect of measures adopted or to be adopted by the Central Bank of Chile under its constitutive law (Law No. 18,840) or other legislation in order to ensure the stability of the currency and the normal operation of domestic and foreign payments. For this purpose the Bank is empowered to regulate the supply of money and credit, international credit, and exchange operations, and to issue regulations governing money, credit, finance, and international exchange. Such measures include *inter alia* the establishment of restrictions or limitations on payments and transfers to or from Chile, as well as transactions relating to them, such as the requirement that deposits, investments, or credits coming from or going to a foreign country be subject to a reserve requirement.

Foreign investors who participate in the financial services sector may transfer their capital abroad two (2) years after bringing it in.

Canada-Chile FTA (1997): Annex G-09.1 (to Article G-09: Transfers)

1. For the purpose of preserving the stability of its currency, Chile reserves the right:
   (a) to maintain existing requirements that transfers from Chile of proceeds from the sale of all or any part of an investment of an investor of Canada or from the partial or complete liquidation of the investment may not take place until a period not to exceed
     (i) in the case of an investment made pursuant to Law 18,657 *Foreign Capital Investment Fund Law* ("Ley 18,657, Ley sobre Fondo de Inversiones de Capitales Extranjeros"), five years has elapsed from the date of transfer to Chile, or
     (ii) subject to subparagraph (c),
     (iii) in all other cases, one year has elapsed from the date of transfer to Chile;

(b) to apply a reserve requirement pursuant to Article 49 No. 2 of Law 18,840, Organic Law of the Central Bank of Chile, ("Ley 18,840, Ley Orgánica del Banco Central de Chile") on an investment of an investor of Canada, other than foreign direct investment, and on foreign credits relating to an investment, provided that such a reserve requirement shall not exceed 30 percent of the amount of the investment, or the credit, as the case may be;

(c) to adopt

(i) measures imposing a reserve requirement referred to in (b) for a period which shall not exceed two years from the date of transfer to Chile,

(ii) any reasonable measure consistent with paragraph 3 necessary to implement or to avoid circumvention of the measures under (a) or (b), and

(iii) measures, consistent with Article G-09 and this Annex, establishing future special voluntary investment programs in addition to the general regime for foreign investment in Chile, except that any such measures may restrict transfers from Chile of proceeds from the sale of all or any part of an investment of an investor of Canada or from the partial or complete liquidation of the investment for a period not to exceed 5 years from the date of transfer to Chile; and

(d) to apply, pursuant to the Law 18,840, measures with respect to transfers relating to an investment of an investor of Canada that

(i) require that foreign exchange transactions for such transfers take place in the Formal Exchange Market,

(ii) require authorization for access to the Formal Exchange Market to purchase foreign currency, at the rate agreed upon by the parties to the transaction, which access shall be granted without delay when such transfers are:

(A) payments for current international transactions,

(B) proceeds from the sale of all or any part, and from the partial or complete liquidation of an investment of an investor of Canada, or

(C) payments pursuant to a loan provided they are made in accordance with the maturity dates originally agreed upon in the loan agreement, and

(iii) require that foreign currency be converted into Chilean pesos, at the rate agreed upon by the parties to the transaction, except for transfers referred to in (ii) (A) through (C), which are exempt from this requirement.

2. Where Chile proposes to adopt a measure referred to in paragraph 1(c), Chile shall, to the extent practicable:
   (a) provide in advance to Canada the reasons for the proposed adoption of the measure as well as any relevant information in relation to the measure; and
   (b) provide Canada with a reasonable opportunity to comment on the proposed measure.

3. A measure that is consistent with this Annex but inconsistent with Article G-02, shall be deemed not to contravene Article G-02 provided that, as required under existing Chilean law, it does not discriminate among investors that enter into transactions of the same nature.

4. This Annex applies to Law 18,840, to the *Decree Law 600* of 1974 ("Decreto Ley 600 de 1974") to Law 18,657 and any other law establishing a future special voluntary investment program consistent with sub-paragraph 1(c)(iii) and to the continuation or prompt renewal of such laws, and to amendments to those laws, to the extent that any such amendment does not decrease the conformity of the amended law with Article G-09(1) as it existed immediately before the amendment.

5. For the purposes of this Annex:
   - *Chilean juridical person* means an enterprise that is constituted or organized in Chile for profit in a form which under Chilean law is recognized as being a juridical person;
   - *date of transfer* means the settlement date when the funds that constitute the investment were converted into Chilean pesos, or the date of the importation of the equipment and technology;
   - *existing* means in effect on October 24, 1996;
   - *foreign credit* means any type of debt financing originating in foreign markets whatever its nature, form or maturity period;
   - *foreign direct investment* means an investment of an investor of Canada, other than a foreign credit, made in order:
     (a) to establish a Chilean juridical person or to increase the capital of an existing Chilean juridical person with the purpose of producing

an additional flow of goods or services, excluding purely financial flows; or

(b) to acquire equity of an existing Chilean juridical person and to participate in its management, but excludes such an investment that is of a purely financial character and that is designed only to gain indirect access to the financial market of Chile;

- *Formal Exchange Market* means the market constituted by the banking entities and other institutions authorized by the competent authority; and
- *payments* for current international transactions means "payments for current international transactions" as defined under the *Articles of Agreement of the International Monetary Fund*, and for greater certainty, does not include payments of principal pursuant to a loan which are not made in accordance with the maturity dates originally agreed upon in the loan agreement.

Chile-Mexico FTA (1998): Annex 9–10 (to Article 9–10: Transfers)
Same text as Canada-Chile FTA.

Central America–Chile FTA (1999)
The agreement has no investment chapter; thus, it does not contain an obligation regarding transfers.

Chile-EU Association Agreement (2002): Annex XIV (Regarding Articles 164 and 165)
Regarding Current Payments and Capital Movements
     With respect to its obligations under Articles 164 and 165 of this Title, Chile reserves:

1. The right, without prejudice to paragraph 3 of this Annex, to maintain existing requirements that transfers from Chile of proceeds from the sale of all or any part of an investment of an investor of the Community or from the partial or complete liquidation of the investment may not take place until a period not to exceed:
   (i) in the case of an investment made pursuant to Decree Law 600, Foreign Investment Statute (Decreto Ley 600, Estatuto de la Inversion Extranjera), one year has elapsed from the date of transfer to Chile, or
   (ii) in the case of an investment made pursuant to Law 18,657, Foreign Capital Investment Fund Law (Ley 18,657, Ley sobre Fondo

de Inversiones de Capitales Extranjeros), five years have elapsed from the date of transfer to Chile and

2. The right to adopt measures, consistent with Articles 2 and 3 and this Annex, establishing future special voluntary investment programs in addition to the general regime for foreign investment in Chile, except that any such measures may restrict transfers from Chile of proceeds from the sale of all or any part of an investment of an investor of the Community or from the partial or complete liquidation of the investment for a period not to exceed five years from the date of transfer to Chile.

3. The right of the Central Bank of Chile to maintain or adopt measures in conformity with the Constitutional Organic Law of the Central Bank of Chile (Ley Orgánica Constitucional del Banco Central de Chile, "Ley 18,840" (hereinafter, "Law 18,840") or other legislation, in order to ensure currency stability and the normal operation of domestic and foreign payments. For this purpose, the Central Bank of Chile is empowered to regulate the supply of money and credit in circulation and international credit and foreign exchange operations. The Central Bank of Chile is empowered as well to issue regulations governing monetary, credit, financial, and foreign exchange matters. Such measures include, *inter alia*, the establishment of restrictions or limitations on current payments and transfers (capital movements) to or from Chile, as well as transactions related to them, such as requiring that deposits, investments, or credits from or to a foreign country be subject to a reserve requirement ("encaje"). Notwithstanding the above, the reserve requirement that the Central Bank of Chile can apply, pursuant to Article 49 No. 2 of Law 18,840, shall not exceed 30 percent of the amount transferred and shall not be imposed for a period which exceeds two years.

4. When applying measures under this Annex, Chile, as established in its legislation, shall not discriminate between the Community and any third country with respect to transactions of the same nature.

Note: Articles 164 and 165 are, respectively, the provisions on the current account and the capital account of title V, Current Payments and Capital Movements.

Chile-U.S. FTA (2003): Annex 10–C Special Dispute Settlement Provisions—Chile

1. Where a claimant submits a claim alleging that Chile has breached an obligation under Section A, other than Article 10.3, that arises from its imposition of restrictive measures with regard to payments and transfers, Section B shall apply except as modified below:

   (a) A claimant may submit any such claim only after one year has elapsed since the events giving rise to the claim;

   (b) If the claim is submitted under Article 10.15(1)(b), the claimant may, on behalf of the enterprise, only seek damages with respect to the shares of the enterprise for which the claimant has a beneficial interest;

   (c) Loss or damages arising from restrictive measures on capital inflows shall be limited to the reduction in value of the transfers and shall exclude loss of profits or business and any similar consequential or incidental damages;

   (d) Paragraph 1(a) shall not apply to claims that arise from restrictions on:

      (i) transfers of proceeds of foreign direct investment by investors of the United States, excluding external debt financing covered in subparagraph (d)(ii), and excluding investments designed with the purpose of gaining direct or indirect access to the financial market; or

      (ii) payments pursuant to a loan or bond issued in a foreign market, including inter- and intra-company debt financing between affiliated enterprises made exclusively for the conduct, operation, management, or expansion of such affiliated enterprises, provided that these payments are made in accordance with the maturity date agreed on in the loan or bond agreement;

   (e) Excluding restrictive measures referred to in paragraph 1(d), Chile shall incur no liability, and shall not be subject to claims, for damages arising from its imposition of restrictive measures with regard to payments and transfers that were incurred within one year from the date on which the restrictions were imposed, provided that such restrictive measures do not substantially impede transfers;

   (f) A restrictive measure of Chile with regard to payments and transfers that is consistent with this Annex shall be deemed not to contravene Article 10.2 10–30 provided that, as required under existing Chilean law, it does not discriminate among investors that enter into transactions of the same nature; and

(g) Claims arising from Chile's imposition of restrictive measures with regard to payments and transfers shall not be subject to Article 10.24 unless Chile consents.

2. The United States may not request the establishment of an arbitral panel under Chapter Twenty-Two (Dispute Settlement) relating to Chile's imposition of restrictive measures with regard to payments and transfers until one year has elapsed since the events giving rise to the dispute.

3. Restrictive measures on payments and transfers related to claims under this Annex shall otherwise be subject to applicable domestic law.

Notes

1. This section is based on Sáez and Sáez (2006). For a detailed analysis of financial liberalization in Chile, see Marshall (1991) and Reinstein and Rosende (2001).
2. The state also guarantees a minimum pension. All dependent workers have to contribute 10 percent of their salaries to such a fund until their retirement age. The pension obtained on retirement depends on the funds accumulated. The retiree has three options: (a) to contract an annuity with an insurance company, (b) to program the monthly withdrawal of the fund, or (c) to contract an annuity with an insurance company starting at a date later than the retirement date while withdrawing from the fund between retirement and the starting date of the annuity. Individuals can also contribute to a voluntary savings account by having the employer withhold an additional percentage of their salaries.
3. From 1981 to January 1983, six banks and five financial companies had already been liquidated.
4. Foreign banks can also open representative offices, but these offices cannot provide banking services.
5. See Reinstein and Rosende (2001) for more details of the changes in the regulatory framework.
6. These statistics are taken from Reinstein and Rosende (2001).
7. Decree Law 600 of 1974, or the Foreign Investment Statute, is a voluntary regime for investing in Chile under which foreign investors sign a contract with the state of Chile for the transfer of capital or other forms of investment

into Chile in exchange for certain guarantees, such as the right to repatriate capital one year after entry, the right to remit profits at any time with free access to freely convertible currencies, and the invariability of the tax regime prevailing when the investment is made. Some of these guarantees were important at a time when uncertainty remained regarding Chilean economic policies and exchange controls were extensively used. Foreign investors can also enter capital into Chile through the general foreign exchange norms contained in chapter XIV of the Central Bank Compendium of Foreign Exchange Norms, but none of the guarantees contained in Decree Law 600 apply to such investments.

8. Hence, any reform to the Central Bank Act requires a special quorum that is greater than that required for regular legislation for its approval.

9. See article 3 of the Central Bank Act. Italics in this and in the following sentences were added by the author.

10. See article 3 of the Central Bank Act.

11. See article 49 (and also 42) of the Central Bank Act for a complete listing of the measures that the Central Bank can adopt regarding foreign exchange transactions.

12. See article 49, paragraph 2, of the Central Bank Act.

13. In 2001, the government introduced a fiscal policy rule according to which the government was obligated to run a structural surplus of 1 percent of GDP. That is, if GDP were at its full-employment level and the price of copper (an important contributor to government revenue) at its estimated long-term level, then the government would be running a surplus equivalent to 1 percent of GDP. The government's actual balance would depend on where the economy was in the cycle. With GDP below its full-employment level and the price of copper below its expected long-term level, the government would run a deficit, and vice versa. Accordingly, with the low levels of GDP and historically low copper prices, the government ran deficits in the 2000–03 period.

14. The creation was very timely because it allowed Chile to make commitments on the management of these funds as an alternative to the mandatory pension system.

15. Previously, mutual funds, investment funds, and housing funds had to be managed by separate entities.

16. ALADI replaced an older integration effort called the Latin American Free Trade Association.

17. In both agreements, the government procurement chapter was also left for future negotiation. In neither case was the deadline respected. Only in 2006 did Canada and Chile begin to negotiate a financial services chapter.

The negotiations were concluded in 2007. Negotiations with Mexico started in 2007 and are still ongoing.

18. Chile's financial services commitments in the Uruguay Round are described in more detail in annex 5C. They can be found in GATS/SC/18/Suppl.3 of February 28, 1998.

19. At the time, the banking act had not been reformed, and foreign banks could access the Chilean market only through the Decree Law 600 foreign investment mechanism.

20. These areas were mainly agriculture, forestry, fishing and aquaculture, food and beverages (mostly wine), some textiles, and professional services.

21. Foreign banks can have commercial presence in Chile as branches of foreign corporations, but for regulatory purposes, they are completely separate entities from their parent corporations, and the limits to their operations are based on their local capital. Thus, in practice, they are not direct branches.

22. This decision was facilitated by the politically very controversial nature of this topic. The government had introduced legislation to increase the percentage of pension funds that could be invested in foreign securities more or less at the same time as the negotiations with the EU and the United States were undertaken; therefore, there was concern that one would interfere with the other.

23. At the time, it was called the Superintendency of AFPs.

24. Isapres are regulated by the Superintendency of Isapres, whose relationship with the government is with the Ministry of Health. Even though Isapres provide health insurance coverage, their regulator was not considered a financial services regulator.

25. Negotiations began in April 2000 in the case of the EU and in December 2000 in the case of the United States.

26. However, experts from the pension regulator, the SP, participated in the preparatory technical work.

27. No consultations took place with other potential stakeholders regarding the financial services negotiations with the EU and the United States, including civil society in general.

28. The text of the Chile-EU financial services chapter and Chile's commitments can be found in http://trade.ec.europa.eu/doclib/docs/2004/november/tradoc _111620.pdf and http://trade.ec.europa.eu/doclib/docs/2004/november/ tradoc_111635.pdf, respectively.

29. Chile reserved the right to introduce specific regulation for the application of this commitment.

30. These provisions differ from those in GATS.

31. These provisions are very similar to those contained in articles 59 and 60 of the Maastricht Treaty.

32. The annex is titled "Annex XIV: Regarding Current Payments and Capital Movement." It can be accessed at http://trade.ec.europa.eu/doclib/docs/2004/november/tradoc_111641.pdf.

33. The measures have to be applied on a nondiscriminatory basis, and the URR is limited to a rate of 30 percent and a two-year maximum period of application.

34. The text of the Chile-U.S. financial services chapter and Chile's schedule of commitments can be found in http://www.ustr.gov/sites/default/files/uploads/agreements/fta/chile/asset_upload_file306_4006.pdf and http://www.ustr.gov/sites/default/files/uploads/agreements/fta/chile/asset_upload_file591_4029.pdf, respectively.

35. In NAFTA, the provision states that nothing in the agreement prevents a party from determining that a public entity will perform such activity exclusively.

36. This issue also came up in the negotiations for the Free Trade Agreement between Central America, the Dominican Republic, and the United States (see chapter 7 in this volume).

37. A WTO panel on gambling clearly stated that a "zero quota" is a violation of the market-access article when a specific service has been committed.

38. The exact list of services is explained later in this section.

39. Both the market-access article and the provision on establishment treat the obligation of a juridical form as a limitation on access or establishment.

40. A difference with the Chile-EU chapter is that the specification of "reasonable" measures is not used.

41. However, it is clearly established that such measures do not include measures that impose performance requirements or limitations on transfers related to investment.

42. Interestingly, many, if not most, of the U.S. states themselves could not meet a more specific obligation.

43. In Chile's view, this provision was an improvement over the GATS annex, whose wording in paragraph 4 on dispute settlement is rather ambiguous.

44. Such services refer in particular to the mandatory pension system, but another example is car insurance.

45. Notable inclusions were supply and brokerage of MAT insurance, reinsurance and retrocession services, provision and transfer of financial information, financial data processing, and advisory and other auxiliary services.

46. Interestingly, most of Chile's reservations refer to "right of establishment" and specifically to the juridical form of establishment.

47. The Trade Promotion Authority approved by the U.S. Congress did not allow for the application of such measures.

48. This resolution occurred in the last round, held in Washington, D.C., in November 2002. A few weeks earlier, the Singapore-U.S. agreement had not been fully completed precisely because of the U.S. position regarding the issue of capital controls. Singapore had not yet accepted the U.S. view on capital controls.

49. Although the approach is different, note that to a certain extent this idea is also anchored in the Canada-Chile annex on the authorization of access to the foreign exchange market.

50. This change was included in legislation that introduced a large number of reforms to the capital market discussed later in the National Congress.

51. Although all financial services chapters contain a prudential measures exception, such an exception has yet to be tested in dispute settlement, and therefore its coverage is still uncertain. In fact, WTO members are not unanimous on the coverage of the prudential exception contained in the financial services annex of GATS.

52. For example, the United States asked Chile to commit on an expedited approval of new insurance products—clearly, a request of its industry—even though the United States itself could not meet that standard because of the variety of its domestic state regulations. A truly liberalizing objective would have been for the United States to reciprocate Chile's already very liberal approval system for insurance products.

53. See also chapter 4 in this volume on performing a regulatory audit.

54. This annex describes Chile's Schedule of Specific Commitments in GATS and in no way reflects Chile's official understanding of its commitments and obligations regarding services or financial services in the WTO.

55. The Isapres collect the 7 percent compulsory contribution for dependent workers. Workers can choose an Isapre or they may choose to belong to the state-managed FONASA.

References and Other Resources

Acuña, Rodrigo, and Augusto Iglesias. 2001. "La reforma a las pensiones [The reform of pensions]." In La transformación económica de Chile [The economic transformation of Chile], ed. Felipe Larraín and Rodrigo Vergara, 430–90. Santiago: Centro de Estudios Públicos.

Cowan, Kevin, and José De Gregorio. 2005. "International Borrowing, Capital Controls, and the Exchange Rate: Lessons from Chile." Working Paper 322, Central Bank of Chile, Santiago.

Ffrench-Davis, Ricardo. 2003. *Entre el neoliberalismo y el crecimiento con equidad: Tres décadas de política económica en Chile* [Of neoliberalism and growth with equity: Three decades of economic policy in Chile]. 3rd ed. Santiago: J. C. Sáez.

Livacic, Ernesto, ed. 2003. *La crisis bancaria del '83: 20 años después* [The banking crisis of '83: 20 years later]. Santiago: Facultad de Ciencias Económicas y Administrativas, Universidad Central de Chile.

Marshall, Enrique. 1991. *El sistema financiero y el mercado de valores en Chile* [The financial system and stock market in Chile]. Mexico City: Centro de Estudios Monetarios Latinoamericanos.

Meller, Patricio. 1996. *Un siglo de política económica chilena (1890–1990)* [A century of Chilean economic policy (1890–1990)]. Santiago: Editorial Andrés Bello.

Reinstein, Andrés, and Francisco Rosende. 2001. "Reforma financiera en Chile [Financial reform in Chile]." In *La transformación económica de Chile* [The economic transformation of Chile], ed. Felipe Larraín and Rodrigo Vergara, 341–90. Santiago: Centro de Estudios Públicos.

Sáez, Raúl E., and Sebastián Sáez. 2006. "Las negociaciones de servicios financieros de Chile [Chile's financial services negotiations]." Serie comercio internacional 75, División de Comercio Internacional e Integración, United Nations, Santiago.

Sáez, Sebastián, Juan Salazar, and Ricardo Vicuña. 1995. "Antecedentes y resultados de la estrategia comercial del Gobierno Aylwin [Antecedents and results of the commercial strategy of the Aylwin Government]." *Colección Estudios CIEPLAN* 41 (December): 41–66.

Stephanou, Constantinos. 2005. "Supervision of Financial Conglomerates: The Case of Chile." Policy Research Working Paper 3553, World Bank, Washington, DC.

CHAPTER 6

Financial Services in the Colombia–United States Free Trade Agreement

María Angélica Arbeláez, Andrés Flórez, and Natalia Salazar

The negotiating process for the free trade agreement (FTA) between the Colombian and U.S. governments was completed in February 2006.[1] Among the many topics discussed and negotiated was a chapter on financial services. This chapter has two main objectives: first, to evaluate the FTA's effect on financial services liberalization on the Colombian economy, and second, to analyze the negotiating process and highlight key lessons learned.

The chapter places special emphasis on the achievements in the negotiation with the United States, relative to the Colombian government's initial objectives, expectations, and strategy. The chapter also evaluates the coherence of the results obtained in relation to the government's vision of the financial sector and, in particular, in the effort to

The authors thank Alejandra González, research assistant at Fedesarrollo, for her valuable contribution in writing this chapter. They also thank Roberto Echandi, Pierre Sauvé, Sergio Clavijo, and Constantinos Stephanou for their comments and suggestions.

further the development of a more open and globally integrated economy with greater international competitiveness. With these objectives in mind, the chapter seeks to shed light on the Colombian financial sector's degree of openness before the FTA and to evaluate whether the FTA maintained the status quo or took liberalization a step further. In addition, it asks whether the outcome of the negotiations is the result of a deliberate policy choice on the part of Colombian authorities or the result of demands made by the United States.

The main conclusion is that the FTA will foster domestic reform in the financial sector, particularly in the area of collective investment schemes and insurance, and will trigger a broader debate on domestic financial reform.

The chapter is organized as follows. It first briefly describes the Colombian financial sector in the past few decades, highlighting the situation before the 1990s and the reforms that took place during that decade, as well as the financial sector's conditions at the time FTA negotiations were entered with the United States. Next, it evaluates the FTA negotiating process, highlighting the preparation and organization within the government and in relation to the private sector and civil society, the different sectors' approaches and actions during the process, and the Colombian government's negotiation strategy in financial services. Subsequently, the chapter analyzes the results of the negotiation in financial services, particularly emphasizing the differences between the government's initial strategy, which was coordinated with the other Andean countries, and what was obtained in similar agreements with the United States. Finally, the chapter investigates the changes foreseen for the Colombian financial sector because of the FTA and the lessons learned from the negotiating process.

Recent Evolution of the Colombian Financial Sector

The efforts to liberalize financial services in Colombia occurred unilaterally at the beginning of the 1990s. Such efforts formed part of a large package of structural reforms that aimed at more openness and flexibility. In addition, this unilateral financial liberalization provided a framework for the negotiation of multilateral trade agreements that took place in the 1990s, especially the commitments acquired through the General Agreement on Trade in Services (GATS); the Andean Community (Comunidad Andina, or CAN); and the Group of Three (G3) free trade agreement between Colombia, Mexico, and the República Bolivariana de Venezuela. In fact, instead of advancing the liberalization of financial services, these agreements merely consolidated what had been accomplished in the process of financial reform at the beginning of the 1990s.

Overview of the Colombian Financial Sector

Overall, as noted in tables 6.1 and 6.2, the Colombian financial sector is relatively small compared with that of other countries. In Latin America, Colombia's financial sector is larger than Mexico's and Peru's but smaller than Chile's. In general, Colombia's banking sector—which includes commercial and housing banks as well as other deposit-taking institutions—traditionally has been larger than the nonbanking sector. The assets of the banking sector are about 45 percent of GDP, and the credit granted to the economy is about 23 percent of GDP. The insurance sector (life and non-life companies) has been small, and its assets are between 4 and 5 percent of GDP. Finally, private pension funds created in 1993 have grown significantly, with a portfolio value approaching 10 percent of GDP. Despite the creation and growth of large institutional investors, the equity market and private bond market are still small, illiquid, and concentrated in a small number of issuers (about 100).

Until the beginning of the 1990s, a scheme of *specialized banking* operated in Colombia. This system was characterized by (a) specialized legal vehicles created for different financial objectives and with specific permissible activities, (b) isolation between different financial system

Table 6.1   Size and Depth of the Colombian Financial System: Banking and Nonbanking Sectors, 2002–04

	Percentage of GDP		
Indicator	2002	2003	2004
Total commercial bank assets[a]	43.8	42.6	45.2
Domestic credit to the private sector	24.9	22.7	22.8
Total insurance company assets	4.0	4.1	4.2
Total pension fund assets	7.7	8.9	10.3
Domestic outstanding government debt	23.5	28.2	30.3
Domestic outstanding private sector debt[b]	8.3	8.6	8.2
Stock market capitalization	11.8	17.8	25.8
Stock market turnover	0.3	0.5	1.5

Source: Data from the World Bank.
a. Figures include all credit institutions (not just commercial banks), excluding financial cooperatives and second-tier development banks.
b. Figures include outstanding financial sector bonds.

Table 6.2   Bank Credit, Stock Market Capitalization, and Outstanding Domestic Debt as a Share of GDP, 2004

Economy	Bank credit (percent)	Stock market capitalization (percent)	Domestic debt (percent)		
			Government	Financial	Corporate
Mature markets					
Japan	94.4	78.5	141.0	25.6	16.3
United States	45.8	129.0	47.1	94.4	22.0
Euro area	103.9	54.6	53.6	29.8	10.0
Emerging markets					
Asia	103.6	74.1	22.3	13.4	6.9
Europe	24.3	34.1	26.9	0.5	1.0
Latin America	20.9	40.2	28.9	5.3	2.6
Argentina	10.4	30.7	5.8	3.4	6.4
Brazil	25.2	50.0	44.7	10.8	0.6
Chile	56.8	114.8	19.6	10.2	11.3
Colombia	18.0	24.3	22.8	4.3	3.9
Mexico	14.3	25.4	22.6	0.8	2.7
Peru	17.6	28.3	5.6	1.3	3.1

Source: Aguilar and others 2006.

vehicles, and (c) severe investment restrictions for deposit-taking institutions in the real sector (de la Cruz and Stephanou 2006).

Law 45/1990 introduced changes to this scheme by adopting a system similar to multibanking (matrix-subsidiaries) and by promoting the creation of financial conglomerates. Despite these efforts, which have aimed at greater flexibility, the structure of the system has not changed much. Within the group of credit institutions (deposit-taking institutions), both commercial and housing banks have been the largest, followed by the financial corporations (investment banks) and companies of commercial financing (finance companies) (table 6.3).

As noted in figure 6.1, over the past 20 years, four phases can be distinguished in the evolution of the financial system of Colombia—financial repression, flexibility and expansion, financial crisis, and recovery.

Financial repression. Prior to the 1990s, the Colombian financial sector operated under a system of specialized banking and was subject to a high degree of financial intervention. This period was marked by high levels of reserve requirements and forced investments, regulated credit policies and interest rate controls, high government participation in financial activity, and strong limitations on the entrance of foreign capital into the sector. In

Table 6.3   Structure of Banking (Deposit-Taking) Institutions, 1995 and 2005

	1995		2005	
Banking system	Share of GDP (percent)	Share of deposit-taking institutions' assets (percent)	Share of GDP (percent)	Share of deposit-taking institutions' assets (percent)
Total system	59.1	100.0	55.3	100.0
Total system, excluding second-tier institutions and cooperatives	52.7		47.2	
Banks	41.0	69.3	41.6	75.2
Commercial	26.9	45.5	30.7	55.4
Housing	12.6	21.3	10.9	19.8
Cooperatives	1.5	2.6	0.2	0.4
Investment banks	6.8	11.4	1.9	3.4
Finance companies	4.9	8.3	3.7	6.7
Traditional	3.1	5.3	1.3	2.4
Leasing	1.8	3.0	2.4	4.3
Second-tier state-owned institutions	6.4	10.9	7.9	14.4
Financial cooperatives	0.0	0.0	0.2	0.3

Source: Author calculations based on data from the Superintendencia Financiera.

Figure 6.1   Main Phases of Colombian Financial Development, 1982–2006

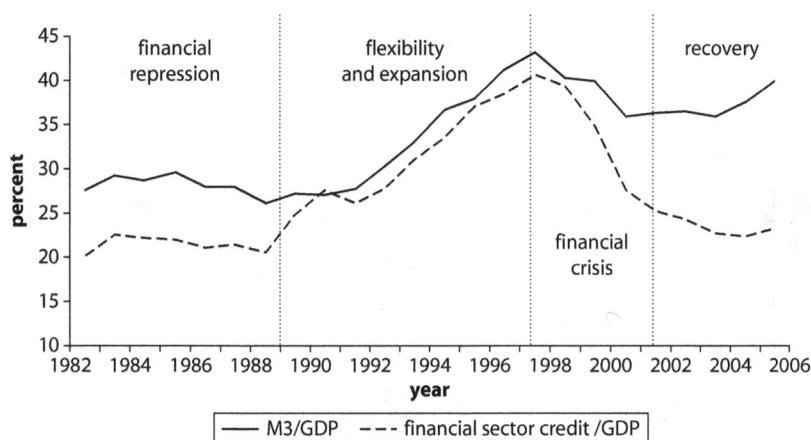

Source: Data provided by the Banco de la República.

the late 1980s, the M3-to-GDP ratio was comparatively low by international standards, oscillating around 30 percent, and the credit-to-GDP ratio was nearly 20 percent. Inefficiency and intermediation spreads remained high (Barajas, Steiner, and Salazar 1999b).[2]

Flexibility and expansion. Early during the period from 1990 to1998, a wave of structural reform involved important changes in the organization and operation of the financial sector. Between 1990 and 1995, the Colombian economy grew at an average rate of 4.5 percent, enhanced by the growth of private consumption and investment. The period also saw significant expansion of the banking sector. The positive economic development and financial liberalization process led to an important improvement in financial deepening. The M3-to-GDP ratio increased from 28 percent of GDP in 1990 to 43.2 percent of GDP in 1997. The number of financial institutions increased, which advanced privatization and reduced government participation in financial intermediation.

In the banking sector, the ratio of public bank to total bank assets fell from 37 percent in 1991 to 11 percent in 2004, whereas the share of foreign bank assets increased from 7 percent to 18 percent in the same period (figure 6.2). Nevertheless, despite increased inflows of foreign investment to the banking sector, such investment is still smaller than in other Latin American countries. For instance, in Argentina, Chile, Mexico, and Peru, foreign bank assets represent nearly 60 percent of the total assets of the banking system, and even in Brazil, a less open economy, this percentage is slightly higher than in Colombia. The entrance of foreign capital into the financial sector occurred in three different ways

Figure 6.2   Assets of Public and Foreign Banks, 1991–2004

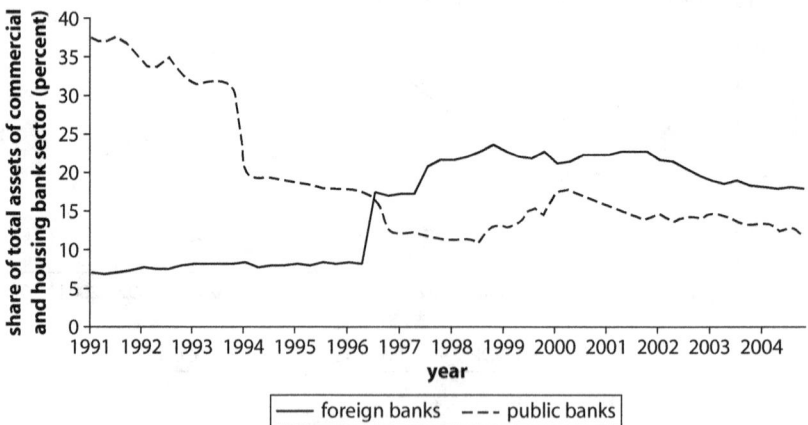

Source: Data provided by the Superintendencia Financiera.
Note: Data on Banco Agrario and BCH are excluded from the calculations. All dates are as of March of the year shown.

(Barajas, Steiner, and Salazar 1999a): (a) repurchase of banks by the old foreign owners (Brazilian, French, Italian, U.K., and U.S. investors) that had been nationalized in the 1970s under Law 75/75; (b) purchase of existing local banks (by Peruvian, Spanish, and Venezuelan investors); and (c) establishment of new foreign subsidiaries (by Ecuadoran, Netherlands, and U.S. investors).

In the insurance sector, foreign ownership also increased, both in life and nonlife activities. Currently, 31 percent of the assets in this sector belong to foreigners, whereas in 1991 foreigners owned only about 15 percent (Vera 2006). In the pension funds subsector, the foreign asset share of around 50 percent has always been higher than in banks and insurance companies.

Financial crisis. Colombia experienced a financial crisis from 1998 to 2001, marked by poor economic performance and weaknesses in regulation and supervision. Most prudential indicators, such as solvency and asset quality, deteriorated significantly. The recession of these years was accompanied by a phase of credit stagnation without precedent in recent economic history. The gains in financial deepening achieved between 1990 and 1997 were practically lost; the credit-to-GDP ratio returned to a level of 20 to 25 percent.

The ratio of nonperforming loans (NPLs) to total loans rose from 6 percent before the crisis to 16 percent in 1999, and the sector's losses represented almost 40 percent of the equity of the system between 1998 and 2000 (Salazar 2005; figure 6.3). The financial crisis affected two segments in particular: housing and government-owned banks.

Recovery. After the crisis, from 2002 to the present, a period of financial adjustment occurred in which a significant amount of public and private resources had to be allocated for the system to recover. Since 2002, the system has improved considerably, although financial deepening is still below the levels registered before the crisis.

Economic growth reached a rate of 5.1 percent in 2005, the highest in the past decade. Internal factors, such as the recovery of household consumption and increased investment, supported this performance. Externally, exports grew rapidly, partly offset by a large increase in imports. Government spending also contributed to domestic economic expansion, and because of increased revenues, a balanced budget was achieved in 2005.

Figure 6.3   Profitability and the Ratio of Nonperforming Loans to Total Loans in the Banking Sector, 1996–2006

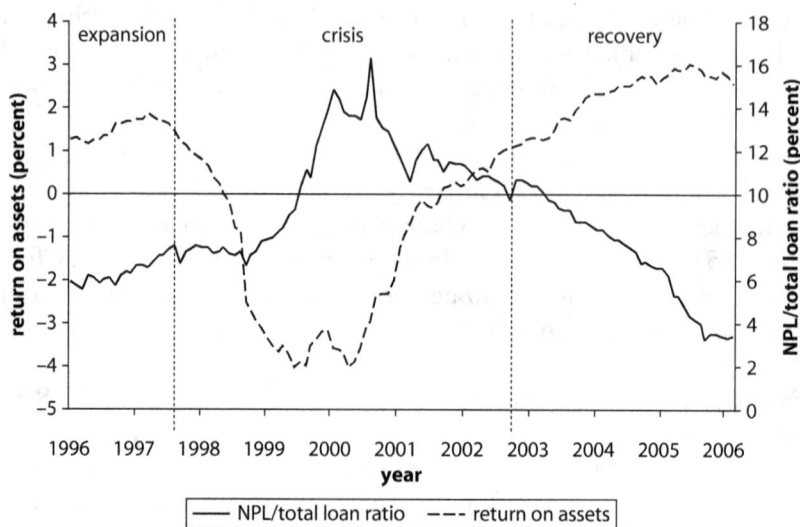

Source: Author calculations based on data from the Superintendencia Financiera.
Note: NPL = nonperforming loans. All dates are as of April of the year shown.

By the time the negotiations with the United States had ended, the Colombian financial sector had also recovered from the crisis, evidenced by bank profitability, solvency, and asset quality indicators. In fact, the return on assets reached 2.8 percent in 2005, which is comparable to the period before the crisis. Similarly, the ratio of NPLs to total loans and provisions for NPLs reached levels of 4 percent and 116.6 percent, respectively. These figures suggest a strong recovery and a more sound footing than during the mid-1990s.

By contrast, as shown in figure 6.4, Colombia's efficiency indicators still appear weak compared with those of other developed countries. For example, the ratio of operating expenses to assets dropped from 6.0 percent in 1996 to 4.8 percent in 2005, which is still higher than in countries such as Chile (de la Cruz and Stephanou 2006), and the existing literature on the subject indicates that there is room for further improvement. X-efficiency research also shows that, given the current situation, the sector could still lower its operating spending (ANIF 2006).

In recent years, significant mergers have taken place within the banking sector, and the number of financial institutions has declined (table 6.4).

Figure 6.4   Ratio of Operating Expenses to Assets in the Banking Sector, 1996–2006

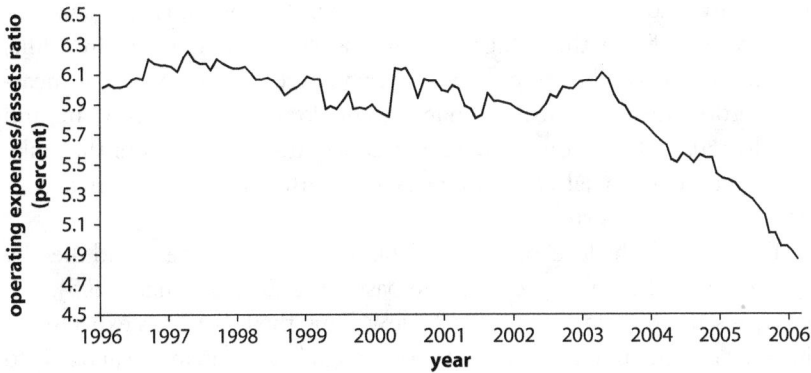

Source: Author calculations based on data from the Superintendencia Financiera.
Note: All dates are as of April of the year shown.

Table 6.4   Number of Financial Institutions, 1995–2005

Number of institutions	1995	2000	2005
Total	279	196	154
Commercial and housing banks	41	30	21
Private domestic	21	15	12
Public	5	4	3
Foreign	12	11	6
Cooperative	3	0	0
Other credit institutions	98	54	32
Investment banks	24	8	2
Finance companies	73	32	24
Financial cooperatives	0	13	5
Cooperatives superior grade[a]	1	1	1
Second-tier state-owned institutions	6	9	10
Bonded warehouse companies	11	9	6
Insurance companies	68	55	49
Life	35	27	24
Nonlife	25	23	20
Capitalization societies	8	5	5
Pension funds	9	6	6
Asset management/trust companies	46	33	30

Source: de la Cruz and Stephanou 2006.
a. *Organismos cooperativos de grado superior* (OCGS)

The consolidation process has led to increased concentration indicators. Yet the conventional indicators show that concentration levels are still low relative to other countries in the region. In Colombia, the share of total assets of the three biggest banks is 40 percent, while in Chile, Mexico, and Peru, the same share is over 50 percent. However, this measure ignores the existence of financial conglomerates.[3] De la Cruz and Stephanou (2006) show that market concentration indicators that take into account financial conglomerates are considerably higher than conventional measures suggest.

Even though the level of liberalization of financial services—and thereby competition—has increased over the past 15 to 20 years (figure 6.5), foreign presence has remained generally low. Thus, the U.S. FTA is expected to increase competition from the entry of foreign banks, forcing local banks to prepare accordingly.[4]

Stages of Financial Services Liberalization in Colombia
In the past 50 years, Colombia underwent a slow process of financial services liberalization, which can be summarized as the following stages.

Unilateral reforms until the end of the 1980s: Strong restrictions on foreign competition. In 1967, in the midst of a severe balance-of-payments crisis, Colombia adopted strict exchange rate controls to prevent a massive devaluation. Through this measure, the central bank (Banco de la

Figure 6.5   Financial Liberalization Index, by Country, 2001

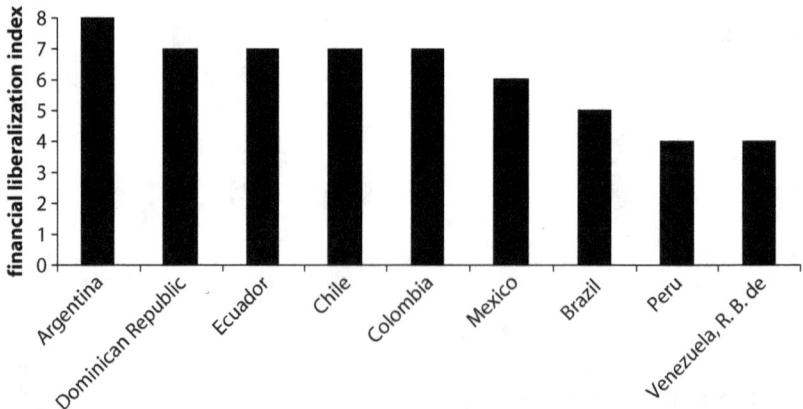

Source: Mattoo, Rathindran, and Subramanian 2001.
Note: The index runs from 0 to 8, with 0 showing a low degree of financial liberalization, and 8 a high degree of financial liberalization.

República) established a total monopoly over the foreign exchange market, becoming the only entity authorized to buy and sell international reserves within the country. In addition, to promote nontraditional exports, the government adopted an exchange rate regime of mini-devaluations. Besides the dampening effect that exchange controls had on the movement of capital, this policy significantly restricted short-term foreign indebtedness, and it would remain in force until 1990.

With regard to foreign investment, these measures, as well as the ones adopted in the Treaty of Cartagena (the Andean Pact, which later became the Andean Community, or CAN[5]), severely restricted foreign investment in the financial sector (Barajas, Steiner, and Salazar 1999a). In the Treaty of Cartagena, the parties agreed to establish strong barriers against the inflow of foreign investment, especially in the financial sector. In Resolution 24 of 1969, the treaty required new foreign companies to become companies with mixed national and foreign ownership (foreign capital ownership could not exceed 49 percent) within a maximum of 15 years. It imposed limits on the remittance of earnings and reinvestment and established controls on contracts for the transfer of technology. In addition, the treaty reserved certain sectors for national capital, including the financial sector. The rule established in the agreement was even stricter for foreign investment in the financial sector, because foreign entities had to become national companies, and no more than 20 percent of the total capital could be owned by foreigners. Moreover, it prohibited further foreign investment in the financial sector from countries that were not part of the agreement.

Colombia was able, however, to exempt itself from this last obligation under article 44. Nevertheless, the rules on foreign capital in the Colombian financial sector gradually approached the rules of the Cartagena agreement. At first, the government tried to induce the transformation of foreign financial entities into mixed organizations through individual "friendly" agreements, but only some banks agreed to make this transformation voluntarily. Hence, the government issued a general regulation regarding the presence of foreign capital in banks and other financial institutions.

In 1975, the Law for the Colombianization of the Banking Sector was issued. It obliged foreign-owned companies to transform themselves into mixed companies within a maximum period of three years. To achieve this transformation, foreign-owned companies had to create a new entity in which no less than 51 percent of the shares belonged to national citizens. In addition, the law prohibited new foreign investment in banks and other credit establishments and in insurance companies.

Since the beginning of the 20th century, several foreign banks—mainly French, Italian, Netherlands, U.K., and U.S.—had been operating in Colombia. The obvious consequence of the Law for the Colombianization of the Banking Sector was the stagnation of new foreign capital inflows. Indeed, foreign bank assets never reached more than 8 to 10 percent of total bank assets. A similar result occurred in the insurance sector. The law did not have the desired effect, however, and the total Colombianization of the financial system did not actually occur. In the case of banks, for example, the forced sale of 51 percent of foreign shares to national citizens was done not as a single block but in fractions or small sales (Superintendencia Bancaria 1989). This strategy allowed foreign owners to maintain control over financial entities and to reacquire the banks more easily when the sector opened for foreign investment in 1990.

At the beginning of the 1980s, macroeconomic conditions deteriorated significantly. Colombia suffered from the effects of a debt crisis that the entire region was undergoing. Sizable fiscal and external deficits had accumulated, and the country entered a period of economic deceleration. Between 1982 and 1984, the Colombian financial sector went through a crisis that in addition to recession was caused by a poor prudential framework, weak regulatory enforcement, and bad management of some entities. The deterioration made evident the existing inefficiencies in the banking sector's operation and resulted in the nationalization of various intermediaries as well as in a major increase in the government's participation in financial activities. The crisis also highlighted the need for improvements in prudential norms (higher solvency requirements and the creation of a deposit-insurance scheme managed by a new government institution, among others) and supervision (unification and improvement of information and transparency norms).

During this period, the banking sector operated under a rather specialized structure. Commercial banks were the only entities authorized to offer checking accounts, and they specialized in offering credit to businesses and consumers. Savings and loan associations (*corporaciones de ahorro y vivienda*, or housing banks) were entrusted with the task of operating the housing financing system. Their deposits and allocations were indexed to the UPAC (*unidad de poder adquisitivo constante*, or constant purchasing power unit), which, in turn, was tied to the Consumer Price Index (CPI) inflation rate. The objective behind the implementation of the UPAC system was to create a financing scheme for housing that ensured a constant real interest rate on both loans and deposits. However, on various occasions, the central bank had to adjust the formula, because under specific macroeconomic conditions, some intermediaries without indexed deposits perceived disadvantages in the deposit market. Thus, the UPAC formula was gradually linked to certificate of deposit interest rates instead of CPI inflation. This scheme was sustainable as long as interest rates and inflation moved in the same direction. In the late 1990s, however, the inflation rate and house prices fell significantly, whereas interest rates rose abruptly, making the problems of the UPAC system more evident.

The reforms in the 1990s. The 1998–99 foreign debt crisis in Latin America, the closing of international markets, and the effects these events had on growth highlighted the failure of the restrictions on the inflow of foreign investment as specified in the Andean Pact. The countries had to relax their policy in this area, attracting foreign investment as a mechanism for complementing the low level of domestic savings.[6] The economic crisis turned out to be less severe in Colombia than in other countries in the region. Colombia's efforts, taken during the crisis between 1982 and 1984, to make its policy more flexible to foreign investment proved important for the financial sector. In fact, the change in this policy allowed some foreign banks to receive additional capital from their headquarters, thereby reducing the fiscal cost that the government would eventually have had to bear for maintaining confidence in the system.

Not until the beginning of the 1990s, however, did Colombia embark on significant financial liberalization. This effort was not an isolated measure, but rather part of a plan to make the economy as a whole more open and flexible. In fact, even though the financial sector reforms were a key part of the overall reform efforts, sensible changes affecting the labor market, the exchange rate and foreign investment, and the institutional policies of the central bank were introduced at the same time. Tariffs and barriers to foreign trade were significantly reduced as well.

Changes in the structure and operation of the financial sector were a response to the growing recognition of the inefficiencies in financial intermediation. This recognition was, to a large extent, the result of the government's high degree of financial repression. Limited competition existed between local entities—and between those entities and foreign providers (Hommes 1990; Ortega 1990).

In 1991, the country adopted new regulations on the exchange rate and foreign investment that allowed greater flexibility in the movement of capital. The central bank abandoned its monopoly over international reserves and allowed banks to buy and sell foreign currency. Likewise, checking accounts could be established abroad, and the policy on short-term foreign debt was made substantially more flexible. The "crawling-peg" exchange rate regime was maintained until 1994, when it was replaced by a "crawling-band" regime.

A new regulation also made the policy for short-term foreign investment more flexible.[7] It granted equal treatment to foreign and domestic investment and allowed an unrestrained inflow of capital for all economic activities.[8] Moreover, it relaxed legal restrictions on foreign exchange and eliminated the maximum limits on the repatriation of earnings, capital reimbursements, and payments for technology transfer contracts (Alonso, Montes, and Varela 2003; Garay 2004). In addition, foreign portfolio investments were permitted. The main implication for the financial sector was that foreigners were permitted to take full ownership of local institutions (banks, other deposit-taking institutions, financial services companies, insurance and reinsurance companies, and securities firms). However, this law maintained certain market-access restrictions, particularly the need to constitute financial institutions as legal entities under Colombian laws, which made having commercial presence through direct branching legally impossible.

Although the norms for private foreign indebtedness were made more flexible at the beginning of the 1990s, in 1993 a nonremunerated deposit in dollars based on short-term foreign debt was established. This deposit was similar to a tax, and its purpose was to reduce the inflows of short-term capital, which had increased significantly at that time. Initially, the tariff of the deposit was set at 47 percent of the value of credits for periods under 18 months (Alonso, Montes, and Varela 2003). As the capital inflows increased, the conditions of the deposit became stricter in terms of its tariff (which was increased) and indebtedness term (which was reduced). Then, in the late 1990s, the authorities reduced the tariff on the deposit in response to a change in the direction of capital flows; the tariff was further reduced to 0 percent in May 2000.

The tendency of public expenditure to grow was reinforced during the period from 1995 to 1997, supported and manifested by an expansionary monetary and fiscal policy. Because of the excess of private expenditure over savings, public and foreign deficits reached 4.5 percent of GDP in 1997. The unstable foreign environment, the disequilibrium of the Colombian economy, and the internal political instability caused frequent attacks on the exchange rate. The central bank's defense of the exchange rate band increased domestic interest rates, which were also affected by an increase in foreign interest rates after the financial crises in Asia and the Russian Federation. Toward the end of 1998, the country underwent a period of economic crisis, and the economy strongly contracted in 1999 (–4.2 percent of GDP). During the same year, the crawling-band regime was abandoned, and a floating exchange rate was adopted. Also in 2000, the central bank formally adopted a strategy targeting inflation.

The increase in interest rates, the recession, and the devaluation had negative repercussions on the stability of the financial sector and resulted in a significant deterioration in its main indicators. Flaws in the regulation and supervision of the financial sector also became evident, especially with regard to risk assessment and risk management. In particular, although the requirements in terms of solvency seemed strict and adequate, once the crisis began it was clear that reserve levels were very low. The housing financing scheme (the UPAC system) also revealed regulatory flaws of the financial sector. The capitalization of interest, the inadequate assessment of collateral, and the level of household indebtedness made the UPAC system unsustainable. Finally, the poor management of public financial entities revealed the deficiencies of the system overseeing them, and substantial government expenditure was required to ensure their reorganization.

The crisis forced the adoption of changes in the financial system. In 1999, a new strategy to finance housing was adopted, and the old savings and loan associations were converted into banks. In addition, regulation and supervision were strengthened, primarily to ensure better evaluation and risk management by credit institutions. At the same time, minimum capital requirements were adjusted. However, the model of specialized financial services provision was not significantly affected, except that the specialized housing bank vehicle was eliminated (de la Cruz and Stephanou 2006).

As of 2005, two institutions in charge of regulation and supervision existed: the Banking Superintendency (Superintendencia Bancaria) oversaw deposit-taking institutions, pension funds, insurance companies, and fiduciaries, and the Securities Superintendency (Superintendencia de Valores) was in charge of mutual funds, stock market traders, and all activities related to the issuance of equity and bonds in the capital market. The different levels of regulation and supervision exercised by the two superintendencies generated regulatory arbitrage problems. To remedy this, the two institutions were, at the beginning of 2006, merged into the Financial Superintendency (Superintendencia Financiera).

Some of the measures taken as a result of the crisis have been associated with financial repression. Certainly the forced investment, which was created to finance part of the mortgage crisis, and the introduction of a financial transaction tax suggest repression. But perhaps the main regulatory weakness of the financial system to date concerns several institutional aspects. In particular, Colombia has weak protections of creditors' rights (Galindo and others 2005), an obstacle that became clear during the 1999 mortgage crisis, when intermediaries experienced serious difficulties recovering their loans and guarantees. Furthermore, the great amount of accumulated, unresolved processes revealed important inefficiencies in the judicial branch. In fact, the protection of creditors' rights in Colombia is lower than other developing countries and other countries in Latin America.

Bilateral, regional, and multilateral commitments. Since the financial reform of the early 1990s, and notwithstanding the changes brought about by the financial crisis, Colombia stayed on a stable liberalization path that lasted through to the U.S. FTA negotiation. However, no commitments on new financial liberalization were undertaken at the international level, and as such, the status quo was consolidated.

First, in the G3 agreement, which was signed in 1994 by Colombia, Mexico, and the República Bolivariana de Venezuela, Colombia and the República Bolivariana de Venezuela would not accept financial services commitments that exceeded what was already covered by existing legislation, even though Mexico tried to negotiate an agreement as broad and ambitious as the North American Free Trade Agreement (NAFTA). The chapter on financial services makes evident that the status quo was unchanged and, accordingly, in the list of commitments, Colombia's reservations were all based on the legislation existing at the time.

The Colombian government had no particular interest in going further in financial services negotiations in the G3 agreement because the government preferred to wait for the results of the then-ongoing multilateral negotiations on financial services under GATS. In addition, the government considered that because of the unilateral reforms previously undertaken, the financial sector was open enough to foreign competition.[9] Given that the agreement involved many economic sectors and was expected to have far-reaching implications that coincided with a period of strong foreign exchange rate revaluation, both the private sector and the Colombian Congress strongly opposed the signing of the agreement. Therefore, the government considered it appropriate to limit the liberalizing commitments to topics related to trade in goods.

The commitments made under GATS in 1997 were also in line with domestic regulation in the financial sector. Regarding commercial presence,

Colombia committed to grant equal treatment to foreign and domestic investors, consolidating what was already included in domestic legislation.[10]

In terms of market access, foreign financial services providers were allowed to establish in Colombia, but only in the legal form of subsidiaries. Commercial presence in the form of either representative offices or branches was not permitted. Colombia's schedule also specified that the supply of financial services in Colombia required prior government authorization, which must be granted in accordance with the criteria and requirements contained in Colombian laws and regulations. Authorization for financial services providers to operate in Colombia was subject to the corresponding superintendency's verification of the character, responsibility, and competence of the people acting as owners, directors, and managers.[11]

In September 2003, Colombia presented an initial offer on financial services trade similar to the Doha Round commitments undertaken in 2001. Several countries requested that Colombia fully consolidate its financial internationalization process and eliminate national treatment limitations. Specifically, the main request of Mexico and the United States was to allow financial entities commercial presence in the form of direct branching without minimum capital requirements.

Finally, the CAN member countries still had not made any commitments regarding liberalization of financial services or any other service. In 1998, the countries expressed their willingness to liberalize subregional services trade, including the financial sector, by the end of 2005, a deadline that was later postponed to September 2007.[12] With this objective, they agreed on a General Framework for Services Trade in which the four modes of supply were to be addressed,[13] together with comprehensive coverage in terms of sectors (to be specified later). Moreover, the countries were to make a commitment to grant all members most-favored-nation (MFN) treatment, and each of them would be required to list the restrictive measures to services trade under a negative list scheme.

During the FTA negotiations, the commitments that Colombia, Ecuador, and Peru had acquired under CAN became problematic. If the United States was given unrestricted MFN treatment, it would fully enjoy the CAN benefits once trade within the Andean Community was liberalized. The inconvenience was resolved as follows: first, the Andean member countries agreed to postpone the services negotiation (including financial services) until November 2007, setting a work timeline.[14] Second, they included in the FTA a clause stating that the commitments would not extend to services provided by North American companies.

The launch of FTA negotiations with the United States. The initiative to sign an FTA with the United States emerged in Colombia, aided by a number of coincidental factors.

First, after the crisis of 1998–99, the economy recovered slowly. In the following three years, growth averaged between 2 and 3 percent, a rate that was considered low in comparison to the historical average and the needs of the country. The idea of encouraging foreign trade as a way of achieving higher growth rates began to be discussed in the government, in the private sector, and among economic think tanks.

Second, the United States was Colombia's most important trading partner, accounting for about 50 percent of Colombian exports, 30 percent of imports, and 20 percent of annual foreign direct investment (FDI) flows. Therefore, if better international trade and investment relationships were to be achieved, the United States would naturally be the candidate of choice.

Third, historically, the relationship with the United States had not been limited to the commercial area. The political relationship between the two countries was important and dynamic, especially with regard to fighting drug trafficking and terrorism. The Andean Tariff Preferences Act (ATPA), Andean Trade Promotion and Drug Eradication Act (ATPDEA),[15] and "Plan Colombia" illustrate the importance of the diplomatic and political relationship between the countries. The idea of signing an agreement with the United States had much to do with the perceived need to give permanency to ATPA-ATPDEA tariff preferences, which were limited to a 10-year period ending in 2002. In 2000, as the expiration date neared, Colombia asked the United States to renew the ATPA-ATPDEA program and to broaden its product coverage. The U.S. Congress approved the renewal in 2002 and then further extended it in 2009, thus leaving the program in force until the end of 2010. Nevertheless, the uncertainty over the permanence of the program and the growing conviction among Colombian decision makers about the positive direct and indirect effects for the country's trade and investment performance encouraged Colombian president Álvaro Uribe to propose the possibility of an FTA during a visit to the United States in 2003. Moreover, the U.S. negotiations on the Free Trade Agreement between Central America, the Dominican Republic, and the United States (CAFTA-DR-U.S.) spurred fears in Colombia that if tariff preferences were not made permanent through an FTA with the United States, Colombia could end up at a competitive disadvantage in the region. In November 2003, at the Summit of the Americas in Miami, Florida, the launching of negotiations between the two countries was announced.

From the beginning, one could foresee that the FTA with the United States would not result in significant reforms in the financial sector comparable to those of the previous decade. First, the Chilean side thought the sector was already sufficiently liberalized, at least with respect to commercial presence. Changes might occur in the areas of cross-border supply and movement of natural persons. Second, as previously discussed, the sector had already consolidated its recovery after the 1998–99 crisis through significant adjustments and increased foreign competition. Although additional changes would be discussed, they would clearly be minor in scope. Third, although the financial sector played an important role in the reform process in the 1990s, other economic sectors, such as agriculture and intellectual property rights, would occupy the main part of the discussions in these negotiations.

As the following sections indicate, given the situation of the financial sector, the negotiations would be conducted to maintain the status quo, a goal that was shared by the government and the financial industry itself.

The FTA Negotiating Process

It is important to recall that neither the G3 agreement nor GATS had involved changes in the openness of Colombia's financial sector. However, both negotiations contributed significantly to the learning process of financial services reform and negotiations in three dimensions: (a) both the government and the financial private sector became familiar with the technical issues of financial services agreements, (b) the two previous negotiations improved coordination within the government and between it and the private sector, and (c) the negotiations helped Colombia develop a sound negotiating strategy. In particular, the experience of the G3 negotiation laid the foundations of the government's strategy for the FTA with the United States, since the text agreed on by Colombia, Mexico, and the República Bolivariana de Venezuela was based on NAFTA's format and contents. Moreover, Colombia adopted organizational schemes for the negotiation that were similar to those used by Mexico in NAFTA.

The Government's Strategy for the FTA

Because the U.S. FTA is a broader and more ambitious agreement than the ones previously signed by Colombia, the government instituted a stricter strategy, including very detailed procedures for each of the steps to take during the negotiation.

The Colombian government created a negotiating team, which was coordinated by the Ministry of Trade, Industry, and Tourism and made up of public sector officials.[16] A chief negotiator, in charge of overseeing the overall negotiation, was assigned as well. The chief negotiator was in permanent contact with the various issue-area coordinators and with the vice ministers or directors of relevant governmental agencies.

Thematic Negotiating Committees were created for the technical preparation. These committees were charged with evaluating Colombia's interests, aspirations, and sensitivities. In addition, a diagnosis was made of each topic, which later helped in discussions with the private sector, workers, civil society, the media, the regions, and other social and political stakeholders throughout the negotiation process. The negotiating team used the Thematic Negotiating Committees to construct the country's negotiating position.

The Ministry of Finance led the negotiating process for financial services, rather than the Ministry of Trade, Industry, and Tourism, which oversaw the other negotiating areas. This decision, which had precedence in previous trade negotiations involving financial services, took into account that financial services negotiation was directly related to the Ministry of Finance's functions and, in particular, that intervention in the financial, insurance, and securities markets would have macroeconomic implications on the financial sector's performance.[17] The central bank also played an active role in the negotiation process, partly because of its concern about capital controls and other aspects of monetary, credit, or foreign exchange policy. The Colombian government has traditionally been averse to dollarization, a stance that has shaped the country's financial strategy as well as the financial sector's negotiations and the control of capital inflows and outflows.

The Banking Superintendency and the Securities Superintendency played an important role in the Financial Thematic Negotiating Committee. They helped the Ministry of Finance assess the various proposals and draft the main documents used in the negotiation, including specific commitments and nonconforming measures. They also supported the review of the financial system legislation.

Other public financial institutions completed the Financial Thematic Negotiating Committee. The Fondo de Garantías de Instituciones Financieras (Financial Institutions Guarantee Fund, or Fogafin—an institution equivalent to the U.S. Federal Deposit Insurance Corporation) and the Banco de Comercio Exterior de Colombia (Colombian Foreign Trade Bank, or Bancoldex—a second-tier public bank specializing in export-import banking operations) also played an important role in advising on technical issues related to their own responsibilities.

The Financial Thematic Negotiating Committee met periodically. These meetings were extremely useful in preparing the government positions, analyzing the documentation, setting out a strategy, preparing for the coming negotiating rounds, and helping to construct a unified position toward the private sector. A secretary, assigned by the Ministry of Trade, Industry, and Tourism, maintained written records of the meetings, keeping track of the discussions.

Coordination with negotiators of other relevant chapters required additional general and specific meetings, mainly for cross-border trade and investment. The Thematic Negotiating Committees of each of these chapters met regularly, discussing, among other issues, those related to investment in financial institutions, social security, public debt, and capital controls.

In this way, the government's decision on the country's negotiating position in financial services involved a consultation process with members of the Colombian Congress and representatives of various state entities such as the central bank, the Securities Superintendency, and the Banking Superintendency. Although there were concerns that trying to arbitrate among so many and diverse interests would cause problems, the Ministry of Finance's strategy promoted the exchange of opinions among all interested state entities, thereby allowing the consolidation of a unified position in the financial services negotiation.

The Decision-Making Procedures

The government set strict decision-making procedures for the negotiating team because of and depending on the complexity of the issue. The decision-making process was subject to the following rules:

- For the most important issues identified by the Thematic Negotiating Committees (commonly known by the negotiators as the "red lines"), the team had to follow the president's direct instructions (adopted by the Foreign Trade Superior Council, which was led by the president and included several ministers). These instructions were established after consultations with the private sector and civil society, as described in more detail later.

- For less relevant topics, the negotiators made decisions within a strict and limited framework (the "green lines"). An issue could be negotiated or decided directly by a negotiator as long as a consensus on the positions was reached at the Thematic Negotiating Committee level and the chief negotiator had agreed to it previously.

If a consensus on the interests and negotiating positions could not be reached in the committees, the issue was referred to the negotiating supervisor. If a consensus could still not be attained, the vice minister of foreign trade would take it up with the vice ministers or officers responsible for the subject at this level. If disagreements persisted, the minister of foreign trade, industry, and tourism would call a ministerial-level meeting to unify the government's position. If the differences still could not be resolved, they would be taken up with the Foreign Trade Superior Council.

Yet throughout the negotiation of financial services, all agreements were reached at the Financial Services Thematic Negotiating Committee's level, so referral to higher interests was not necessary. A general consensus always existed among the different government authorities and even between them and the private sector, except on a few specific topics that will be discussed later in this chapter.

Before the negotiations began, the government hired Tandem Insourcing, a consulting firm, to complement the strategy in the decision-making process. At the outset, Tandem Insourcing began with a needs assessment, which took the form of written questionnaires and in-person individual and group interviews. On the basis of the needs assessment and in partnership with the negotiating team, a plan was developed that included the following types of activities:

- Running practice negotiation simulations for the negotiators
- Facilitating the assessment of previous negotiating rounds
- Training in negotiation skills
- Holding cross-cultural briefings on issues relevant to negotiation styles
- Developing a comprehensive strategy
- Consulting during the negotiating rounds
- Providing individual or group coaching throughout the process.

Tandem Insourcing provided the government with software (called the Tandem Methodology), which the negotiators used throughout the negotiation process. This software tracked issues, potential trade-offs, and variables that needed to be considered, providing the chief negotiator, the Thematic Negotiating Committees, and the consultants with a clear overview of the state of the negotiation. The software was used to measure performance, track progress during negotiation rounds, and determine how well goals were reached during the postnegotiation evaluation stage. In addition, Tandem Methodology provided negotiators with a complete catalogue of the offensive and defensive interests in each of the negotiation topics, ranked according to their importance. Tandem Methodology thereby helped build the "negotiation map" as it identified the negotiation's various alternatives in each of the topics, assigning superior or inferior grades to each alternative depending on how well they represented Colombia's interests. This map allowed objective measurement of results and helped set boundaries beyond which negotiations should not go.

In the specific case of financial services, the negotiation map served the following purposes:

- Controlling the negotiation strategies and avoid imbalances
- Coordinating the financial services topics with those of other related negotiating tables (for example, cross-border services with the investments table and the dispute settlement table)
- Facilitating a quick response to proposals from other Andean countries and the United States
- Articulating the interaction between the private sector, the Colombian Congress, and the authorities
- Allowing the transparent and objective evaluation of the negotiation's progress and of the decisions made at the financial services negotiation table
- Determining which decisions could be made directly by the negotiators without submission to higher authorities.

Coordination with Andean Countries

From the beginning, the U.S. government showed interest in negotiating an FTA with the Andean countries (Colombia, Ecuador, and Peru) as a group. After some discussions within CAN, these countries agreed to negotiate jointly with the United States.

For this purpose, Colombia, Ecuador, and Peru held coordination meetings a few days before the negotiating rounds with the United States. The idea behind these meetings was to reach consensus on a single negotiating position with the United States, starting from the assumption that negotiating as a bloc with the United States would improve the countries' positions and allow them to obtain better results than if they carried out negotiations individually.

On several occasions, single negotiating positions were agreed on and jointly presented to the United States by the three Andean countries, such as the commitments on social security and collective investment schemes. However, the three countries could not reach an agreement on all topics. Nonetheless, even in those cases, the meetings were useful because the differences could be discussed and managed in such a way that the United States could not later take advantage of divergences within the Andean bloc. An example is the commitments regarding branches of banks and insurance companies; only Colombia had defensive interests in this area, since Ecuador and Peru already allowed this type of commercial presence in their territories. Whereas Colombia hoped to receive some compensation for such a commitment, Ecuador and Peru wanted Colombia to grant the same treatment that Colombian investors were already getting in their countries. This difference in position led Ecuador and Peru to support the U.S. position more than the Colombian one, because eventual access to the Colombian markets would be in their favor as well.

A comparison of the commitments undertaken by Colombia, Ecuador, and Peru shows that the three countries assumed very similar obligations in the financial services chapter. The differences among the Andean countries were more on the strategic side. Colombia wanted to use its financial commitments to receive more favorable treatment on the investment chapter, whereas Ecuador and Peru held that each chapter should be negotiated individually. This strategy difference explains why Colombia wanted to take all the time needed to ensure that it would get favorable results in the investment chapter (those requests are detailed later), whereas Ecuador and Peru wanted to close the negotiation of the financial services chapter regardless of the outcome of the negotiation of the investment chapter. In addition, differences in the degree of dollarization or the need for capital controls led to divergent negotiation perspectives.

Interaction with the Private Sector, the National Congress, and the Civil Society

The Colombian government was actively seeking the participation of the private sector, Congress, and civil society for two main reasons. First, their support was needed to gain acceptance of the FTA on the domestic level. Second, their knowledge and experience were perceived as crucial for achieving the best agreement for the country. To enhance such participation, the government set up a series of consultations and permanent discussions with these stakeholders.

To coordinate the private sector's participation in the negotiating process, the government made an agreement with the Associations Council[18] (Consejo Gremial), a body that unites different private associations in the country. This agreement's purpose was to serve as a transmission channel of the private sector's interests to the government, foreseeing that the interests of private organizations, as well as of people not belonging to the council, were equally important in attaining a good agreement. Diverse financial institutions' positions were also taken into consideration through the various financial associations.

Additionally, during the negotiations, a direct channel for consultation between the negotiating team and the private sector was created—a space parallel to the negotiating tables referred to as the *side room*. The side room was up and running during all the negotiating rounds, and in the case of financial services, it helped negotiators consult with and present information to the associations and financial institutions throughout the course of the negotiations.

Through its side room, the financial sector witnessed firsthand the evolution of the negotiations and contributed input, data and other information, and arguments to defend Colombia's negotiating standpoint. Research tasks were assigned to private sector representatives during the meetings, which gradually became clarifying documents that Colombia presented at the negotiating table. Thus, Colombia was able to present documents to the agreement's signatories that explained how the social security system works in Colombia, what types of operations trust funds have and the size of the market in which they operate, what types of insurance are mandatory and their characteristics, and what investment regimes are permitted for pension funds and insurance companies. The private sector's contributions turned out to be crucial throughout the negotiation, allowing negotiators to identify problems and solutions during the rounds in real time.

For the broader public, the negotiating team organized presentations that were conducted the week after each negotiating round and that typically took about two days. The chief negotiator, supported by the negotiating team, made a general presentation about the negotiation and highlighted the main progress in each chapter. These presentations were meant to give an informative summary of each of the topics discussed in the FTA.

The general overview was followed by more specific and detailed presentations carried out by each Thematic Negotiating Committee. These presentations were conceived as in-depth meetings where civil society could interact directly with negotiators of the different topics. They were scheduled to last for one complete morning or afternoon, and the negotiators were obliged to give due consideration to all proposals or questions posed by civil society.

Regarding financial topics, a good example of civil society participation was the specific request made by the productive sector to accept the U.S. proposal under which Colombia should permit its residents to buy insurance products abroad. The argument was that a change of Colombian legislation to allow different industries to choose where to buy their insurance products (locally or in the United States) would enhance industry efficiency and competitiveness. The negotiators took the request into account, and the government undertook commitments that allowed Colombian residents to buy most insurance products from insurance companies established in Ecuador, Peru, or the United States, beginning four years after the agreement came into force.

The Private Financial Sector's Preparation and Position Regarding the FTA

In preparation for the negotiations on financial services and to ensure coordinated and frequent interaction with the government's negotiating team at various levels, the associations representing the financial sector formed a group led by the Banking Association (Asobancaria). The Colombian Insurance Federation (Fasecolda); the Trusts Association (Asofiduciarias); the Colombian Stock Exchange (Bolsa de Valores de Colombia, or BVC); the Exchange Institutions Association (Asocambiaria); the Colombian Federation of Leasing Companies (Fedeleasing); and the Association of Commercial Financing Companies (Asociación de Compañías de Financiamiento Comercial) were all part of this group. Not all financial associations had equal importance and representation; in some cases, conflicting interests resulted in their taking different positions regarding the FTA negotiations. For instance, in capital markets, the BVC asked for some degree of protection for market infrastructure or at least a gradual liberalization process, whereas the remaining bodies supported greater foreign competition. In the end, evidence showed that the most active associations during the negotiations were Asobancaria, Fasecolda, and Asofiduciarias.

Additionally, to prepare technically for the negotiation and to have their own position on defensive and offensive interests, the associations hired Fedesarrollo[19] and the Asociación Nacional de Instituciones Financieras (National Association of Financial Institutions, or ANIF) to undertake a research project that would cover all financial services areas and that would present positions on the FTA. The effort became relevant because it was the first detailed technical approach to this type of agreement in financial services, making it an important tool not only for the financial sector and academia, but also for the government. In fact, the report's recommendations were subject to discussion between (a) Fedesarrollo and ANIF and (b) each of the financial associations, and they were presented to the Ministry of Finance's negotiating team. In general, everyone agreed with the conclusions that subsequently constituted the financial sector's positions.

The report (Junguito and Gamboa 2004) covered topics related to deposit-taking institutions, insurance, pension funds, capital markets, and trust funds. In general terms and on the basis of previous trade negotiations (CAFTA-DR-U.S., Chile-U.S., and NAFTA), the study did not identify any major downside risks for the Colombian financial sector, given that the sector already had adequate levels of openness to foreign investment and liberalization of the capital account compared with other countries that had negotiated with the United States. Rather, it insisted on the need to preserve macroeconomic stability and to promote a competitive environment, which, aside from not putting national entities at a disadvantage vis-à-vis foreign entities, would also respect the conditions under which foreign investors were already operating in Colombia. In addition, the report recognized that the agreement had to protect consumers of financial services (including insurance). In very broad terms, the report was more inclined toward maintaining the status quo than advancing an aggressive liberalization agenda.

Regarding its macroeconomic aspects, the report did point out that a deeper commercial liberalization of financial services could lead to greater dollarization and capital movements, particularly in the case of cross-border trade, which was not considered desirable for the country. It argued that dollarization—which could increase, for example, if management of dollar-denominated checking accounts were allowed—might not bring about better results in financial intermediation and economic growth. Moreover, reversing dollarization is difficult and expensive in terms of macroeconomic stability, particularly because it reduces the government's control over monetary policy and may exacerbate exchange rate vulnerability. Regarding the increase in the degree of capital inflows and outflows, the report stated that this process could bring about difficulties in short-term macroeconomic management, given the exchange rate's instability and contagion risks (massive capital outflows), and because such an increase would make avoiding amplification of capital movements by the domestic financial sector more difficult. For these reasons, the study considered it best for liberalization to take place through increased commercial local presence (FDI) rather than cross-border trade, all under the regulatory framework applicable to local providers. The convenience of maintaining Colombia's ability to mitigate capital movements (that is, to preserve the capital inflow-outflow control instruments) was highlighted, particularly in the case of short-term capital flows.

The report was emphatic in reference to commercial presence, recommending that foreign financial and insurance companies looking for business opportunities in Colombia do so as subsidiaries (with contribution of their own capital) and not as branches (with no capital assigned to the country), because the latter might create unfair competitive conditions,[20] decrease foreign capital income, relax prudential norms (because minimum capital could not be made mandatory), and hinder controls if different requirements were established for each type of entity. In addition, the report suggested that the government should preserve the possibility of regulating subsidiaries with local capital, defining their characteristics, relation to headquarters, capital requirements, technical reserves, and investment regime (particularly for insurance companies and funds). Competitive conditions for domestic companies and for foreign companies that were already operating would be unequal in the absence of the ability to regulate such factors; the result might be to promote national savings drainage and reduce income tax receipts because branches would not have the same tax burden as local companies.

In this direction, the report also recommended limiting and regulating cross-border trade and financial services consumption abroad. For the banking sector specifically, the report proposed that cross-border consumption services be provided by entities subject to prudential norms in their country of origin. Moreover, for stability and efficiency of monetary policy to be achieved, the ability to limit the level of individuals' indebtedness abroad would be necessary, whether such indebtedness resulted from cross-border trade or from consumption abroad. All banking operations carried out by Colombian nationals in the U.S. market, in any of these supply modes, should be registered by the Colombian authorities to prevent asset laundering, an aspect also applicable to Colombian investments in foreign funds. Finally, the report suggested negotiating positive lists in both of these services supply modes, which would better ensure those aspects that Colombia really intended to include in these obligations.[21]

As regards Colombia's pension system, given that the social security scheme is supported by public guarantees, the report recommended that it would be crucial for the government to maintain autonomous management of mandatory pensions. Thus, maintaining commercial presence for this activity was suggested.

For the securities market and trust funds, even though no great threats were identified, the report called attention to the difficulties that could arise with the United States with reference to collective investment schemes, given that in Colombia such schemes can be managed only by trust funds or securities broker-dealers (*firmas comisionistas de bolsa*). This setup is a very different from that operating in the United States. The securities sector expressed concern about the U.S. stock market infrastructure—securities transaction, deposit, compensation, and settlement systems[22]—but the report showed that, contrary to this concern, such an infrastructure could benefit the country.

Few offensive interests on Colombia's part were identified because of the very limited Colombian presence in U.S. financial markets. Colombian banking entities are present only through agencies, because the requirements for opening subsidiaries in the United States are extremely strict, and even the approval procedures for opening agencies are complex and require a lot of effort. Moreover, even if the Colombian population that was legally resident in the United States were a potential market for insurance companies, that market potential would be very difficult to exploit because of how regulation varies across the U.S. states. For those reasons, the report recommended not sacrificing any defensive interests, notwithstanding that Colombia should try to improve the current conditions for Colombian providers that wished to open agencies in the United States.

The study concluded that Colombia's FTA negotiation with the United States offered significant opportunities, such as enhanced access to foreign capital, reduced cost of capital, and a chance to improve know-how. Nonetheless, the FTA also implied important challenges, for which the government was advised to modify the internal regulatory framework to put domestic financial entities in a better competitive position. For example, the report insisted on the need to revise the investment regime on insurance companies' technical reserves as well as regulation on pension funds, which are considered to hinder industry competitiveness with their investment management restrictions.

The Colombian government was fully aware of the need to carry out domestic regulatory changes, as evidenced by the discussions within the financial sector, which were held simultaneously with the negotiation process, under the Internal Agenda framework, and led by the National Planning Department.[23] In general terms, the objective of the Internal Agenda was to achieve a greater degree of competitiveness and efficiency for the economy's productive sectors.

The discussion of the Internal Agenda for the financial sector included several subjects. A main point was the financial system's structure—specifically the need and advisability for the banking system to move toward a multibanking structure and for a merger between the Banking Superintendency and the Securities Superintendency. Other legal issues were elimination of the financial transactions tax, mandatory investments, and directed credit; lower commercial presence of publicly owned banks; and the legal rights of creditors, efficiency of judicial administration, and elimination of interest rate ceilings.

However, the Ministry of Finance was even more ambitious, pointing out the need for comprehensive financial sector reform, which materialized as an ongoing process after 2005 with the support of the World Bank and the U.S. Agency for International Development. The project aims to develop solid technical fundamentals to design financial reform aimed at modernizing the financial sector and fixing any failures that today keep it from being more competitive.[24]

The Financial Sector's Biggest Fears

Financial institutions had two big concerns regarding the U.S. FTA. First, they feared the agreement would put the Colombian financial sector at a disadvantage vis-à-vis financial institutions of other signatories. Second, they worried about the possibility that the changes brought about by the agreement would engender financial reform that could be detrimental for the sector's interests.

Regarding the first concern, the financial industry feared that the FTA would favor foreign financial entities. Insurance companies, for example, were worried that Colombia would allow its residents to purchase insurance from Ecuadoran, Peruvian, or U.S. companies, thereby allowing them to circumvent the value added tax on insurance in the Colombian market (which in many countries either is not levied on insurance or is levied at less than the Colombian tax rate). As a result, Colombian insurance companies feared that domestic consumers might end up seeking insurance with foreign companies. In general, however, Colombian financial institutions thought that greater foreign competition would have positive effects, as long as equal conditions for competition were guaranteed to all.

Regarding the second concern, financial institutions looked apprehensively at the fact that the FTA would allow presentation of a legislative plan in the Colombian Congress, either because the agreement needed it for its future implementation or because the government considered a parallel financial reform to be necessary. Colombian financial institutions viewed with suspicion a legal plan for financial reform based on the FTA because the sector is not particularly popular among congressional representatives.[25] The financial sector feared that Congress might change proposed measures in a way that could adversely affect them.

The Government's Strategy for the FTA on Financial Services

The government's strategy took shape in a "negotiation map" for financial services.[26] Using Tandem Methodology, the government defined and pursued the following Colombian defensive interests at the financial services table during the negotiation:

- Protecting domestic financial services consumers from financial services providers based outside the country, in case problems were encountered in the services or products provided
- Guaranteeing the constitutional right for a minimum pension for social security pension contributors
- Not extending to FTA signatories benefits deeper than those agreed on in other multilateral agreements, such as those reached or to be reached with members of CAN
- Facilitating access for the establishment and operation of Colombian financial entities in Ecuador, Peru, and the United States by eliminating restrictions and speeding up processes[27]
- Maintaining an acceptable level of central bank supervision of cross-border indebtedness with foreign financial entities to prevent asset laundering[28]
- Protecting national savings and avoiding a cash drain[29] (especially the case for pension funds)
- Preserving the ability to determine whether certain insurance products could not be acquired outside the country, such as mandatory insurance, products related to social security, or products for which there is a national guarantee (such as pensions for life insurance)[30]
- Guaranteeing transparency in regulatory changes and minimizing the administrative load and costs of regulation and supervision
- Maintaining discretionary powers over the control of capital inflows and outflows to preserve macroeconomic stability

- Preserving the right to grant advantages to state financial entities (such as Banco Agrario or the National Savings Fund) to address market failures
- Protecting local financial services consumers from foreign financial institutions' mistakes if they had been subcontracted by a financial institution with commercial presence in Colombia.[31]

Another important aspect of Colombian negotiation strategy was placing conditions on concessions for direct branching and the cross-border provision of insurance concessions. The first condition was retaining the central bank's ability to maintain controls on capital flows—specifying that such control would not be permanent and control measures could be applied for a maximum of only one year without compensation.[32] The second was ensuring that the investment chapter would take into account the special particularities of investments in public debt securities.[33]

The U.S. FTA's Financial Services Chapter

The Andean financial services chapter is self-contained, which means that it deals with all issues related to financial services. When some aspects of other chapters apply to financial services, the financial services chapter makes a concrete reference. This is the case for the provisions in the dispute settlement chapter and the investment chapter that apply to financial services, which are modified by the relevant articles in the financial services chapter. The chapter itself is composed of the following general provisions, annexes, and understandings:

- *General provisions.* Such provisions regulate the scope and coverage of the chapter; provide for the disciplines of national treatment, MFN treatment, market access for financial institutions, and cross-border trade; regulate the supply of new financial services, the treatment of certain information, and the treatment of senior management and board of directors of financial institutions; regulate the application of nonconforming measures and exceptions; provide for the transparency and administration of certain regulation, supervision, and self-regulatory measures; regulate the dispute settlement procedure and the investment disputes settlement in financial services; and, finally, contain definitions applicable to the chapter.

- *Understanding concerning social security financial services.* This annex sets up the understanding among the parties of the application of the scope and coverage of the chapter with regard to the provision of services related to social security. This annex is the first of its type in an FTA.

- *Cross-border trade annex.* This annex contains the positive list of insurance and insurance-related services, banking services, and other financial services that can be offered across borders.

- *Transparency annex.* This annex specifies the regulation and supervision transparency measures contained in the chapter that may require legislative and regulatory changes.

- *Expedited availability of insurance services annex.* This annex provides that the parties should endeavor to maintain existing opportunities or may extend them (for instance, by not requiring product approval for insurance, by allowing the introduction of products unless those products are disapproved within a reasonable period of time, and by not imposing limitations on the number or frequency of product introductions).

- *Specific commitments annex.* This annex provides specific commitments regarding portfolio management, branching of banks and insurance companies, and (in the case of Colombia) consumption abroad of insurance products.

- *Financial Services Committee annex.* This annex provides the composition of the Financial Services Committee. The committee is charged with supervising the implementation of the financial services chapter and its further elaboration, considering issues regarding financial services that are referred to it by a party, and participating in the dispute settlement procedures in accordance with the chapter.

- *Understanding regarding financial services.* This understanding clarifies, among other issues, that nothing in the chapter prohibits a party from requiring the issuance of a decree, resolution, or regulation by the executive branch, regulatory agencies, or central bank to authorize new financial services not specifically authorized in its law. It also clarifies that a party may adopt excise or other taxes levied on cross-border services insofar as such taxes are consistent with national treatment and MFN treatment. Finally, it specifies that a party may require the authorization of cross-border financial services suppliers and of financial instruments.

The following are important topics negotiated in the FTA related to commitments on right of establishment, cross-border insurance trade, cross-border trade in financial services other than insurance, collective investment schemes, and social security.

Right of Establishment

Right of establishment refers to the rules for establishing financial institutions in a given country. Such rules include freedoms as well as restrictions on financial institutions established in the country regarding full or partial ownership by a foreign company and the legal forms for purposes of establishment.

As already mentioned, before the FTA negotiations, Colombia had norms that established a certain degree of freedom for setting up foreign financial institutions in its territory. Since 1991, in fact, all financial institutions established in Colombia generally could be of foreign ownership without limitations regarding the amount or percentage of equity owned by foreign investors. The unrestricted and nondiscriminatory foreign ownership of several insurance companies, pension funds, and banks also indicates the regime's openness.

Colombia has, however, maintained certain market-access restrictions—particularly the need to constitute financial institutions as legal entities under Colombian laws—and it has specified the legal forms in which such entities could be constituted. Thus, no commercial presence was legally possible through direct branching, and foreign institutions could not simply open a branch dependent on the head office and its capital while offering financial services domestically. Colombia, therefore, allowed the presence of foreign financial institutions but required the creation of subsidiaries that had to operate autonomously in Colombian territory and comply with the domestic ownership regime (such entities had to have a board of directors, physical address, and commercial registration number; publicly swear in their management officers; and so on). This aspect changed with the FTA negotiation, when the United States asked the three Andean countries to agree to complete freedom of establishment in their territories, including the possibility for market access through branches, and to eliminate the imposition of specific legal forms for the establishment of financial entities.

As for the entry of Andean financial institutions to the U.S. market, the U.S. proposed a nonconforming measure—in the end accepted by the Andean countries—under which access to the U.S. market for financial services providers from Colombia, Ecuador, or Peru would be subject to nondiscriminatory legal measures at the state and federal levels. Such institutions would be subject to prudential measures and other types of customary limitations applicable to financial institutions. In a footnote to appendix III of the financial services chapter, however, the United States clarified that, for example, partnerships and sole proprietorships are not generally legal forms under which diverse financial institutions can be constituted. Through its nonconforming measures, the United States also made clear that access to its markets in the form of branches was subject to limitations related to its federal and state legislation.[34] Thus, there will not be reciprocity because the United States would have complete access to the territories of Colombia, Ecuador, and Peru, whereas these countries' banks and insurance companies will not be able to open branch offices in several U.S. states.

Yet this commitment does not imply big changes for Ecuador or Peru because before the FTA, they already allowed such an establishment. For them, this commitment brings about consolidation at an international treaty level of their internal legislation's status quo. The commitment, however, requires a legislative change for Colombia, because it implies accepting a new way to access its market that was *not* previously permitted. As compensation, Colombia's commitment to allow access through branches will be limited to banks and insurance companies and will become effective only four years after the treaty comes into effect.

The domestic industry accepted these commitments because it perceived that branches with capital assigned would not be a threat, since establishing a subsidiary in the country does not accrue much advantage. Banks and insurance companies, however, wanted to have time to prepare in case competition increased, which was achieved with the four-year period negotiated, giving them enough time to prepare for this new type of commercial presence.

In the FTA, Colombia retained the right to determine conditions under which branches could be established. According to the corresponding specific commitment, Colombia could regulate branches, including their characteristics, structure, relationship to their parent company, capital requirements, technical reserves, and obligations regarding risk patrimony and their investments. This regulation, however, could not nullify or impair the commitment or unduly restrain market access.

Finally, the three Andean countries made their respective nonconforming measures clear: even though they accepted banks' and insurance companies' access to their markets as branches, in every case a minimum capital had to be assigned to banks, and minimum capital and technical reserves had to be assigned to insurance companies, which had to be effectively incorporated in the country where the branch operated and the amounts concerned converted to local currency.

With these nonconforming measures and through the creation of legal entities under local laws, Colombia looked to guarantee equal conditions for banks established in Colombia and foreign financial institutions' branches in the country. Colombia also sought to protect local consumers in case of foreign financial entities' bankruptcy, ensuring that assets would always be available in Colombia that, according to local laws, could be used to pay for the companies' liabilities. This point was reinforced by the right of the government to provide that the capital required for setting up a branch be equivalent to that required to set up a bank or insurance company, which also eliminated any advantages of a branch office over a subsidiary. These measures reassured the local industry that foreign bank branches and banks established in Colombian territory would not benefit from unequal treatment.

Clearly, the United States would have preferred a negotiation in which Colombia accepted the establishment of branches with no assigned capital. Nonetheless, what was negotiated provided new opportunities for the U.S. banking industry. First, a subsidiary usually has to organize a board of directors. Difficulties in coordinating the subsidiary's and parent's board are eliminated by allowing the latter to take direct control of all decisions in all of its branches.

Second, according to Colombian corporate law, a subsidiary can pay dividends only when, among other requirements, it has closed its financial statements, they have been audited, the supervisor has approved them, and the shareholders have met and approved such payment. This procedure is long and expensive. According to what has been negotiated, branches constituted in Colombia may send remittances of their liquid profits, as long as they meet the minimum required solvency margin and other minimum capital requirements. This provision should speed up and make less costly the process of paying the profits.

Cross-Border Trade in Insurance

Before the FTA, Colombia had a highly restrictive regime for cross-border trade insurance. In fact, Colombian legislation prohibited domestic residents from acquiring insurance policies internationally: it prohibited foreign insurance companies from offering cross-border insurance policies to domestic residents as well as the movement of persons (such as visits from foreign insurance companies' representatives) to offer insurance policies.[35] The only exception was for foreign insurance companies offering or Colombian companies acquiring reinsurance policies.

The U.S. FTA will generate fundamental changes in the Colombian market, because it will give way to greater competition for domestic insurance companies in several modes of supply. Similar commitments were undertaken by Ecuador, Peru, and the United States.

Insurance consumption abroad. Until now, Colombian residents had to acquire their insurance policies at locally established companies. The FTA will allow the possibility of acquiring most types of insurance policies from Ecuadoran, Peruvian, or U.S. insurance companies as well as the possibility for those companies to offer such policies four years after the FTA takes effect.[36] This commitment does not, however, allow suppliers to "do business" or "solicit business" in its territory. The country will define the terms *doing business* and *soliciting or advertising* such that the definitions are consistent with the commitment itself.

The commitment to allow consumption abroad is made on the basis of a negative list, meaning that consumption of all insurance policies internationally will be allowed except for those that are explicitly excluded. The list includes the following insurance products: (a) those that are or may become mandatory under Colombian law; (b) annuities in any form related to social security; (c) insurance for disability and survival related to social security;[37] (d) professional risk insurance related to social security;[38] (e) other insurance products related to social security that Colombian law may establish in the future;[39] and (f) all branches when the taker, insured, or beneficiary is a state entity.[40]

Cross-border insurance supply. Under the FTA, Colombia's commitments on cross-border insurance supply turned out to be quite limited. Only Ecuadoran, Peruvian, and U.S. insurance companies will be able to offer a limited number of insurance policies that are fundamentally related to international trade. Finally, the commitments of Ecuador, Peru, and the United States are similar to those of Colombia.

Temporary presence of persons offering insurance services in the Colombian territory. The four countries agreed to allow the temporary presence of persons of another party for offering insurance policies to their residents. In this case, Colombia used the same positive list containing the commitments related to cross-border insurance supply. Thus, the commitments for supply through physical presence of persons are also limited because they are basically connected to insurance policies related to international trade. Moreover, according to this list, the cross-border supply through physical presence of persons of life insurance or insurance covering personal risks will not be allowed, so most consumers will be protected.

Other important issues related to insurance. As for banking services, Colombia will still have the ability to impose taxes, require authorization both for suppliers and instruments, and authorize new financial services.[41]

Cross-Border Trade in Other Financial Services

For cross-border trade of financial services other than insurance, the commitments made were limited and many of them had little effect on Andean countries.

The United States proposed that the four countries should commit to allowing cross-border trade under three modes of supply.[42] The financial services provided under such commitments were (a) financial information transfer and supply; (b) financial data processing and related software; and (c) advisory and other auxiliary financial services, excluding intermediation related to banking services and including reports and credit analysis, investment portfolio analysis, and advisory services related to acquisitions and corporate restructuring.

Commitments related to the supply and transfer of financial information did not generate problems.[43] In Colombia, for example, information vendors (Bloomberg and Reuters) have cross-border operations that do not require commercial presence or the government's authorization to operate, and they do not need to comply with any regulation in particular.[44] Moreover, for good functioning of the market and adequate price setting, vendors need to have this type of information. Thus, this commitment merely meant a consolidation of the status quo.

The commitments related to financial data processing and software did not cause any controversy either, although capital market operators were concerned that such a commitment could be understood as an authorization for stock exchange platforms to have cross-border operations. Local capital market operators thus demanded that these institutions should operate in Colombia under commercial presence and not under cross-border supply. To prevent misunderstandings, the agreement made clear that the supply of either electronic or physical exchange platforms was not contemplated within the supply of cross-border services.[45]

In contrast, the Constitutional Court gave Colombian residents the right to request the review and elimination of negative or mistaken information in any database (normally in credit bureaus) as well as the right, especially for financial debtors, to eliminate information on default payments after a given time. Therefore, the commitment clarified that consumer credit information had to be used according to Colombian legislation, thereby protecting the right to privacy and the integrity of a natural or juridical person's good name.

Finally, the commitments regarding advisory and other auxiliary financial services related to banking services did not present any major problem except on the matter of credit reports and analysis. The concern was that this area included bond issuers' credit ratings. Colombian legislation requires that companies wishing to issue certain securities, particularly those of fixed income, must be rated by agencies established in Colombia and supervised by the Financial Superintendency. This requirement implies that to issue such securities a financial service has to contract with an entity with commercial presence in Colombia, and therefore a cross-border supply of this service is not legal in Colombia.[46] Consequently, it was agreed to exclude from the Colombian positive list a commitment on credit reports and analysis.[47]

Collective Investment Schemes

Collective investment schemes (CISs) in Colombia are structured and managed by trust companies through common ordinary funds and special funds, by securities broker-dealers through equity funds, and by investment management companies offering investment funds. Before the FTA was signed, Colombian legislation did not allow investment fund administrators (of CISs) to outsource the management of any part of those funds to third parties.[48]

Colombia, Ecuador, Peru, and the United States agreed that after the FTA came into effect, they would allow CIS administrators established in their territories to hire other financial institutions for various services. In accordance with specific commitments, Colombia, Ecuador, Peru, and the United States will allow financial institutions organized outside their territories (but in one of the parties) to provide investment advice and portfolio management services to CISs located in their territories.

Colombia, Ecuador, and Peru committed to issue regulations to allow such subcontracting in favor of U.S. companies. In addition, the Andean countries have committed to allow local CIS administrators to hire other local CIS administrators to manage all or part of their portfolio (local portfolio management). In return, the United States agreed to allow its mutual investment funds[49] to subcontract with Colombian, Ecuadoran, or Peruvian CIS administrators for the same services.

This agreement implies significant changes for Colombia, which may even result in a full reconsideration of CISs. Currently, a trust company, for example, cannot subcontract a third party to provide portfolio management services, because a CIS administrator must carry out all tasks in relation to that CIS in-house. After the public's resources are collected, the administrator must make all investment decisions, monitor and value securities positions, and give back the resources at investors' request, according to each scheme's rules. Allowing a third party to carry out any of these tasks, such as investment decisions, is currently considered to be a "delegation or professionalism" subject to Financial Superintendency sanctions.

The FTA changes the current scheme, which is restrictive and inadequate, for the better.[50] Four years after the treaty comes into effect, a CIS may contract tasks with several expert institutions located in that country or in other signatory countries. For example, a Colombian securities broker-dealer would be able to hire a trust company to carry out all its CIS investments. In the meantime, the entity that collected the resources from the public would be able to manage another part of those resources (for example, carry out those investments in which it has more expertise) or simply concentrate on the CIS's marketing and leave the investment task to third parties.

Social Security

The issues that probably commanded the most attention from Colombian negotiators during the negotiating rounds were those related to social security. One reason is that anything that refers to changes in social security is sensitive in all countries, drawing attention from the media and Congress. In addition, the Colombian Constitutional Court is very vigilant about every change made to the system, the system's functioning, and beneficiaries' rights. Proof of the last is that almost every statute modifying the Colombian social security system has been contested in court. In almost all cases, the court has found some part of the modifications unconstitutional or constitutional, depending on its interpretation (normally the most favorable to the users of the system).

Therefore, anything negotiated in the FTA had to be well explained to the Constitutional Court, the Congress, and the media. The easiest course would have been to make no changes to the system and to delay complete autonomy over future changes to the system. However, the United States demanded that the financial services chapter apply to social security services, if they were conducted by financial institutions that were in competition with a public entity or a financial institution.

In the case of Colombia, some services that are part of the social security system are, in fact, conducted by financial institutions that are in competition with a public entity. The pension system comprises two subsystems in competition: a fully funded system administered by private pension funds and a pay-as-you-go system administered by the state-owned Instituto de los Seguros Sociales (Social Security Institute).

The Colombian Financial Sector after the FTA: Impacts and Lessons

Considering the situation of Colombia's financial system at the time of the negotiations, one must conclude that the government's strategy has been mixed. On the one hand, the government adopted some liberalizing steps for certain activities in the FTA. On the other hand, it tackled internal weaknesses in regulation and supervision that negatively affected financial operation, efficiency, and competitiveness.

The U.S. FTA and Domestic Financial Reform

One of the most interesting aspects of the analysis is that the Colombian government took advantage of the FTA in framing domestic structural financial reform, which undoubtedly will significantly affect the sector's operation and structure in the future. Since the launch of the FTA, the government has advocated the need for continued change in the financial sector to enhance market-access conditions, promote greater competition, and increase overall efficiency in financial intermediation. The authorities are conscious of the adjustments that need to take place, such as promoting economies of scale and overcoming regulatory obstacles. Additional aspects related to financial repression, such as financial transaction taxation, forced investment and directed lending practices, weak protection for creditors, and regulation of insurance companies and pension funds, require continued attention.

Taking into account the adjustment pressures and legislative changes flowing from the FTA, the authorities have pursued the discussion of financial reform. With President Uribe's reelection, the continuity of this process is ensured.

The Expected Effect of the FTA on Financial Services

The analysis of the FTA suggests that after the reforms adopted in the 1990s, it is the first step toward greater liberalization of financial services in Colombia, although the changes deriving directly from the treaty's negotiation seem, at first glance, to be relatively modest. However, some elements of the financial services chapter should be highlighted.

With respect to commercial presence, the main change for Colombia was the allowance of branches as a new legal form for foreigners to supply financial services, although foreign branches are required to operate with capital assigned to the country and under Colombia's prudential norms. This change places Colombia in the same situation as most Latin American nations, and the negotiation results are similar to the case of Chile and most CAFTA-DR-U.S. member countries.

In practice, the new situation will not differ much from the current situation. However, the agreement has advantages for the United States, because branches are not required to establish a local board of directors, thus speeding up the process of remitting branch profits. Therefore, this policy change will likely make Colombia more attractive for financial foreign investment. In addition, if greater competition by foreign investment occurs in the local market, the financial sector and the government may develop diverse strategies, such as encouraging mergers with the purpose of increasing the size of the sector and improving efficiency and competitiveness.

Concerning the insurance sector, the FTA was much more ambitious in the sense that Colombian individuals and companies will be able to purchase insurance policies from foreign insurance companies when the treaty enters into effect. Additionally, foreign insurance companies will be able to offer in Colombia insurance services on a cross-border basis and through the presence of natural persons. The liberalization of these two modes of supply may generate significant changes in the insurance market because of increased competition for insurance companies already established in the country. Moreover, from the consumer's viewpoint, the FTA liberalization measures appear positive. Although these changes will be implemented gradually and the effects within the insurance sector should not be abrupt, enhanced efficiency in the insurance sector will be important and constitute a challenge for domestic firms in Colombia.

Finally, the FTA may bring important changes regarding collective investment schemes. The agreement foresees the right of CIS administrators to subcontract with other country's portfolio administrators and, as a consequence, local administrators (a feature prohibited in Colombia before the FTA). This change will take place over a four-year transition period. Several years ago, the financial industry itself and related authorities had made significant efforts to modify the model under which CISs function. As such, the FTA's effects are in line with previous domestic strategy. This change, too, should have positive effects on the Colombian financial system. The legal improvements required by the FTA and the changes noted previously have accordingly been important discussion topics within the agenda of financial reform being pursued.

Beyond the direct changes introduced by the financial chapter negotiations, one cannot underestimate other types of indirect effects that the FTA may have involving FDI. The FTA almost certainly places Colombia in a better position for attracting FDI, including in its financial sector, because of the stabilizing effect that promotes better legal enforcement, more effective information flows, clearer dispute resolution, and a sounder macroeconomic environment. All these factors contribute to improving the country's investment climate and reassuring foreign and domestic investors. Simultaneously, changes introduced though the forthcoming financial reform should support and complement those brought about by the FTA.

Lessons Learned from the U.S. FTA Financial Services Experience

A first element worth mentioning is the adequate preparation and organization of the negotiations by the government. This effort has had positive effects not only for the financial sector's operation, but also for the acceptance of the financial services agreement by key financial representatives. Among the positive effects are the following:

- The coordination between monetary and fiscal authorities—that is, the central bank and the Ministry of Finance and its superintendencies—as well as with financial associations constitutes a positive and important factor, facilitating a consensus on proper negotiation strategies. This situation contrasts with the experience of other key sectors, such as agriculture and pharmaceuticals, where important disagreements emerged inside the government and, in several cases, within the private sector.

- The Ministry of Finance's deliberate decision to isolate the financial sector negotiations—the only issue not negotiated directly by the Ministry of Trade, Industry, and Tourism—from other sectors resolved the problem of sacrificing crucial industry issues in exchange for gains in other sectors. In practice, this strategy allowed the Ministry of Finance to focus on central issues regardless of how the negotiations in the rest of the chapters evolved. In addition, this strategy guaranteed that the negotiators were specialists on the subjects under negotiation.

- Another crucial factor in the negotiation was the joint discussion of issues of public debt, capital flows, and financial services. Such discussion was sensible not only because these topics are in many ways related, but also because the talks were beneficial for Colombia, in particular with respect to investments in public debt securities (which were in the end not covered by the investment chapter).

- For the private sector, communication and information flows between financial associations and the negotiating team were clear and constant, although—and not surprisingly—some individual differences arose, mainly from the insurance sector regarding cross-border trade and foreign consumption. The broad acceptance of the treaty by the Colombian financial industry underscores the success of this effort, especially when one considers that no public debate—which could slow negotiations—ever opened on this subject. Indeed, the financial services chapter was one of the first to be concluded during the FTA discussions.

Annex 6A: Colombia's Schedule of Specific Commitments Undertaken in GATS

Table 6A.1 provides a summary of the specific commitments made by Colombia under GATS.

Table 6A.1　Colombia's Schedule of Specific Commitments Undertaken in GATS

Sector or subsector	Limitations on market access	Limitations on national treatment
All financial services	Mode 3: The national government may require national and foreign financial entities to meet an economic needs test as a condition of operating in Colombia. Factors such as public interest, economic and financial conditions, and local and general conditions will be considered. Establishment of a company as an affiliated company or subsidiary is permitted. Other forms of supply, in particular branch offices, are excluded. The commercial presence must be carried out in accordance with the purpose specifically authorized for the affiliated company or subsidiary, and the affiliated company or subsidiary must adopt the legal status required by the Colombian regulations. Representative offices of foreign financial entities may not supply financial services in Colombia. The supply of financial services in Colombia requires prior government authorization. Such authorization is granted in accordance with the criteria and requirements contained in Colombian laws and in regulation principles that are accepted on an international level that apply to a particular financial entity.	Mode 3: The special conditions on privatization of state-owned companies require that such companies will be exclusively offered to natural persons and national juridical persons.

(continued)

Table 6A.1   (continued)

Sector or subsector	Limitations on market access	Limitations on national treatment
	Authorization for financial services providers to operate in Colombia is subject to the corresponding superintendency's verification of the character, responsibility, and competence of the people acting as owners, directors, and managers.	
	The specific superintendency must verify that the petitioning entities have adequate controls to prevent asset laundering and to manage risks. These entities must have consolidated supervision in accordance with generally accepted international principles.	
Insurance and insurance-related services		
Direct insurance (including co-insurance) different from life insurance	Mode 1: Unbound, except for insurance related to foreign trade operations, exclusively for journeys that begin or end in a Colombian port	Mode 1: Unbound
	Mode 2: Unbound	Mode 2: Unbound
	Mode 3: None	Mode 3: None
	Mode 4: Unbound, except as indicated in the horizontal commitments applicable to all the sectors included in this list	Mode 4: Unbound, except as indicated in the horizontal commitments applicable to all the sectors included in this list
Reinsurance and retrocession	Mode 1: None	Mode 1: None
	Mode 2: None	Mode 2: None
	Mode 3: None	Mode 3: None
	Mode 4: Unbound, except as indicated in the horizontal commitments applicable to all the sectors included in this list	Mode 4: Unbound, except as indicated in the horizontal commitments applicable to all the sectors included in this list

Insurance intermediation, such as brokerage and agency[a]	Mode 1: Unbound Mode 2: Unbound Mode 3: None Mode 4: Unbound, except as indicated in the horizontal commitments applicable to all the sectors included in this list
Services auxiliary to insurance, such as consulting, actuarial, risk assessment, and claim settlement services	Mode 1: Unbound Mode 2: Unbound Mode 3: None Mode 4: Unbound, except as indicated in the horizontal commitments applicable to all the sectors included in this list
Banking and other financial services (excluding insurance)	
Acceptance of deposits and other repayable funds from the public	Mode 1: Unbound Mode 2: Unbound Mode 3: None Mode 4: Unbound, except as indicated in the horizontal commitments applicable to all the sectors included in this list
Lending of all types, including, among others, consumer credit, mortgage credit, and factoring and financing of commercial transactions	Mode 1: Unbound Mode 2: Unbound Mode 3: None Mode 4: Unbound, except as indicated in the horizontal commitments applicable to all the sectors included in this list
Financial leasing	Mode 1: Unbound Mode 2: Unbound Mode 3: None

(continued)

Table 6A.1 (continued)

Sector or subsector	Limitations on market access	Limitations on national treatment
	Mode 4: Unbound, except as indicated in the horizontal commitments applicable to all the sectors included in this list	Mode 4: Unbound, except as indicated in the horizontal commitments applicable to all the sectors included in this list
Guarantees and commitments	Mode 1: Unbound Mode 2: Unbound Mode 3: None Mode 4: Unbound, except as indicated in the horizontal commitments applicable to all the sectors included in this list	Mode 1: Unbound Mode 2: Unbound Mode 3: None Mode 4: Unbound, except as indicated in the horizontal commitments applicable to all the sectors included in this list
Trading specified instruments for own account or for account of customers, whether on an exchange, in an over-the-counter market, or otherwise	Mode 1: Unbound Mode 2: Unbound Mode 3: None Mode 4: Unbound, except as indicated in the horizontal commitments applicable to all the sectors included in this list	Mode 1: Unbound Mode 2: Unbound Mode 3: None Mode 4: Unbound, except as indicated in the horizontal commitments applicable to all the sectors included in this list
Participation in issues of all kinds of securities, including underwriting and placement as an agent (whether publicly or privately) and provision of services related to such issues	Mode 1: Unbound Mode 2: Unbound Mode 3: None Mode 4: Unbound, except as indicated in the horizontal commitments applicable to all the sectors included in this list	Mode 1: Unbound Mode 2: Unbound Mode 3: None Mode 4: Unbound, except as indicated in the horizontal commitments applicable to all the sectors included in this list

Money broking	Mode 1: Unbound Mode 2: Unbound Mode 3: None Mode 4: Unbound, except as indicated in the horizontal commitments applicable to all the sectors included in this list	Mode 1: Unbound Mode 2: Unbound Mode 3: None Mode 4: Unbound, except as indicated in the horizontal commitments applicable to all the sectors included in this list
Provision and transfer of financial information and financial data processing and related software by providers of other financial services	Mode 1: Unbound Mode 2: Unbound Mode 3: None Mode 4: Unbound, except as indicated in the horizontal commitments applicable to all the sectors included in this list	Mode 1: Unbound Mode 2: Unbound Mode 3: None Mode 4: Unbound, except as indicated in the horizontal commitments applicable to all the sectors included in this list
Advisory, intermediation, and other auxiliary financial services on all the activities listed above, including credit reference and analysis, investment and portfolio research and advice, and advice on acquisitions and on corporate restructuring and strategy	Mode 1: Unbound Mode 2: Unbound Mode 3: None Mode 4: Unbound, except as indicated in the horizontal commitments applicable to all the sectors included in this list	Mode 1: Unbound Mode 2: Unbound Mode 3: None Mode 4: Unbound, except as indicated in the horizontal commitments applicable to all the sectors included in this list

Source: World Trade Organization database.

Note: Modes 1 to 4 refer to limitations on market-access and national treatment commitments in the four modes of supply: (1) cross-border supply, (2) consumption abroad, (3) commercial presence, and (4) temporary presence of natural persons). "None" and "unbound" refer to full and no liberalization commitment, respectively, for a specific mode.

a. This information is taken from GATS/SC/20/Suppl.3.

Notes

1. To date, the agreement is still pending congressional approval in the United States.

2. The *intermediation margin* (defined as the net interest margin as a percentage of assets) averaged 6 to 7 percentage points, a level that was similar to the average for the region but practically double that of the level registered for industrial economies.

3. A *financial conglomerate* is a group of companies under common control whose exclusive or predominant activities consist of providing significant services in at least two different financial sectors (de la Cruz and Stephanou 2006).

4. Since 2007, foreign direct investment in the financial sector has increased. In 2006, a Spanish bank acquired a local institution, which had been nationalized during the previous crisis, raising the foreign share to 21 percent. Other sales of state-owned banks to foreign investors are expected in the near future.

5. Member countries at the time were Bolivia, Colombia, Ecuador, Peru, and the República Bolivariana de Venezuela.

6. See the Treaty of Cartagena, Decisions 220 and 244, for the specific policies.

7. This new regulation coincided with the elimination of the few restrictions on foreign investment that were still maintained in the framework of the Andean Pact (Resolutions 291 and 292).

8. National defense and toxic waste were excepted.

9. In any case, the República Bolivariana de Venezuela was the G3 country most strongly opposed to such a negotiation.

10. See annex 6A of this chapter for Colombia's schedule of specific commitments undertaken in GATS.

11. The only limitation regarding national treatment was that natural persons and national juridical persons would exclusively be offered special conditions on the privatization of state-owned companies.

12. Decision 439 in 1998 stated that subregional services trade liberalization should be achieved no later than 2005. This deadline was first modified in January 2006 through Decision 629 and then in June 2006 through Decision 634. Decision 629 extended the deadline to June 30, 2006 for stating working tables, and Decision 634 extended it to November 15, 2006, seeking to end revisions and agreements in September 2007. See http://www.comunidadandina .org/normativa/dec/dectema_servicios.htm for details.

13. These four modes are commercial presence, cross-border trade, foreign consumption, and temporary movement of services suppliers.

14. A high-level working team was created in charge of revising the content of the restrictive measures listed in Decision 510, as well as the services that

would be liberalized. The team was to present to the commission a proposal indicating which measures would be subject to liberalization and sector harmonization. Following the commission's approval, liberalization and harmonization would begin in September 2007 with the adoption of the corresponding decisions.

15. The ATPA-ATPDEA program is the commercial component of the War on Drugs that the United States initiated in 1991. The U.S. legislation entered into force in 1992 for Colombia and Bolivia and 1993 for Ecuador and Peru. Under the ATPA-ATPDEA program, a significant list of Colombian products has benefited from the reduction or elimination of import tariffs in the United States.

16. This team comprised public sector employees, central bank personnel, representatives from the superintendencies, and representatives of the public service commissions.

17. The Ministry of Finance was in charge of the Banking Superintendency and the Securities Superintendency (which have since been merged into the Financial Superintendency).

18. This entity unites 14 associations in Colombia, and its mission is to consolidate the social function of the country's associations by means of coordinating their activity to promote identification and unification criteria on topics of national interest, as well as to stimulate the analysis and search for unified positions in the private sector regarding topics of social interest.

19. The financial associations were seeking to have not only a technical study that could help them in setting a position but also recommendations coming from independent think tanks with credibility within the government and the country.

20. Unfair competition might arise because domestic institutions were exposed to minimum capital requirements and other prudential regulation, whereas branches were not supposed to have local capital.

21. Consumption abroad can be controlled by different means. The government can negotiate using a positive list, which means that only the services contained in the list are allowed to be consumed abroad. To enforce the list, the government can establish exchange rules under which any product consumed abroad not included in the list would be illegal and therefore subject to sanctions (the central bank might deter the entrance to the country of an indemnification or subject it to sanctions if not allowed to be consumed abroad). In addition, parties to a treaty can agree with respect to all modes of cross-border trade in financial services (including consumption abroad) that any party may require the authorization of cross-border financial services suppliers of the other party and of financial instruments before they are actually sold to its residents. This type of measure was actually negotiated in the Andean FTA at the

request of Colombia. The request of authorizations seems to be very difficult to exercise, because it calls in many cases for an extraterritorial application of local law. In addition, consumption abroad can be controlled through the imposition of taxes on such consumption. The Andean FTA uses this method, under which any party may adopt excise or other taxes levied on cross-border services, including consumption abroad. This provision was included in the text at the request of Colombia to give relief to Colombian insurance companies. In Colombia, as a general rule, the consumption of insurance products is subject to a value added tax, which can be up to 16 percent of the price premium paid for the insurance. Because the United States has no value added tax and the tariffs are much lower than the Colombian tariff, Colombian insurance companies were worried that Colombian residents would have extra incentive to consume abroad so that their final cost would be lower.

22. The main concern came from the BVC because it currently has a monopoly. The BVC opposed cross-border trade regarding activities such as securities exchange, deposit, custody, compensation, and settlement, preferring instead commercial presence of foreign providers. However, other stock market participating agents considered having greater choices useful because they would be less dependent on the BVC's infrastructure.

23. Within the process of negotiating a trade agreement, the Colombian government worked domestically along with regional entities, the private sector, political actors, and civil society on an agreement called the *Internal Agenda*.

24. The Colombian government, supported by the World Bank, commissioned studies in different areas to identify the main problems faced by the sector. Some topics covered by research studies included the financial sector structure, organization and multibanking, pension funds, insurance companies, collective investment schemes, and electronic payments. The Ministry of Finance organized seminars where the main results, conclusions, and proposals were discussed with the industry.

25. Among some congressional representatives and other groups, the Colombian financial sector is perceived as a sector that pursues its own interest and profitability at the expense of its clients.

26. During the process, the negotiation map was complemented by Colombia's specific interests, based on an assessment of each sector's (securities, banking, insurance) strengths and weaknesses, which were, in turn, validated in their respective associations and by the higher authorities in the negotiation's decision-making process.

27. Colombian banks were very interested in speeding up the administrative processes for establishing branches or agencies in the United States. Many of them believed that getting approval took too long or that they were rejected without any objective explanation. This information was very valuable for the

negotiators when negotiating the rules regarding the right of establishment. Colombian negotiators focused on two aspects: (a) establishing a fixed time for the supervisors to accept or deny licenses and (b) eliminating any subjectivity in the decision on an application filed. As a result of the negotiations, the parties agreed that (a) a party's regulatory authority should make an administrative decision on a completed application of an investor in a financial institution or a cross-border financial services supplier of another party relating to the supply of a financial service within 120 days and should promptly notify the applicant of the decision; (b) each party's regulatory authorities should make publicly available the requirements, including any documentation required, for completing applications related to the supply of financial services; and (c) on the request of an applicant, a party's regulatory authority should inform the applicant of the status of its application. If the authority required additional information from the applicant, it should notify the applicant without undue delay.

28. This provision would normally be covered by the prudential carve-out and applied on a nondiscriminatory basis, but it was a major concern of the central bank.

29. The government was worried about the possibility that, as a result of the negotiations, scarce national savings would leave the country, especially in the case of pension funds. The government did not want the resources administered by private pension funds established in Colombia, which invest their resources mainly in Colombia, to end up outside the country if, for example, consumption abroad of the mandatory pension services were permitted.

30. With regard to mandatory insurance, the government did not want to allow certain mandatory insurance (for example, car insurance) to be consumed abroad because part of the premium paid for this insurance goes to a public fund (named Fosyga) that covers the payment for accidents caused by cars that unlawfully flee the scene of the accident. If this type of insurance could be consumed abroad, funding Fosyga would be more difficult. With regard to pension funds, the government worried that any additional liberalization might entail new risks that could be a burden on the state. In Colombia, pension funds are guaranteed by Fogafin. According to the Fogafin guarantee, if a pension fund goes into bankruptcy, the pensioners have the right to claim their payments. For the government, any negotiation had to take into account that any exacerbation of such risk might affect Fogafin's finances, which could happen, for instance, if the cross-border portfolio management commitments allowed a Colombian pension fund to give the money to a foreign collective investment scheme that might not adequately manage the funds. Such a scenario might create a higher burden on the Fogafin guarantee, which would be directly affected because it would end up paying the guarantee for mistakes made by someone not subject to local supervision.

31. In this regard, it was important for the government that if a collective investment scheme were allowed to contract with a U.S. portfolio manager, any mistakes committed by the manager could not serve as an excuse in case of a
lawsuit by an investor. For the Colombian government, mistakes made by sub-
contractors had to be borne by the collective investment scheme that subcontracted them and not by the individual investor.

32. This petition was similar to what Chile obtained in the FTA with the United
States.

33. According to the initial U.S. proposal, an investment in public debt securities
should receive the same treatment as any other type of investment. Hence,
any investor in public debt securities would be granted the same rights and
protections as any other type of investor (for example, protection from expropriation). The Colombian negotiators considered such a proposal unaccept-
able because the Investment Chapter covers only political risks and not
commercial risks. When an investor acquires public debt securities, he or she
is assuming commercial risks (such as a default on its payment), which is
reflected in the price paid and on the emerging markets bond index.
Therefore, such public debt acquisition should not be covered by the
Investment Chapter. Because of the negotiation, the parties agreed on a special annex (Annex 10-F). Among its provisions are that (a) the parties recognize that the acquisition of public debt securities issued by one party
presupposes a commercial risk, and therefore, any default should not be considered an expropriation unless the investor proves it, and (b) public debt
restructuring can be subject to an FTA arbitration under section B of the
Investment Chapter because restructuring cannot be considered in itself as an
expropriation.

34. First, federal and state legislation prohibit credit unions, savings banks, and
savings associations from establishing branch offices in the United States
under a foreign law. Second, foreign financial institutions wanting to accept or
keep deposits under US$100,000 in the United States must constitute a sub-
sidiary under federal law. Thus, a foreign bank cannot establish a branch office
dedicated to accepting deposits under this limit, thereby constituting a major
limitation to developing retail markets for Andean citizens, which is what
Colombian, Ecuadoran, or Peruvian banks would naturally be seeking in the
United States. Third, establishing foreign banks as branch offices is not
allowed in the states of Alabama, Delaware, Florida, Georgia, Idaho, Kansas,
Louisiana, Maryland, Mississippi, Missouri, North Dakota, Oklahoma, Texas,
West Virginia, and Wyoming. Fourth, foreign insurance companies' branch
offices are not authorized to sell surety bonds for agreements with the U.S.
government. Finally, the United States included in its nonconforming measures "all the existing nonconforming measures for all states, the District of
Columbia, and Puerto Rico." Some U.S. states prohibit the establishment of
insurance companies through branch offices, which constitutes an additional

limitation for Colombian, Ecuadoran, and Peruvian insurance companies that want to access this market. The states that do not allow initial entry of a non-U.S. insurance company as a branch to supply life, accident, health (excluding workers' compensation) insurance, nonlife insurance, or reinsurance and retrocession are Arkansas, Arizona, Connecticut, Georgia, Hawaii (branching allowed for reinsurance), Kansas, Maryland, Minnesota, Nebraska, New Jersey, North Carolina, Pennsylvania, Tennessee, Vermont, and Wyoming.

35. Interestingly, no cases are known where these regulations actually were enforced.

36. According to article 5 and its respective annex, Colombia will allow individuals living in its territory and Colombian citizens, regardless of their place of residency, to purchase insurance policies from cross-border insurance financial services suppliers of Ecuador, Peru, or the United States located in their territories, including third-country insurance companies established in those three countries.

37. These insurance products are acquired by pension funds for insurance against the risk of contributors' disability and survival, for which pension funds are liable if a contributor becomes disabled or passes away. They were excluded for the same reasons discussed in the case of annuities.

38. These insurance products protect workers if they suffer an accident at work or contract a work-related illness. These products were excluded for the same reasons discussed in the case of annuities.

39. This general exclusion aims to ensure that Colombia can prohibit the consumption abroad of any insurance relating to social security that may exist in the future. The reason for this exclusion is to guarantee for Colombia the greatest possible degree of autonomy in social security matters after signing the FTA, which would have been affected if such insurance services could be consumed abroad.

40. These insurance services were excluded so that the state would remain insured or continue as the beneficiary of policies issued only by Colombian insurance companies, taking into account the state's current prerogatives. An example of these prerogatives is the state's ability, in the case of state agreements, to declare the event of a calamity and effect the policy covering it, by means of an administrative act declaring its expiry. This prerogative, which allows the state to make effective an insurance policy in an expeditious manner, would be lost if the policy were acquired by a foreign insurance company.

41. According to the Andean Financial Services Chapter, each party shall permit a financial institution of another party established in its territory to supply any new financial service that the party would permit its own financial institutions, in like circumstances, to supply without additional legislative action by the first party. Thus a "new financial service" is a service that (a) is not supplied in the territory by any financial institution and (b) would be supplied,

for the first time in the country, by a financial institution of another party without need of additional legislative action.

42. These modes are cross-border, consumption abroad, and presence of natural persons.

43. The general rule is that this service may be supplied in any of the territories without the requirement of a state license or of compliance with strict regulation, which means that such a service does not represent a major interest to the government because it is not subject to state intervention.

44. This financial information is supplied to capital market operators through passive screens (*pantallas pasivas*).

45. These services can be supplied in any of the signatory countries, but only through commercial presence.

46. For an adequate rating of securities issuers, an understanding is necessary of the country's conditions, especially those of its economic sectors. The major concern with this commitment is that the knowledge and understanding of such conditions are almost impossible or very difficult to achieve without a local presence. For this reason, the cross-border supply of this service is not allowed.

47. However, if Colombia in the future allows any other country to supply these services, financial institutions of the signatory countries of this treaty will automatically gain the right to supply the same services under the same mode on a MFN basis.

48. For more details regarding CISs in Colombia, see de la Cruz and Stephanou (2006).

49. These are investment companies registered by the U.S. Securities and Exchange Commission under the U.S. Investment Company Act of 1940.

50. It is restrictive because it does not allow different business models under which a financial institution can, for example, concentrate only on marketing the CIS and collecting the resources from the public, leaving other tasks to other institutions. It is inadequate because it inhibits the achievement of economies of scale based on specialization: because a single CIS administrator must do everything (marketing, resource collection and investment, monitoring of investments, valuation, and so on), the CIS cannot concentrate on what it does best.

References and Other Resources

Aguilar, Camila, Mauricio Cárdenas, Marcela Meléndez, and Natalia Salazar. 2006. "The Development of Latin-American Bond Markets: The Case of Colombia." Fedesarrollo, Bogotá.

Alonso, Gloria, Enrique Montes, and Carlos Varela. 2003. "Evolución de los flujos de capital y de la deuda externa del sector privado en Colombia, 1990–2003

[Evolution of capital flows and external debt of the private sector in Colombia, 1990–2003]." Borradores de Economía 266, Banco de la República, Bogotá.

ANIF (Asociación Nacional de Instituciones Financieras). 1976. *La colombianización de la banca* [The Colombianization of the banking sector]. Bogotá: Ediciones Tercer Mundo.

———. 2006. *Fusiones y adquisiciones en el sector financiero colombiano: Análisis y propuestas sobre la consolidación bancaria (1990–2006)* [Mergers and acquisitions in the Colombian financial sector: Analysis and proposals on bank consolidation *(1990–2006)*]. Bogotá: ANIF.

Barajas, Adolfo, Roberto Steiner, and Natalia Salazar. 1999a. "Foreign Investment in Colombia's Financial Sector." IMF Working Paper 99/150, International Monetary Fund, Washington, DC.

———. 1999b. "Interest Spreads in Banking in Colombia, 1974–96." *IMF Staff Papers* 46 (2): 196–224.

de la Cruz, Javier, and Constantinos Stephanou. 2006. "Financial System Structure in Colombia: A Proposal for a Reform Agenda." Policy Research Working Paper 4006, World Bank, Washington, DC.

Galindo, Arturo, Alejandro Izquierdo, Alejandro Micco, and Mauricio Olivera. 2005. *Desencadenar el crédito: Cómo ampliar y estabilizar la banca— Progreso económico y social en América Latina, Informe 2005* [Triggering credit: How to expand and stabilize the banking sector—Economic and social progress in Latin America, Report 2005]. Washington, DC: Inter-American Development Bank.

Garay, Luis Jorge. 2004. "Colombia: Estructura industrial e internacionalización 1967–1996 [Colombia: Industrial structure and internationalization 1967–1996]." Banco de la República, Bogotá. Electronic edition from the Luis Angel Arango Library.

Hommes, Rudolf. 1990. "Palabras del ministro de hacienda en el XII Simposio sobre el Mercado de Capitales [Remarks by the minister of finance at the XII Symposium on the Capital Market]." In *Apertura económica y sistema financiero* [Economic openness and the financial system], ed. Florángela Gómez Ordóñez. Bogotá: Asociación Bancaria de Colombia.

Junguito, Roberto, and Cristina Gamboa. 2004. "Los servicios financieros y el TLC con los Estados Unidos: Oportunidades y retos para Colombia [Financial services and the FTA with the United States: Opportunities and challenges for Colombia]." *Cuadernos Fedesarrollo* 14, Fedesarrollo, Bogotá.

Mattoo, Aaditya, Randeep Rathindran, and Arvind Subramanian. 2001. "Measuring Services Trade Liberalization and Its Impact on Economic Growth: An Illustration." Policy Research Working Paper 2655, World Bank, Washington, DC.

Ortega, Francisco. 1990. "El sistema financiero ante la apertura económica [The financial system before economic openness]." In *Apertura económica y sistema financiero* [Economic openness and the financial system], ed. Florángela Gómez Ordóñez. Bogotá: Asociación Bancaria de Colombia.

Salazar, Natalia. 2005. "Los bancos extranjeros en la crisis: Colombia 1998–2001 [Foreign banks in crisis: Colombia 1998–2001." Master's thesis, Facultad de Economía, Universidad de los Andes, Bogotá.

Superintendencia Bancaria. 1989. "La inversión extranjera en el sistema financiero colombiano [Foreign investment in the Colombian financial system]." *Revista Superintendencia Bancaria* 5 (October): 3–22.

Vera, Alejandro. 2006. "Supervivencia de las firmas en la industria aseguradora colombiana, 1991–2003 [Survival of firms in the Colombian insurance industry, 1991–2003]." *Carta Financiera* 132 (January–March): 50–59.

CHAPTER 7

The CAFTA-DR-U.S. Negotiations on Financial Services
The Experience of Costa Rica

Roberto Echandi

In January 2003, the United States and the five Central American countries launched the negotiations that would lead to the signing of the Free Trade Agreement between Central America, the Dominican Republic, and the United States (CAFTA-DR-U.S.). This free trade agreement (FTA) contains 22 different chapters regulating a series of subject areas, one of which is trade in financial services.

For two reasons, the experience of Costa Rica on the financial services chapter during these negotiations is particularly noteworthy. First, contrary to many other trade agreements, CAFTA-DR-U.S. includes commitments in financial services that go well beyond the regulatory status quo in Costa Rica. The agreement therefore not only locked in existing standards but also became a source of external pressure for domestic reform. Second, despite being a small developing country, Costa Rica succeeded in defending domestic needs during the negotiations with a much stronger trade partner, the United States. Thus, the case provides some useful policy lessons for future trade negotiations.[1]

The views presented are those of the author and do not represent those of the government of Costa Rica. Raul Sáez and Constantinos Stephanou provided comments and suggestions.

To put the negotiations in context, the next section presents an overview of Costa Rica's financial reform process since the 1980s, followed by a section that analyzes the political and economic factors involved in this process. The third section focuses on the CAFTA-DR-U.S. negotiations on the financial services chapter and the political economy of the negotiations in the case of Costa Rica, analyzing the roles of the different actors involved and their interactions throughout the negotiation process. The fourth section focuses on the contents of the CAFTA-DR-U.S. chapter on financial services, describing the rules and disciplines included therein as well as the liberalization commitments undertaken. This section is followed by a fourth section that addresses the effects that CAFTA-DR-U.S., and particularly its financial services chapter, will have on the Costa Rican financial system. The last section presents some final remarks, drawing on the lessons from the Costa Rican experience in the CAFTA-DR-U.S. negotiations.

The Financial Liberalization Process in Costa Rica, 1984–2006

The Costa Rican financial system could be characterized as "well intermediated, yet centered on traditional banking intermediation, largely dominated by public institutions and still influenced by sizable offshore banks" (IMF and World Bank 2003, 5).[2] Two main variables may explain these key features of the Costa Rican financial system: (a) the relatively small size of the Costa Rican economy and (b) the fact that the Costa Rican financial sector is undergoing a process of market-oriented economic reform that is yet to be completed.[3]

Like most Latin American countries, Costa Rica started a process of deep market-oriented reform after the debt crisis and the collapse of the import-substitution industrialization model in the 1980s. The reform process started in the midst of an economic crisis entailing high inflation rates and sizable external debt, a significant devaluation, and stagnation of economic growth. The reform of the financial sector was clearly one of the main pillars of the subsequent transformation of the Costa Rican economy.

The Costa Rican central bank, Banco Central de Costa Rica (BCCR), used to supervise, through the General Banking Audit Office (Auditoría General de Bancos), only some financial intermediaries. The BCCR imposed credit and interest rate caps, it forbade intermediation in foreign currency (to both private and state institutions), and the incipient private banking sector was not allowed to accept deposits for periods shorter than six months. Monetary policy was even more repressive and relied on statutory minimum cash reserves that reached 50 percent.

In the 1980s, Costa Rica had no private pension fund operators or regulated sector in charge of administering investment funds. The incipient Costa Rican stock exchange and its brokerage houses operated as self-regulatory organizations based on limited provisions included in the Code of Commerce. Financial products used to be even more limited than they are today and consisted mostly of public sector securities in the primary market.

Within this context, the process of financial reform since 1982 pursued three fundamental objectives that were clearly stated by the new authorities in charge of the BCCR: (a) the new policies would provide greater freedom and flexibility to financial intermediaries, (b) they would increase competition within the domestic financial sector (aiming to decrease intermediation margins and to improve capacity to render new services), and (c) policies would aim to improve and to strengthen prudential supervision.

The process of financial sector reform has been gradual and can be distinguished as three stages: (a) preparation for modernization of the financial sector (1984–87), (b) modernization of the regulatory framework (1988–94), and (c) deepening of the process of reform (1995–present).

During the first phase, a number of key measures were adopted. The BCCR established a crawling-peg system, and private banks were allowed to accept deposits for increasingly shorter periods. Furthermore, the process of liberalization of interest rates and credit caps began, and commercial banks were allowed to open new domestic branches without prior BCCR authorization. Finally, the authorities started the practice of demanding loan portfolio classification and its corresponding loan loss provision backing.

The second phase started with the enactment of the Law of Financial Modernization of 1988, which created the General Financial Entities Audit Office (Auditoría General de Entidades Financieras). This new legislation entailed three significant steps in upgrading the regulatory framework: (a) better controls and requirements to allow the operation of nonbanking financial corporations (*financieras*); (b) cooperative savings and credit organizations, as well as mutual housing and loan societies to be brought under the supervisory framework; and (c) minimum regulatory capital for banks and nonbank financial corporations. Another significant step was the enactment of the Law of Public Solicitation of Securities (Ley de Oferta Pública de Valores), which restricted public solicitation for securities to only authorized and supervised entities. This legislation was complemented with the promulgation, in 1990, of the Law Regulating the Stock Market (Ley Reguladora del Mercado de Valores), which regulated what until then was a sector self-regulated through the Costa Rican National Exchange. The reform also entailed the creation of the National Securities Exchange (Central Nacional de Valores); the development of the process of enterprises' risk classification; and the withdrawal of the functions of custody, enterprise control, and arbitration from the National Exchange.

The third phase of the process (1995–present) was initiated with reform of the Organizational Law of the Central Bank (Ley Orgánica del Banco Central) in 1995. This legislation entailed significant transformations toward a more open and market-oriented financial sector. The reform limited the options of the central bank to establishing interest rate caps and fixing interest rates for financial intermediaries. Subject to stringent conditions, private banks were allowed to provide current-account deposit services. Private banks were also provided access to lender-of-last-resort facilities. Finally, the statutory minimum cash reserve rate was significantly reduced to promote the use of indirect instruments of monetary policy.

Regarding supervision and regulation, the General Superintendent of Financial Institutions (Superintendencia General de Entidades Financieras, or SUGEF) was created, replacing the former General Financial Entities Audit Office. Like its predecessor, SUGEF is a body linked to the BCCR, but with greater powers and administrative autonomy through its own executive board. Furthermore, through the new Organizational Law of the Central Bank, the ex post system of regulation, which until then had been the practice, was amended to encourage a prudential ex ante supervisory approach. More attention was given to aspects such as regulatory capital and equity sufficiency and, over the past decade, to the issue of offshore banking and related financial groups.

Also over the past decade, another set of important reforms took place. The Law Regulating the Stock Market was reformed in 1997, leading the National Securities Exchange to become the General Superintendent of Securities (Superintendencia General de Valores, or SUGEVAL), an entity with greater supervisory powers. Furthermore, new legislation was enacted to regulate new financial instruments, such as investment funds, and initial steps were taken to standardize securities.

Regarding pensions, in 1995, both the Pension Superintendent (Superintendencia de Pensiones, or SUPEN) and the regimes of individual capitalization were created.[4] In 2000, the Law for Workers' Protection established a new national pension system, which from then on would be based on three pillars: (a) the traditional social security scheme of the state, the Costa Rican Social Security Institution (Caja Costarricense de Seguro Social, or CCSS), (b) the fund of obligatory pensions, and (c) voluntary complementary pensions.

An area the process of financial reform did not touch was the insurance sector. Since 1924, Costa Rica has maintained a state monopoly, through the National Insurance Institute (Instituto Nacional de Seguros, or INS) for all types of insurance, including reinsurance and insurance for import and export activities. Unlike other financial services activities, insurance does not have a specific monitoring body. As discussed later, the opening and modernization of the insurance sector in Costa Rica is one of the most important results of the CAFTA-DR-U.S. negotiations in financial services.

As part of the modernization of the supervisory framework for the financial sector, the National Council of Supervision of the National Financial System (Consejo Nacional de Supervisión del Sistema Financiero, or CONASSIF) was created in 1997. CONASSIF comprises the three superintendent agencies responsible for the supervision and control of financial intermediaries, the stock market, and pension funds: SUGEF, SUGEVAL, and SUPEN.

Evolution in the Size and Depth of the Financial System

Costa Rica's financial sector today is by far bigger and more sophisticated than in the 1980s. Whereas in 1987 the total assets of financial institutions represented 48 percent of GDP, the size of the Costa Rican financial system in 2005, according to the BCCR, amounted to approximately US$14 billion, equivalent to 71 percent of GDP. Both the number and types of financial institutions have increased after more than two decades of reform and are now subject to supervision. In addition to the different actors participating in the still incipient securities and pensions markets, cooperative savings and credit organizations as well as mutual housing savings and loan societies emerged and were brought under SUGEF's supervision. Furthermore, the financial intermediation market at the beginning of the 1980s comprised 4 state banks, 1 special-chartered bank, 10 private banks, and 36 nonbank financial entities. In 2005, the Costa Rican financial system comprised 3 state banks, 12 private banks, 2 banks created by special law (Banco Popular and Banco Hipotecario de la Vivienda), the ANDE Savings and Credit Bank (Caja de Ahorro y Préstamos de la Asociación Nacional de Educadores), 9 nonbanking financial corporations (*financieras*), 28 cooperative savings and credit organizations, and 3 mutual housing savings and loan societies. The stock market in 2005 had 1 national exchange and 1 securities exchange, 22 equity issuers, 47 bond issuers, 3 classifying companies, 23 brokerage houses, and 22 investment fund administration societies. The pensions sector, which is made up of the general pension scheme—disability, old age, and death; special public sector schemes; statutory contributory and supplementary pension schemes; and voluntary contributory schemes—had nine pension fund operators. The insurance sector remains the least developed area of the Costa Rican financial system.

In addition, large financial groups now dominate the Costa Rican financial sector. They typically include an onshore bank, an offshore bank, a stockbroker, an investment fund, an insurance brokerage firm,[5] a pension fund, and a mortgage company. In 2005, 22 financial groups, 16 of them private, operated in the country. As shown in table 7.1, commercial banks still account for the overwhelming majority of the total assets of the financial sector, reaching 57.9 percent of GDP in 2004, whereas other nonbank credit institutions held a substantially limited share, 9.2 percent of GDP. Since 2005, however, investment funds (both mutual funds and pension funds) have grown very rapidly because of reforms that have clarified the legal and regulatory framework for mutual funds and created a private, second-pillar pension system. Indeed, in 2004, total assets administered by pension funds amounted to 17.1 percent of GDP, representing 24 percent of total financial sector assets and the equivalent of 37.9 percent of bank deposits as of December 2005.

Over the past 20 years, the capital market in Costa Rica has remained narrow and essentially centered on public securities. The main features of the capital market are as follows:

> The capital market is dominated by domestic public debt securities (issued by the Treasury and Central Bank) of short duration (less than one year), with most trading (80 percent) consisting of repo operations. Due to the small size of the country and the lack of adequate infrastructure development, the

Table 7.1   Costa Rica: Domestic Financial System Characteristics, 2002–04

	Percentage of GDP		
Characteristic	2002	2003	2004
Total commercial bank assets	48.9	51.5	57.9
Other credit institution assets	7.0	7.5	9.2
Total insurance company assets	5.36	5.26	5.28
Total net assets of mutual funds	1.0	1.6	0.6
Total assets of investment funds	4.04	3.66	2.62
Total assets administered by pension funds	17.3	19.6	17.1

Sources: BCCR; INS; Investment Company Institute; Sociedad de Seguros de Vida del Magisterio Nacional; SUGEVAL; SUPEN.

market for private securities is essentially underdeveloped, with only a handful of securities, mainly issued by the financial sector, trading very limited amounts in the open market. The equity market is nearly nonexistent. The capital market has performed basically two functions, orthodox finance of public debt and money market activity. Brokerage houses have played an important role in both of these markets. (IMF and World Bank 2003, 14)

Within this context, private financing through the stock market is, not surprisingly, practically nonexistent; in 2004, trade in stock on the National Exchange represented only 3.6 percent of GDP.

Evolution in Concentration and State Ownership in the Financial System

After more than two decades of financial reform, despite significant progress, the Costa Rican financial system is still highly concentrated and characterized by deep-rooted state participation. This situation is evident not only in banking but also in the pension and insurance sectors.

As table 7.2 shows, the top three banks accounted for 62.4 percent of total assets of the banking sector in 2005. Excessive concentration is also present in the other intermediaries that comprise the national banking system: financial corporations, cooperative savings and credit organizations, and mutual housing savings and loan societies. Given that regulations

Table 7.2   Concentration and State Ownership in Costa Rica's Domestic Financial System, 2002–05

Indicator	2002	2003	2004	2005
Concentration ratio				
Top three commercial banks (percentage of total assets)	59.0	57.3	56.9	62.4
Top three insurance companies (percentage of total premiums)	100	100	100	100
Top three pension funds (percentage of total assets)	87.0	81.1	74.4	72.6
State ownership				
Commercial banks (percentage of assets)	54	53	56	57
Insurance companies (percentage of total premiums)	100	100	100	100
Pension funds (percentage of total assets)	64	67	76	78

Sources: BCCR; INS; SUPEN.

allow commercial banks to create pension operators and investment fund management societies (*sociedades administradoras de fondos de inversión*), concentration in pensions and investment funds,[6] although showing a declining trend, is also very high. For instance, in 2005, three of nine operators of pension funds accounted for 72.6 percent of total assets in that sector.

Concentration in insurance is even higher, given the state monopoly controlling the sector. In 2004, total assets of insurance companies in Costa Rica represented 5.3 percent of GDP, of which practically 100 percent belonged to the INS (5.2 percent of GDP).

Since 1984, government participation in the Costa Rican financial system, albeit declining, continues to dominate the banking and pension sectors. Despite the greater openness and participation of the private sector within the Costa Rican financial system, state banks controlled 57 percent of total assets in 2005. Furthermore, state ownership of pension funds represented 78 percent of total assets.

The process of financial liberalization has led the banking system to become more diversified, with private banks continuing to gain market share. Indeed, between 1998 and 2001, private banks increased their market share from 33 percent to 42 percent. Furthermore, between 1990 and 2003, private banks' assets have grown at an average annual rate of 28.1 percent, almost twice as fast as those of state banks. This trend has increased the relative participation of private banks in total bank assets from 12 percent in 1990 to 34 percent in 2003. Total deposits attracted by private banks, including deposits in national and foreign currency, increased from 7 percent to 29 percent between 1990 and 2003, leading to an average annual increase equivalent to 32.6 percent, a rate significantly higher than the 17 percent experienced by the state banks. However, the state banks continue to dominate; their market share had a marginal reduction from 67 percent in 1993 to 56 percent in 2002.

The relative importance of the private banking sector in Costa Rica is, however, greater if the resources mobilized through offshore banking are taken into account. The limited depth in the Costa Rican banking system, in particular the development of competitive financial services, has encouraged the growth of financial activities through entities established abroad (in The Bahamas, the Cayman Islands, and Panama) with holding companies based in Costa Rica (that is, offshore banks). Offshore banks are a predominant feature among private financial groups in Costa Rica. They have been widely used as a conduit for tax and regulatory evasion, with limited physical presence in the offshore centers and a very similar profile of intermediation to that of their onshore counterparts. Thus, most loans are to Costa Rican customers. Offshore banks expanded very rapidly in the early development of private banking, and the size of the offshore operations is almost identical to local mobilization in Cost Rica, mainly as a response to high unremunerated reserve requirements (reaching 28.3 percent in December 1995) and a search by private banks for a competitive edge against public banks (IMF and World Bank 2003, 16).

Despite these problems, a positive feature of the process of financial reform in Costa Rica is that the gradual opening of the sector to private competition has been based on a nondiscriminatory approach that does not distinguish between foreign and domestic banks.[7] Thus, the increasing participation of the private sector in the Costa Rican financial sector has been allowed regardless of the origin of its capital. Consequently, foreign ownership has increased simultaneously with the growth of private sector participation. Historically, Costa Rica has been a country open to foreign investors. It has never had a specific law regulating foreign investment in particular and, thus, has allowed foreign investors to benefit from the same legislation applicable to Costa Rican private entrepreneurs. Moreover, Costa Rica does not have any screening mechanism or any registration requirement applicable to foreign investment, which explains why the calculation of foreign participation in the Costa Rican financial system is based on unofficial data: no official information on foreign capital in the Costa Rican financial system or on the number of foreign-controlled banks is published.

Unofficial data provided by banking groups to SUGEF indicate that foreign participation in the financial system, albeit far from dominant, is not negligible, especially in the banking sector. In 2005, of the 12 private banks operating in Costa Rica, 9 had at least a 50 percent share of foreign capital,[8] indicating that about 27 percent of total bank assets were foreign owned. The significant share represents foreign investment from other Central American countries, in particular El Salvador, Nicaragua, and Panama. However, Canadian and U.S. investment has been growing in recent years, mainly through multinational banks such as Scotiabank and Citibank. In the securities market, about 36 percent of the firms registered on the National Exchange are owned by financial groups controlled by foreign investors. The degree of foreign ownership is considerably lower in the pension sector, where pension operators controlled by foreign interests own less than 10 percent of total pension assets. However, the limited degree of foreign ownership is a side effect of sector domination by public financial groups and not the result of any protectionist policy against foreign capital participation. The same trend is evident in the insurance sector, where the state monopoly has prevented any private participation in the market (except for the possibility of trading the state monopoly's insurance products).

Evolution in the Performance of the Financial System

In addition to the effects already explained, the process of financial reform has also meant a significant transformation in the structure of credit activities. Up to the 1980s, the BCCR used to enact the credit program for commercial banks, determining how much to lend to each productive activity and at what interest rate. The reform has allowed the intermediaries to make those decisions by themselves, according to the risk and credit policy of each financial institution. As a result of better financial supervision, the need to improve financial indicators, and the imperative to reduce the nonperforming loans in credit portfolios, banks have been more cautious in financing activities that in the past had been traditional for state banks, such as providing credit to the agricultural sector and domestic industries. As the relative importance of services has grown over the past two decades, the structure of the loan portfolios has tended to mirror that trend. Thus, nowadays, along with housing financing, trade and services dominate credit portfolios in both state and private banks.

Another important transformation of the Costa Rican financial system since the 1980s relates to the phenomenon of dollarization.[9] Before financial sector reform and modification of the Organizational Law of the Central Bank in 1995, commercial banks could not undertake any transactions in foreign currency. Even private contracts in U.S. dollars were illegal. The BCCR was the only entity allowed to effect any transaction in foreign currency. After the reform in 1995, commercial banks were allowed to receive deposits in U.S. dollars (subject to the restriction of the statutory minimum cash reserve). Today almost half of deposits are denominated in foreign currency. The commercial banking sector's ability to intermediate in foreign currencies and the access of private banks to resources abroad have led to an increasing dollarization of the credit structure. Whereas in 1990 only 4 percent of banks' total credit was denominated in U.S. dollars, in 2003 this figure had increased to 56 percent. Yet the stability of the Costa Rican financial system has been assessed positively:

> Subject to important caveats on the quality and completeness of the information, the supervised Costa Rican financial system exhibits some strengths. The onshore banking system generally reports relatively high liquidity, moderate

profitability, high ratios of capital to risk-weighted assets (about 15 percent on average), and limited nonperforming loans. The strong participation of public banks, which enjoy the trust of the public and whose liabilities are fully guaranteed by the state, provides an additional measure of stability in the short run. (IMF and World Bank 2003, 5)

If one analyzes the structure of credit from a different perspective, the Costa Rican debt market has tended traditionally to concentrate on short-term operations. After more than two decades of reform, this trend has not changed. Although in 1997 90.5 percent of fixed-term deposits in local currency were deposited for periods shorter than a year, in 2000 that figure was equivalent to 76.6 percent. Dollar-denominated fixed-term deposits have evidenced the same trend. In 1997, 90 percent of total fixed-term deposits in U.S. dollars were deposited for periods shorter than a year, whereas in 2000, the figure amounted to 90.1 percent.

At least in principle, these important transformations in the financial system should lead to greater levels of competition and lower interme-diation margins. Despite significant progress, however, financial interme-diation margins remain high. Even though financial reform has led to an important reduction in the difference in the margin of intermediation between state and private banks—from 10.1 percent in 1996 to a little less than 5 percent in 2002—the absolute margins of intermediation con-tinue to be high. For state banks, the difference between the active rate and the cost of funds decreased from 18.9 percent in 1990 to 10.2 percent in 2002. Private banks reduced that margin from 9.8 percent to 6.0 percent. The difference in the margin of the reduction stems from the price-taker position that private banks have assumed, benefiting from less efficient state banks.

Financial System Regulatory Framework: Supervision

As mentioned earlier, CONASSIF comprises the three superintendent agencies responsible for the supervision and control of financial inter-mediaries (SUGEF), the stock market (SUGEVAL), and pension funds (SUPEN). Given the overwhelming importance of the banking sector within the Costa Rican financial system, the focus here is on the main challenges of SUGEF when supervising banking groups.[10]

For the first time in Costa Rica, the Organizational Law of the Central Bank of 1995 regulated the constitution, operation, and supervision of financial groups. The law requires foreign banks to form part of a national financial group and obliges those groups to submit accounts subject to audit. These reports are required for the supervision of the national financial group and are not published.

In 2001, CONASSIF enacted a series of recommendations based on the Basel I recommendations regarding credit and capital adequacy requirements and following the "building blocks" model. Furthermore, on the basis of an expansive interpretation of this legislation, SUGEF signed in 2002 memorandums of understanding (MOUs) with the supervisory authorities. Under those MOUs, SUGEF was allowed to conduct, together with the local supervisors, on-site inspections of affected banks.[11] However, in September 2005, the Attorney General's Office put into effect an interpretation of the Organizational Law of the Central Bank, stating that SUGEF does not have the authority to supervise banks domiciled abroad, even though those banks may be part of a Costa Rican financial group.[12]

According to the Attorney General's Office, SUGEF can have access to only four types of information: (a) financial statements; (b) aggregated data on quality, risks, and concentration of assets; (c) operations performed by entities domiciled abroad with other entities of the group; and (d) the composition of social capital. The interpretation of the Attorney General's Office was that the Organizational Law of the Central Bank prohibited SUGEF from verifying on site or requiring the presentation of further detailed information.

Of course, banks can still voluntarily submit to SUGEF all disaggregated information necessary for effective consolidated supervision. However, the decision has meant that a substantial part of the financial system—particularly offshore banking—remains inadequately regulated and supervised by the Costa Rican authorities.[13]

Conditions Affecting Competition in Trade in Services

Among the aspects still pending is the uneven competition between state and private banks. State banks enjoy advantages over their private competitors because, by law, the former have the guarantee and fullest cooperation of the state and all its departments and institutions. The executive board of each state bank is appointed by the government's cabinet, and these banks' capital may be increased by law or by capitalization. Public deposits in state banks are fully guaranteed by the state, whereas private banks do not have any kind of insurance to protect public deposits.[14]

The discussion on leveling the playing field between state and private banks has also stemmed from the different conditions that private banks must comply with for access to sight deposits. In Costa Rica, only banks—public and private—are authorized to take deposits in current accounts.[15] However, under the 1995 reforms, private banks were permitted to accept deposits in current accounts only if they satisfy certain requirements.[16]

Private banks, whether owned by foreigners or nationals, must fulfill the same requirements. With respect to ownership of individual investments, a financial entity must be formed in accordance with the legal requirements for the formation of a joint stock company in Costa Rica, which requires at least two shareholders. Although there are no formal requirements concerning percentages owned by investors in a joint stock company, the requirement to set up an entity in Costa Rica precludes foreign banks from establishing branches, because they are regarded as part of the parent company. Besides these shortcomings, foreigners can freely enter the banking services market, a situation that also applies to capital markets and pension schemes.

In capital markets and pension schemes, private and state operators compete on an equal footing. Here, Costa Rican laws allow private participation, subject only to the establishment of a legal entity under Costa Rican law. Foreign investors can own 100 percent of pension operators and brokerage houses in Costa Rica.

In sharp contrast, the state monopoly affects the insurance market in Costa Rica. Problems include the high cost and narrow range of services, the lack of a specialized monitoring mechanism and external audit of financial results, the poor development of insurance as an instrument for promoting national savings, and the distortions caused by the INS investments, which meet the needs of public sector financing rather than profitability criteria.

The Pending Reform Agenda in the Costa Rican Financial System

Financial reform in Costa Rica has begun, but the process is obviously still far from being completed. In 2003, the IMF and the World Bank identified four main shortcomings: (a) measures related to macroeconomic and monetary policy;[17] (b) measures related to the quality of supervision of financial institutions in Costa Rica;[18] (c) measures to improve the financial infrastructure, affecting the business climate necessary for an adequate development of the financial system;[19] and (d) measures that (directly or indirectly) affect the liberalization of trade in financial services. Within this last group, the assessment considered that Costa Rica should address three main issues: (a) the requirement for foreign banks to enter the Costa Rican market only through subsidiaries, (b) the need to liberalize the insurance sector, and (c) the need to level the playing field between state and private banks.

As is noted later in this chapter, the CAFTA-DR-U.S. negotiations played a key role in fostering continuation of financial system reform in Costa Rica. Although an FTA could not address all the issues of concern, the CAFTA-DR-U.S. negotiations certainly became a venue for discussing and addressing the issues included in the reform measures related to the liberalization of trade in financial services.

Evolution of Trade Policy Reform in Financial Services in Costa Rica since the 1990s

Since the 1980s, international trade and investment policy in Costa Rica, together with the process of financial liberalization, has been among the main pillars of the new export-led development strategy. Trade and investment policy has been oriented toward promoting the country's role in international markets, mainly by expanding and diversifying the export base and linking that process to the attraction of increasing inflows of foreign direct investment (FDI).

Costa Rica has consequently become more assertive in penetrating international markets. This attitude has been reflected not only in the magnitude and composition of its trade in goods and services with the rest of the world, but also in the way the country has financed the excess of domestic investments over domestic savings. In addition, using fiscal incentives and its exchange rate policy, Costa Rica established an environment favorable to the exporting sector and foreign investment.

The negotiation of the CAFTA-DR-U.S. chapter on financial services represents a watershed in the evolution of trade policy reform with respect to the financial sector in Costa Rica. Until CAFTA-DR-U.S., international rules and disciplines included in trade and investment agreements fell under one of two categories. The first category simply lacked any specific provision directly applicable to trade in financial services and did not bind any level of liberalization of trade in financial services. The FTAs negotiated with Mexico in 1994, Chile in 1998, the Dominican Republic in 1998, Canada in 2000, and the Caribbean Community (CARICOM)[20] in 2004 fall within this category. Numerous factors, both domestic and external, explain the motivation of Costa Rica to negotiate these FTAs.[21] Similarly, none of the bilateral investment treaties negotiated by Costa Rica between 1996 and 2004 includes binding commitments (see table 7.3 for the country details).

Table 7.3   Regional Trade Agreements and Bilateral Investment Treaties Negotiated by Costa Rica

Regional trade agreements	Year[a]	Bilateral investment treaties	Year[a]
Central America	1963	France	1997
Mexico	1995	Germany	1997
Canada	2002	United Kingdom	1997
Chile	2002	Chile	1998
Dominican Republic	2002	Canada	1999
CARICOM	2005	Spain	1999
CAFTA-DR-U.S.	2009	Taiwan, China	2000
		Argentina	2001
		Czech Republic	2001
		Netherlands	2001
		Paraguay	2001
		Venezuela, R. B. de	2001
		Korea, Rep. of	2002
		Switzerland	2002

Source: Costa Rica Ministry of Foreign Trade.
Note: CARICOM = Caribbean Community; CAFTA-DR-U.S. = Free Trade Agreement between Central America, the Dominican Republic, and the United States.
a. Year of approval in the Costa Rican Legislative Assembly.

A second category of instruments did include specific rules and disciplines applicable to financial services. The only such agreement applicable to Costa Rica is the financial services agreement negotiated under the umbrella of the General Agreement on Trade in Services (GATS) in 1997.[22] Within this context, for the first time ever, Costa Rica undertook international obligations binding a certain level of liberalization of trade in financial services. The timing is no coincidence: in 1996, the state monopoly over sight deposits was finally dismantled. With the opening of the state monopoly, the legislation regulating financial services in Costa Rica was significantly liberalized,[23] giving the country the possibility of undertaking commitments in the context of GATS. Costa Rica undertook commitments with respect to the following five financial services: (a) acceptance of deposits and other repayable funds from the public; (b) lending of all types, including consumer credit, mortgage credit, factoring, and financing of commercial transactions; (c) credit card services consisting of the financing of the purchase of products using credit cards or other types of plastic money; (d) provision and transfer of financial information and financial data processing and related software by providers of other financial services; and (e) financial leasing services. The level of liberalization of investment bound in those services was significant, because practically no specific measure was exempted from the national treatment and market-access obligations. See table 7.4 for summary information.

Such commitments had, however, two important caveats. First, in the section on horizontal measures, Costa Rica reserved its prerogative to forbid branching. A second important caveat was the evident lack of any obligation with respect to insurance services. Not surprisingly, those two caveats would later become the two key issues of contention between Costa Rica and the United States at the financial services negotiation table of CAFTA-DR-U.S.

Five major factors help explain the lack of a chapter on financial services in all six regional trade agreements negotiated by Costa Rica between 1995 and 2004, as well as its inclusion in CAFTA-DR-U.S.

- The Costa Rican experience shows that for a country to be able to participate in financial services negotiations, a certain degree of previous domestic financial liberalization is necessary. Because of the legal limitations on branching and the state monopoly in insurance in place before 1995, Costa Rica's negotiation could not offer any substantial status quo commitments to foreign services providers. In addition, political factors came into play. The ongoing process of domestic financial liberalization faced strong political opposition, and the inclusion of a chapter on financial services could have been seen as an imposition of foreign trade partners.

- The Costa Rican experience also suggests that once domestic financial liberalization has reached a certain level, international negotiations on trade in financial services not only may be possible, but also may be perceived as conducive to the reform. Indeed, after a politically contested reform has taken place, governments may wish to lock in the reforms that were so painfully obtained. Hence, just after the financial reforms of 1996 had passed, Costa Rica was not only able but also willing to make an interesting offer to other World Trade Organization members in the context of the 1997 financial services negotiations under GATS. Within this context, however, it must be noted that international agreements tend only to bind the existing legal status quo, but often fail to lead to effective new trade liberalization.

- The Costa Rican experience shows that for a country to actively pursue financial liberalization, an aggressive domestic constituency

Table 7.4 Summary of Financial Services Commitments Undertaken by Costa Rica under GATS

Financial services sector	Mode 1: Cross-border supply	Mode 2: Consumption abroad	Mode 3: Commercial presence	Mode 4: Presence of natural persons
All sectors and subsectors			Only the establishment of companies in the form of affiliated companies or subsidiaries is permitted, and other forms are excluded, particularly branches	
Banking and other financial services (excluding insurance): acceptance of deposits, lending of all types, and credit card services	Unbound	Unbound	No national treatment or market-access restriction	Unbound, except horizontal restrictions on temporary entry
Provision and transfer of financial information and financial data processing and related software by providers of other financial services	No national treatment or market-access restriction	No national treatment or market-access restriction	No national treatment or market-access restriction	Unbound, except horizontal restrictions on temporary entry
Financial leasing services	Unbound	Unbound	No national treatment or market-access restriction, except that commercial banks and financing enterprises cannot provide leasing services	Unbound, except horizontal restrictions on temporary entry

Source: Data from the World Trade Organization Secretariat.

needs to push the government in that direction. This factor comes into play particularly when the other party to the negotiations is not a demandeur in favor of including financial services within the agreement. In the context of international trade negotiations, if a small developing economy has very limited bargaining power, governments have to clearly identify priorities and use their scarce negotiation capital to pursue those priorities. Domestic constituents then can become decisive in the choice of these priorities, as illustrated by the Costa Rican experience.

• The Costa Rican experience suggests that power matters. It is no coincidence that CAFTA-DR-U.S. is the first international agreement Costa Rica negotiated to include liberalization commitments that go beyond existing domestic legislation. The United States is by far Costa Rica's most important trade and investment partner, comprising about half of Costa Rica's trade and being the source of more than half of its FDI inflows. Within this context, the bargaining position of the United States vis-à-vis Costa Rica was formidable and enabled the United States to frame the liberalization of trade in insurance services as a deal breaker for the agreement. As the negotiation of the FTA with Mexico illustrates, such a result would have been unlikely in the negotiation with a trade partner with less bargaining power.

• The Costa Rican experience also shows a most important and yet often less noticed aspect of negotiations of FTAs, which is the key role that such processes may play in fostering domestic economic reform, particularly in the context of small developing countries.

One main rationale behind CAFTA-DR-U.S. is to create a certain degree of external pressure, which may help overcome domestic political opposition and support new reforms. In this sense, the agreement is about domestic reform, a catalyst for internal change aimed at modernizing the economies of the region. This rationale is illustrated by how CAFTA-DR-U.S. affected the process of financial reform and Costa Rica's commitment to open the state monopoly on insurance services. Clearly, as already mentioned, the likelihood for an FTA to become an instrument to foster domestic reform depends on the weight of the negotiating counterpart. For example, in 1993, Mexico requested that Costa Rica include a financial services chapter in the Costa Rica–Mexico FTA. Because of the limited relative importance of the trade and investment flows with

Mexico, Costa Rica had a stronger bargaining position vis-à-vis Mexico and was able to resist that demand. The situation was clearly different when the United States sat across the negotiating table.

Since the 1990s, Costa Rica has been immersed in a domestic debate about the role of the state in the economy and, in particular, about the possibility of opening several state monopolies remaining in strategic sectors, of which insurance is one. However, the strong resistance from public unions to any opening of state monopolies has paralyzed the political debate. Within this context, CAFTA-DR-U.S. became a key tool in breaking the impasse and in forcing Costa Rican society to make a decision on the matter. Hence, CAFTA-DR-U.S. has been quite controversial in Costa Rica.

The Negotiation of the CAFTA-DR-U.S. Chapter on Financial Services

Because of its market size and geographic vicinity, the United States has always been an important trade partner for Central America. However, the preferential trade relationship between the Central American countries, the Dominican Republic, and the United States started only in the 1980s, with the enactment of the U.S. Caribbean Basin Recovery Act,[24] most commonly known as the Caribbean Basin Initiative. Under this legislation, most exports from Central America and the Caribbean countries benefit from duty-free treatment in the U.S. market. Despite the existence of this preferential scheme, the Central American countries expressed their concerns about the potential negative impact that the North American Free Trade Agreement (NAFTA) would have in terms of erosion of market-access preferences and investment diversion.

Consequently, the Central American countries expressed their interest in negotiating a separate FTA with the United States. It was, however, a decade later, in January 2002, that President George W. Bush announced the U.S. intention to negotiate an FTA with the countries of Central America. The goal was to strengthen their relationship with the United States; to support the process of economic, political, and social reform undertaken by these countries since the 1980s; and to contribute to the process of establishing the Free Trade Area of the Americas (White House 2002).

Between November 2001 and September 2002, the Central American countries and the United States organized a series of workshops to exchange information about their respective trade regimes and discuss a series of topics to be addressed in the later negotiations. This preparatory stage proved to be extremely useful for Costa Rica, because it enabled the negotiation team to collect information not only about U.S. legislation, but also about the negotiation priorities of the United States and how it had pursued such interests in previous negotiations. This information was key in the preparation of the Costa Rican team's negotiation roadmap.

The Structure: Calendar, Number of Rounds, and Groups

During the preparatory stage, the Central American countries and the United States agreed on the timing, organization, and structure of the negotiations.[25] The parties agreed that negotiations would be launched in San José, Costa Rica, in January 2003, and that they would hold nine negotiating rounds, one approximately every month and a half, leading to the conclusion of the final agreement in December 2003 in Washington, D.C.

To conclude the agreement within that period was an ambitious endeavor. However, the Central American countries clearly understood the importance of sticking to this schedule for two main reasons. First, 2004 was going to be an election year in the United States, and the Central American countries did not want the agreement to become a pawn in the U.S. electoral process. Second, it was clear by then that the Office of the U.S. Trade Representative was planning to start negotiating FTAs with other countries, such as Australia, Morocco, and the Andean countries, which because of their market dimensions could be more attractive for the U.S. private sector. Thus, there was a real risk that if the negotiation of CAFTA-DR-U.S. proved too cumbersome for the United States—something that was quite possible, because the negotiation entailed dealing with five countries at the same time—the U.S. government could turn its attention to negotiations with other attractive markets.

In addition to the time frame and number of negotiating rounds, one of the most important aspects of the negotiations was its structure. Indeed, for small developing countries, the structure may be of major importance, because they may lack numerous personnel specialized in the disciplines of trade law and policy. This was certainly the case for Costa Rica, where the group of negotiators capable of leading the national delegation was quite small. Consequently, the Central American countries had difficulty participating in more than a few negotiations simultaneously.

To overcome this challenge, the Central American countries strongly argued for and obtained a simple negotiating structure. In addition to the lead negotiators from the five Central American countries and the United States overseeing the progress of the negotiation process, five main negotiation groups were agreed on: (a) market access for goods, (b) trade in services and investment, (c) government procurement and intellectual property, (d) dispute settlement and institutional issues, and (e) labor and environment. The negotiation of the financial services chapter fell under the aegis of the negotiation group on services and investment, which, in addition to the chapter on financial services, discussed the chapters on cross-border trade in services, investment, telecommunications, temporary entry, and electronic commerce. Whereas the United States had different teams for different subjects, the core of the Central American negotiation teams was fundamentally the same for all the topics addressed.

The CAFTA-DR-U.S. Countries and Their Interests in the Financial Services Chapter

CAFTA-DR-U.S. has seven signatories. However, the agreement was negotiated between two parties: the five Central American countries and the United States.[26] Such a negotiation scheme required a high degree of coordination among the Central American countries.

Thus, before the negotiations were launched, the Central American countries agreed among themselves not only on the parameters for organizing their joint participation in the negotiation, but also on the main substantive objectives and principles that would be pursued. Among the most important organizational rules were the following[27]: (a) the negotiation team would be exclusively composed of government officials and not private sector representatives; (b) the private sector would participate in the negotiations only under the side-room format;[28] (c) each negotiation group would designate a Central American speaker, but such designation would not impede any country from participating in the negotiation if necessary; and (d) before each negotiating round, the Central American countries would hold a coordination meeting to agree on the specific points to be taken to the negotiation table. Later, the Central American countries agreed that Costa Rica would act as the secretariat of the negotiation process, putting the country in charge of forwarding the proposals and counterproposals to the United States and circulating among the five Central American countries any communication transmitted by the United States.

For trade in financial services, the common objectives agreed on for the negotiation, at a general level, were the following (Ministerio de Comercio Exterior 2003a):

- Clearly determine the scope of application of the chapter, comprising both productive investment in the financial sector and those cross-border financial services of interest to the Central American countries.

- Agree on provisions that do not erode the supervisory powers of the various superintendent agencies regulating the domestic financial sector in each country.
- Provide national treatment and most-favored-nation (MFN) treatment to investors and investments in financial institutions as well as to financial services providers.
- Include provisions to ensure that all measures of general application affecting trade in financial services are administered in a reasonable, objective, and impartial manner.
- Promote the transparency of measures of general application affecting trade in financial services.
- Include a list of reservations allowing the parties to bind the level of access granted to the domestic financial services market according to the legislation existing at the start of the negotiations.
- Allow financial supervisory authorities of each party to apply any prudential measure necessary to safeguard the integrity and stability of the financial system.

The general common objectives referred to here did not mean that all five Central American countries had exactly the same interests in the negotiation of the CAFTA-DR-U.S. financial services chapter. Whereas the interests of Costa Rica, Honduras, and Nicaragua tended to be defensive,[29] those of El Salvador and Guatemala were offensive.[30]

This disparity in specific interests did not prevent the Central American countries from agreeing on a common negotiating strategy vis-à-vis the United States. Although Costa Rica, Honduras, and Nicaragua were more concerned with the defense of their legal status quo, they considered that an initial offensive posture in the negotiations could be useful because it would highlight U.S. resistance to modifying its own laws, which, in turn, would weaken U.S. demands for reforms in the domestic systems of Central American countries. At the end of the day, this strategy did not prove particularly effective. Clearly, with CAFTA-DR-U.S., the Central American countries were getting preferential access to one of the biggest markets in the world, which also happened to be the main destination for their exports. Central America, in contrast, did not represent a significant market for the United States. Thus, the United States could afford not to be 100 percent conceptually consistent in its negotiation positions.

An analysis of the interests of the parties shows that trade in financial services was not the most controversial issue in the negotiations. By the time the negotiations started, most Central American countries had progressed significantly in liberalizing their financial systems, giving them significant leeway to undertake the rules and disciplines included in a NAFTA-like chapter on financial services. Costa Rica was the only country that had lagged in the liberalization process and, not surprisingly, was the country with which the United States had the most difficulty reaching an agreement.

The Political Economy of the Negotiation Process in Costa Rica: Main Actors and Their Interests

The negotiation of FTAs has been a key component of Costa Rican international trade policy over the past two decades. Convinced of the importance of fostering financial liberalization and liberalization of trade in financial services to promote a better overall investment climate, Costa Rican authorities recognized the importance of including a chapter on financial services in the country's FTAs. However, given the lack of a domestic constituency pushing for liberalization of trade in financial services in markets overseas, Costa Rica readily dropped this objective when the other negotiating party objected.

In the case of CAFTA-DR-U.S., the United States had indicated its interest in including a financial services chapter even before launch of the negotiation process. Such inclusion was not a controversial issue for Costa Rica. By the time the negotiations started, Costa Rica had reached a significant level of liberalization of its financial sector. However, Costa Rican authorities were aware that during the negotiations the United States would likely request further concessions that were highly controversial and politically sensitive for Costa Rica.

According to the preparatory work undertaken by the Costa Rican negotiation team, three main points of contention were expected: (a) opening the state monopoly on insurance; (b) allowing financial services providers to establish branches, rather than subsidiaries, in Costa Rica; and (c) leveling the playing field between public and private banks in Costa Rica. In the end, the original diagnosis proved to be correct, and the three issues were the last to be resolved in the very last round of negotiations between Costa Rica and the United States.[31]

Before negotiations began, each of these issues had already been subject to political debate in the Legislative Assembly of Costa Rica. Although the government was in favor of liberalization, other sectors— in particular public unions and left-wing-oriented political parties—not only strongly objected to the reform bills but also submitted their own proposals to push in the opposite policy direction, leading to a political impasse.

These very politically sensitive issues would become even more challenging because the financial services negotiations were not the only highly contested topic of CAFTA-DR-U.S. In addition, such controversial issues included market access in agriculture and protection of intellectual property rights, as well as the request by the United States to open the state monopoly in telecommunications, a key pillar of the Costa Rican welfare state.[32]

The last issue was particularly sensitive in 2000, three years before the CAFTA-DR-U.S. negotiations started. Public unions and left-wing nongovernmental organizations (NGOs) successfully organized an opposition campaign against opening the telecommunications monopoly. Even though the legislation was approved by an overwhelming majority of votes—45 of 57—civil unrest reached such a magnitude that the Legislative Assembly opted to withdraw the bill from discussion. The reform had been halted, and as a result, public unions, anti–free trade NGOs, and left-wing political parties had strengthened their influence on Costa Rican politics.

Within this context, proposing liberalization of trade in services had become a political liability, leading practically all candidates in the presidential election of 2000 to promise to keep all of the state monopolies. Thus, from the outset, CAFTA-DR-U.S. clearly would entail reforms very objectionable to strong members of the Costa Rican political spectrum. This situation substantially affected the negotiations. For the agreement to be approved in the Costa Rican Legislative Assembly, it had to be politically palatable. Within this context, the main strategy of the Costa Rican negotiation team was thus to convince their U.S. colleagues that only some of the U.S. requests could be included in CAFTA-DR-U.S.

In addition to public unions, anti–free trade NGOs, and left-wing political parties, all of which strongly opposed the CAFTA-DR-U.S. negotiations from the beginning, the five main Costa Rican actors were the president, the Ministry of Foreign Trade (Ministerio de Comercio Exterior, or COMEX), the BCCR and the financial supervisory authorities, the domestic financial sector, and the INS.

As the highest authority to which the Costa Rican negotiation team was accountable, President Abel Pacheco was one of the key players in the CAFTA-DR-U.S. negotiations. As a candidate of a center-right political party, he was elected in April 2002 with a weak political mandate. His team of economic advisers shared the basic market-oriented principles that had guided the four previous administrations, ensuring the continuation of the reform process begun in the 1980s. Consequently, at the beginning of his term, President Pacheco strongly backed Costa Rica's participation in CAFTA-DR-U.S. However, the political commitment to economic reform and free trade was not very strong, and later he was not willing to assume the political cost of explaining to the citizenry the importance of opening the existing state monopolies to competition.

COMEX, which formed the Costa Rican negotiation team for CAFTA-DR-U.S., was obviously another key actor of the process. Established in the early 1990s, COMEX became one of the main forces within the government pushing for the completion of market-oriented economic reform. Over the years, it had managed to attract and develop a team of specialized professionals, most of whom had obtained postgraduate degrees in top European and U.S. universities and participated in prior trade negotiations. By the time the CAFTA-DR-U.S. negotiations were launched, the COMEX negotiation team had developed the reputation of being capable of adequately defending the national interests, a factor that proved key in reassuring the private sector and some segments of civil society that the best possible results would be obtained in the negotiations with the United States. Nevertheless, for those sectors opposing market-oriented reform, COMEX represented the main enemy of the welfare state.

Following the instructions of the president, COMEX would attempt to avoid agreeing on any commitment affecting the state monopolies. Except for insurance, COMEX envisaged that Costa Rica would not have any problem subscribing to most of the commitments derived from the financial services chapter. The two other issues that would be kept away from the negotiation table were the imminent requests of the United States to (a) allow financial services providers to establish branches and (b) level the playing field between public and private banks.

Unlike branching, leveling the playing field between public and private banks was an objective the Costa Rican private financial sector explicitly supported. However, if CAFTA-DR-U.S. was used as an instrument to level the playing field, the United States would bring other issues to the negotiating table—in particular the opening of the insurance monopoly. During the last phase of the negotiations, both COMEX and the BCCR considered that including these reforms in an already loaded reform agenda would certainly decrease the viability of CAFTA-DR-U.S. in the Legislative Assembly.

Indeed, by the last negotiation rounds, CAFTA-DR-U.S. clearly would entail a considerable package of highly sensitive political reforms. In addition to convincing all Costa Rican productive sectors to be exposed to U.S. competition, the agreement would involve (a) opening the state monopoly on telecommunications, (b) opening the state monopoly on insurance, (c) dismantling the preferential regime existing for local dealers representing foreign companies, and (d) increasing the disciplines and tightening enforcement measures on intellectual property rights. As such a "megatreaty," the agreement risked becoming a formidable magnet enabling vested interests to easily build a strong opposing coalition.

The two other key actors in the domestic political economy of the negotiations were the BCCR and financial supervisory authorities (SUGEF, SUPEN, and SUGEVAL) and the INS. The BCCR and the financial supervisory authorities developed an excellent working relationship with COMEX and were incorporated in the negotiation team. They had a common interest not only in familiarizing the supervisory authorities with the contents and reach of an international trade negotiation in financial services, but also in ensuring that the structure, contents, and administration of the financial services chapter were fully compatible with Costa Rican supervisory legislation.

The INS did not get involved in the negotiations until a late stage, when the United States brought to the table the issue of insurance.[33] At a very late stage of the negotiation process, the United States requested the opening of Costa Rica's state insurance monopoly and explicitly stated that the issue was a deal breaker. Within this context, the president had to weigh the cost of staying outside CAFTA-DR-U.S. against the political cost of undertaking the requested reforms. Considering the dependence of Costa Rica's economy on the United States, leaving Costa Rica marginalized from an FTA with its major trade and investment partner was clearly not an option.

The Costa Rican negotiators succeeded, however, in convincing the United States that an agreement comprising the entire U.S. "wish list" would not be politically viable in Costa Rica. They insisted that if a deal were to be concluded, the United States would have to clarify its priorities and understand that in every negotiation no party can obtain 100 percent of what it originally envisioned. This argument was difficult to reject.

In the context of the negotiations, the argument meant that the United States would have to decide between (a) obtaining access to the Costa Rican insurance market or (b) giving U.S. financial institutions the possibility of establishing branches and leveling the playing field between state and private banks. In addition, Costa Rica made clear that to make any opening of the insurance sector politically viable, the United States would need to accept that the process would follow principles of gradualism and prudential regulation and would not entail any obligation to privatize the INS. In the end, the United States opted for gradual access to the Costa Rican insurance market and gave up its intention of obtaining branching with respect to any other financial services and leveling the playing field between public and private banks in Costa Rica.

Domestic events facilitated this decision. Even before the negotiations began, several bills were introduced in the Legislative Assembly that aimed at leveling the playing field and allowing branching. Thus, through a side letter to the agreement, the Costa Rican government confirmed to the United States that Costa Rica would make "reasonable efforts" to pursue those reforms in the Legislative Assembly.

This understanding enabled U.S. negotiators to sell the outcome of the negotiations to their own constituency. Together with making the United States identify its main priorities, this argument influenced the results on the three main contentious issues at the financial services table. Although branching and leveling the playing field would not be obtained through "hard law" commitments in CAFTA-DR-U.S., these issues were going to be fostered through domestic political channels. Furthermore, the United States obtained a significant concession in return: opening of the state monopoly in insurance.

Of all the participants in the negotiations, the INS—in particular its executive president—proved to be the most controversial. Despite being an autonomous state enterprise, the INS board of directors is still appointed by the government, and in theory, its interests should coincide with those of the government. However, as the CAFTA-DR-U.S. experience demonstrated, state monopolies tend to acquire a life of their own, becoming a pressure group in their own right. Instead of complying with the directives of the president of the republic, the INS, led by its executive president, became an obstacle to orderly conduct of the negotiations.

Taking advantage of the political controversy that opening the state monopolies would generate, the INS executive president found a formidable opportunity to position himself in the Costa Rican political arena.[34] Instead of acting as an ally to the government, he opted to object to the negotiations and accuse the government of relinquishing its duty to protect the monopoly, which he considered to be one of the fundamental pillars of the welfare state. He knew that siding with the public unions, anti–free trade NGOs, and left-wing political parties would make remaining in office difficult for him. Nevertheless, attempting to remain in charge of the INS, he publicly announced that if the president asked him to leave, it would be because the government had betrayed its original Social Christian ideological roots by negotiating CAFTA-DR-U.S. In the wake of the conclusion of the negotiations,[35] this situation led to a confrontation within the government, which became public because of the INS executive president's strategy to make as much use as possible of the mass media.

Clearly, the quarrel between the INS and the government generated some anxiety and doubts in the public. Public unions immediately began to attack the agreement. Anti–free trade NGOs and several left-wing academics followed suit, starting a widespread campaign at the national level, which has lasted until today, calling on civil society to resist what they perceive to be an attempt to destroy the Costa Rican welfare state. Interestingly enough, however, contrary to the state monopoly in telecommunications, the INS monopoly on insurance did not have much popular support, as gradually became evident. Although the campaign against the agreement continued, it did not gravitate around defense of the INS. Thus, the financial services chapter was not the center of controversy in Costa Rica's political debate over CAFTA-DR-U.S.

In 2004, public unions started to threaten the government with generating social confrontation if the agreement was sent to the Legislative Assembly for discussion. President Pacheco therefore opted to refrain from sending the agreement to the Legislative Assembly and gradually began to distance himself from COMEX and the negotiation team he had previously backed. Almost two years passed before the Pacheco administration finally decided to send CAFTA-DR-U.S. to the Legislative Assembly in October 2005, with the clear intention of leaving the task of pursuing its approval to the next presidential administration, which would start in May 2006.

CAFTA-DR-U.S. became one of the main issues in the 2006 presidential race. Despite the overwhelming campaign undertaken by the alliance opposing the agreement—comprising the Partido Acción Ciudadana (Citizen's Action Party) and other left-wing parties, public unions, anti–free trade NGOs, and some public universities—by early 2006, the majority of the Costa Rican population still supported the approval of the treaty and the opening of state monopolies to competition. In February 2006, following a contested election, Óscar Arias was again elected president of the republic. He clearly advocated the approval of CAFTA-DR-U.S., and the treaty was finally accepted in October 2007.

The Negotiation Process: Organization and Lessons from the Costa Rican Experience

Another important aspect of the negotiation of the financial services chapter is how the Costa Rican government organized its negotiation team, planned the negotiation process, and handled the difficult political dynamics. This section addresses those aspects.

Organization within the Costa Rican negotiation team. Unlike in other developing countries, the COMEX negotiation team did not have a high level of turnover, enabling the ministry to develop a cadre of negotiators who had gathered experience over more than a decade of negotiation practice. This element proved to be very important from two perspectives. First, the Costa Rican negotiation team easily gained the confidence of their Central American negotiation colleagues, enabling the development of a positive working relationship within the Central American group. This relationship was a key aspect in a negotiation process in which the Central American countries negotiated jointly as one party with the United States. Second, because Costa Rican negotiators were not amateurs in international trade and investment law, U.S. negotiators could feel that despite the substantial differences in political and economic power existing between the countries, at least from a technical perspective they had a counterpart capable of arguing and defending positions and interests as well as any other U.S. major negotiating partner.[36]

In addition to the president, who was ultimately responsible for making political decisions, the core of the Costa Rican negotiation team comprised seven persons: the COMEX minister, the general lead negotiator, and the lead negotiators of the five negotiating groups.

The substantive preparation for the subject matter of the negotiations was pivotal. Each lead negotiator clearly understood that the key for a successful negotiation was to avoid any surprise during the negotiation process. The negotiation objectives that Costa Rica opted to pursue in each topic had to correspond to the economic and political realities of the country and could not generate misleading expectations among any sector of the Costa Rican constituency. Thus, from the outset, using a carefully conducted assessment of the interests and constraints of each negotiating party, each lead negotiator had to be able to predict how the negotiations in each particular chapter would evolve and to envision the most likely scenarios that Costa Rica would face in the later stages of the process. For this purpose, each lead negotiator prepared a roadmap for the negotiations.

These roadmaps anticipated which positions the United States would submit to the negotiating table, what the advantages and disadvantages of every proposal would be for Costa Rica, which issues were going to be the most controversial, and what strategy could be devised to lead to the most politically palatable outcome for Costa Rica. All of this had to be done before the negotiations started. Having such a detailed roadmap was the only way Costa Rica could identify not only how best to defend its interests, but also how to adequately manage the anxieties and expectations of the different stakeholders.

Thus, preparing the negotiation road map entailed a significant amount of research in multiple areas—not only about Costa Rica but also about the United States. Most of the research and studies were done within COMEX, but because of time constraints, the ministry commissioned a couple of studies from outside experts.[37]

Preparation of the substantive aspects of the negotiation was just part of the story. As mentioned before, after the negotiation roadmap was drawn, each lead negotiator also had the responsibility to set up a network of contacts with various government agencies and private sector groups for consultations. These points are further developed in the following sections.

Organization within the government. The coordination mechanisms established within the government led to a pyramidal decision-making structure. At the top was the president of the republic, who would make the final political decisions and who had to be constantly briefed on the progress of the negotiations by the minister of foreign trade.

A second working level was ministerial, for which COMEX requested the president to constitute an advisory group of other ministers who were related to the matters subject to negotiation. This level proved very useful in maintaining the cohesion and coherence of government positions regarding CAFTA-DR-U.S. and, in particular, in avoiding the intergovernmental divisions that pressure groups often seek to generate to pursue their vested interests. The ministerial advisory group, headed by the minister of foreign trade, included the minister of foreign affairs, the minister of agriculture, the minister of commerce and industry, and the minister of finance. When required to comment on specific issues, other ministers were invited to participate. For instance, some intellectual property matters were discussed with the minister of health, while the chapters on labor and environment required consultation with the minister of labor and the minister of energy, mining, and natural resources, respectively.

In the case of the financial services chapter, in addition to the minister of finance, the president of the central bank was consulted.

The third working level within the Costa Rican organizational structure was technical. Each of the five lead negotiators was responsible for organizing and setting up a network of contacts and working relationships with the diverse government agencies related to the subject matter under his or her responsibility. In the case of the negotiation of the financial services chapter, COMEX contacted the BCCR, the Ministry of Finance, and the three existing supervisory authorities for the financial sector in Costa Rica (SUGEF, SUPEN, and SUGEVAL)—and, at a later stage, the INS.[38]

The main objective of the working relationship among COMEX, the BCCR, and the financial supervisory institutions was to fully integrate the other government agencies into the negotiation process to ensure that the chapter on financial services was fully compatible with Costa Rican prudential legislation and the powers that each of these supervisory agencies had in their respective fields. The working relationship entailed interaction at three different levels. First, a technical working group comprising staff from all the institutions involved was established. This working group met regularly to discuss and evaluate the negotiation roadmap proposed by COMEX and to review the negotiation texts. The different agencies distributed their responsibilities as follows: COMEX was responsible for leading the negotiation, with the technical support of the different regulatory agencies in each of their respective fields of expertise (that is, SUGEF for banking issues, SUGEVAL for matters related to securities, and SUPEN for matters related to pensions). The BCCR was consulted on all issues covered by the chapter, in particular prudential safeguards. Under this scheme, no decision on the financial services chapter was ever made without involvement of the regulatory agencies.

A second level of interaction between COMEX and the regulatory agencies was through the negotiation rounds. The staff of the regulatory institutions was invited to be part of the Costa Rican delegation to the negotiation rounds. However, the agencies soon discovered that they had very limited funding available to finance participation of their staff in every negotiating round. The negotiation roadmap became particularly useful in this context, because the team could predict which specific issues would be brought to the table in each particular negotiating round, thereby enabling the various regulatory institutions to decide the specific rounds in which they wanted to participate.

Besides the two levels just discussed, a third level of interaction was a direct communication channel that was opened between the lead negotiator of the CAFTA-DR-U.S. Negotiation Group and the heads of the regulatory authorities. COMEX would directly and regularly brief the latter on the overall evolution of the negotiations. This high-level communication channel proved to be particularly useful, because the technical staff of the regulatory authorities did not always keep their supervisors duly informed. Furthermore, rather than focusing on specific technical issues, the heads were interested in having a broader picture of the negotiation process. This point proved particularly important. If asked by the press or the private sector about their opinion on the evolution of the negotiations, regulatory authorities would be able to make not only an informed comment but, more important, a comment that was coherent with the general discourse of the government on the process, thus providing evidence that the government was acting in an articulate and coordinated manner.

Consultation Mechanisms with the Private Sector and Civil Society

During the CAFTA-DR-U.S. negotiations, COMEX set up the widest and most comprehensive consultation and information mechanisms with the private sector ever implemented in the context of a Costa Rican international negotiation. The main objective was not only to inform and receive inputs from those consulted, but also to adequately manage the expectations of the private sector and civil society. In this regard, avoiding surprises was important, and the negotiation roadmap prepared by COMEX proved particularly useful for this purpose. Allowing the private sector and the public in general to observe step by step how the negotiations unwound, without unexpected surprises, was key to maintaining a calm environment, to generating confidence in the negotiation process, and to gradually allowing the different sectors to get used to the idea of the reforms that the agreement would entail. Thus, transparency, certainty, and predictability are necessary aspects of consultation mechanisms.

The consultations with the private sector were carried out in four ways. First, even before the negotiations were launched, the legislation constituting COMEX established the Foreign Trade Advisory Council, comprising representatives of each of the main producers' associations, unions, and cooperatives. The council is a permanent instance of dialogue between the minister of foreign trade and the private sector on trade issues. Consequently, once the CAFTA-DR-U.S. negotiations started, it became one of the main channels of dialogue between COMEX and the productive sector.

Especially for the negotiations, a series of meetings was held with representatives of enterprises and producer associations who wanted to participate in the consultation process. In the agriculture and manufacturing sectors alone, COMEX held 360 meetings with representatives of more than 900 enterprises and 57 associations of producers, covering 49 different productive sectors. In the area of services and investment, COMEX consulted 87 associations and 27 private institutions. In addition to the sectoral consultation process, COMEX maintained a permanent dialogue with major representative organizations. Consultations were held through the mechanism of side rooms whereby the private sector was briefed, as often as three times a day during a negotiating round, about the specific issues that had been addressed or agreed on in the different negotiating groups. These side rooms were open to everybody, both the private sector and the civil society. Because not every interested person could travel to the negotiation rounds held overseas, COMEX opted to organize an open side room in San José before and after each round of negotiations. During the negotiations, more than 60 side-room meetings were organized. In those meetings, 313 representatives of 84 different organizations, 61 members of the productive sector, and 23 members of civil society participated.

In addition to these general consultation mechanisms, COMEX set up a direct working relationship with the financial sector. One of the main communication vehicles was the Costa Rican Banking Association, which comprised both state and private financial groups and established a separate working group on CAFTA-DR-U.S. The mission of this working group was to meet regularly with COMEX before, during, and after each round of negotiations and to keep the association appropriately briefed on the evolution of the process. Given the smooth and direct working relationship established between the Costa Rican Banking Association and the negotiation team, the former never felt the need for active participation in the general consultation mechanisms set up by COMEX for the private sector.

A consequence of all these efforts to engage the private sector in the discussions on the negotiations is that the domestic financial sector, both public and private, became one of the most enthusiastic supporters of CAFTA-DR-U.S. in Costa Rica. It publicly defended the transparently designed negotiation process and supported the agreement after the negotiations were concluded.[39]

COMEX also attempted to fully inform and engage civil society in the negotiations. This effort proved to be the most difficult of all, because the battle for CAFTA-DR-U.S. would have to be fought before the public. COMEX opted to establish a group of government officials whose main mission was to design and implement a communication strategy. The goal was to inform the public not only about the objectives, contents, and merits of CAFTA-DR-U.S. in general, but also about each of the negotiation topics, including financial services. This communication strategy entailed numerous mechanisms. During the year of the negotiations, COMEX carried out the following activities:

- Through the main national newspapers, it issued a public invitation to all citizens to comment on any aspect of the agreement.
- On the COMEX Web page, it posted basic information about the origin, contents, and progress of the negotiations and the profiles of the parties involved in the negotiations, and it updated this information daily.
- Through free CDs, it distributed to the public a bibliography and compilation of relevant information.
- Through the Internet, it set up a permanent hotline to answer questions from the public, leading to more than 20 daily requests (and responses) on average.
- It distributed nationwide more than 100,000 copies of 11 different explanatory documents addressing different aspects of the negotiations.
- It organized and participated in more than 103 seminars and dialogues with civil society on the agreement.
- Through the main mass media, it released at least two daily reports on the evolution of each round of negotiations.

From the Costa Rican experience with the mechanisms of information and dialogue with civil society and the private sector, two important lessons can be drawn. For the success of the negotiation process on the domestic front, setting up proactive consultations, engaging the private sector in the negotiations, keeping it informed, and consulting it on its interests and needs are fundamentally important. Today, CAFTA-DR-U.S. has strong support from the private sector, which is badly needed to counterbalance the passionate resistance from other sectors.

A second important lesson from the Costa Rican experience is that despite the titanic efforts undertaken by the government, important segments of civil society will not be interested in learning about trade agreements. However, the use of mass media campaigns becomes pivotal for success, in that such campaigns not only can help demonstrate the benefits of reform, but also can show transparency and wide public participation during the negotiation process. The task is important because many opponents attack reforms not only because of their contents but also on the basis of their negotiation process.

The CAFTA-DR-U.S. Chapter on Financial Services

The CAFTA-DR-U.S. provisions regulating financial services are set out mainly in chapter 12 of the agreement, although two other chapters are also relevant: chapter 10 on investment and chapter 11 on cross-border trade in services. Chapter 12 basically follows the logic and structure of NAFTA's chapter 14. In this regard, it balances two potentially conflicting objectives. Chapter 12 promotes the liberalization of international trade in financial services, but at the same time, such liberalization must not erode the capacity of the national competent authorities to adequately supervise their respective financial systems. These two policy objectives explain the structure and main features of chapter 12.

In fostering liberalization of trade in financial services, the provisions of chapter 12 are based on nondiscrimination principles of national and MFN treatment and are similar to those in the chapters on investment and cross-border trade in services. Chapter 12, however, operates independently from those chapters, and financial services are exempt from their rules and disciplines. The scope of chapter 12 thus depends on the meaning of *financial institution* and *financial service*, as will become clear later.[40]

To safeguard the appropriate supervision of financial services in each of the contracting parties, chapter 12 also differentiates between the rules and disciplines that apply to investment in financial institutions and those that apply to cross-border trade in financial services. Although the reach and depth of the obligations applicable to investment in financial institutions are significant, those applicable to cross-border trade in financial services are much more limited. The reason for such differentiation stems from the fact that international trade in financial services is more likely to raise conflicts among the different applicable laws and jurisdictions of the countries involved and thus is more likely to affect negatively adequate financial supervision by competent national authorities.

Effect of CAFTA-DR-U.S. on the Costa Rican Financial System

The effect of the agreement on the financial system of Costa Rica can be assessed from two different perspectives. One is to assess the effect that the rules, disciplines, and market-access commitments undertaken by Costa Rica in chapter 12 may have on the financial sector. The other is to assess the effect that the creation of the FTA as whole may have on the Costa Rican financial system. As explained later, one can reasonably expect, from both vantage points, that the agreement will have a significantly positive effect on Costa Rica.

Effect of the Chapter on Financial Services

The CAFTA-DR-U.S. commitments undertaken by Costa Rica have started to generate a series of positive effects on the Costa Rican financial system. The most obvious one has been the significant push that the agreement has generated toward reinvigorating the process of financial liberalization that had stagnated for almost a decade.[41] After a heated presidential election in which CAFTA-DR-U.S. became one of the main issues, and especially after the victory of the party advocating the FTA, new political alliances have regrouped in favor of modernization of the country in general and of the financial sector in particular.

Chapter 12 did what several domestic political groups could not do for more than a decade: it prompted Costa Rica to decide whether the state monopoly on insurance will be opened for competition. Chapter 12 initiated legislation on a modern regulatory framework to ensure competition in the insurance sector, something the country should have done decades ago.

Thus, from this perspective, the effect of chapter 12 on the Costa Rican financial system is twofold: the chapter not only has fostered the liberalization of the insurance sector—and the liberalization of trade in services in the same field—but also will affect the insurance market's structure and performance.[42] In addition, chapter 12 has a direct effect on the sector in the sense that it is fostering an upgrading of the legal framework used to regulate the financial system. For the first time ever, Costa Rica will have a supervisory authority for insurance. Furthermore, although chapter 12 does not entail any legal reform with respect to any other financial service, it will trigger the political momentum necessary for further reforms.

Effect of CAFTA-DR-U.S. as a Whole

The other perspective from which to assess the effect of the agreement on the financial sector is in terms of the effects of the FTA as a whole.

From this broader perspective, the contribution of CAFTA-DR-U.S. toward fostering a more modern and competitive market for financial services in Central America stems from three main results the FTA will likely generate.

First, one can reasonably expect that CAFTA-DR-U.S. may generate significant dynamic effects on trade and investment in Costa Rica and in Central America as a whole. Over the past two decades or so, FDI inflows into Costa Rica have multiplied by a factor of 10. The overwhelming share of those FDI inflows are export oriented, and for every U.S. dollar Costa Rica receives in FDI, the country increases its exports by US$18.[43] More than 70 percent of that FDI is concentrated in the high-tech and services sectors, leading, in turn, not only to a significant increase in value-added jobs, but also to the diversification of the Costa Rican export base. Within this context, the potential for fostering backward links is significant, and small and medium-size Costa Rican enterprises have already started to integrate with multinational corporations. Thus, Costa Rica is gradually being brought into the international production supply chains of numerous multinational corporations.

The Costa Rican experience shows the role that long-term, preferential access to the U.S. market can have in attracting FDI inflows. Thus, CAFTA-DR-U.S. should represent a strong and positive signal for international investors by securing and improving the access that Costa Rican exports have already enjoyed in the U.S. market as a result of the Caribbean Basin Initiative. By establishing a legal framework regulating its trade and investment relations with the United States, Costa Rica is likely to become an even more attractive place for export-oriented FDI in the near future. Furthermore, the significant reforms that Costa Rica will undertake in various services sectors, such as telecommunications, distribution services, and insurance, will improve the business environment in the country, serving as an additional incentive to attract FDI inflows. Within this context, the financial sector of Costa Rica has a lot to gain, not only in terms of the likely growth of its current client base, but also in terms of the likely increase in the demand for financial services resulting from the new productive activities.

Second, a key aspect of the agreement that will likely significantly affect the Costa Rican financial system is the dynamic effect that the multilateral character of the agreement will generate. CAFTA-DR-U.S. will establish an expanded regional market in which trade in goods and services is governed by a common legal framework. The practical effect of such a scheme is that foreign investors will be able to conceive of

Central America, the Dominican Republic, and the United States as one integrated market, attracting market-seeking FDI and increasing the demand for logistical services within the region.

This integration scheme will generate greater opportunities for financial services suppliers in Costa Rica and the region. However, it will also likely generate greater competition among them by fostering the integration of financial markets in Central America. As a result, the pressure for harmonization of regulations, including those dealing with supervision of financial activities, will increase. With the United States as a key player in this integration scheme, this harmonization can be expected to proceed upward, prompting the authorities of the Dominican Republic and the Central American countries to gradually adopt internationally accepted standards for financial regulation.

Third, one of the most important contributions of CAFTA-DR-U.S. will be strengthening of the rule of law and transparency in the public administration of the region's countries. The different chapters contain several provisions on transparency and the rule of law, and once public institutions have acknowledged and internalized them, spillover effects in other areas may occur.

This outcome can be expected in most countries of Central America, in particular, where CAFTA-DR-U.S. will directly affect the domestic legal system, enabling every resident to invoke any right derived from the agreement in local courts. Thus, for instance, the obligations included in article 12.11 of chapter 12, although originally crafted with international investors in mind, will also apply to national citizens and residents in each Central American country and the Dominican Republic. Although the transparency standards set out in article 12.11 may seem basic and fundamental, national authorities in many of these countries have not always granted such rights to their constituents. With CAFTA-DR-U.S., this situation will change for good. There are reasons for confidence about positive developments in the region. One is that the standards of protection and treatment included in chapter 12 will definitely have an effect, and those standards will have teeth because financial investors will be able to enforce most of the guarantees included in chapter 12 through international arbitration, without requiring their home state to sponsor their claim against the host country. Another reason to be confident about the strengthening of transparency and the rule of law in the region is that the agreement will set a precedent in trade negotiations. Negotiations of future trade agreements between Central America and other countries, such as the already announced negotiations with the

European Union, will certainly use CAFTA-DR-U.S. as a normative floor. Given the increasing attention of the international debate on trade and development to recognizing the importance of fostering transparent and responsible governance institutions in developing countries, these issues are likely to remain crucial in the future.

Conclusions

The Costa Rican experience in the negotiations of CAFTA-DR-U.S., and in particular of the chapter on financial services, can be assessed to draw some policy lessons that may be of use in other negotiation contexts.

One aspect illustrated by the Costa Rican experience in CAFTA-DR-U.S. is that the rationale of this FTA—contrary to those of many other developing countries—is not limited to improving market-access conditions for key export markets, increasing exports, or attracting increased FDI inflows and diversifying the export supply. Without any doubt, all these objectives were part of the story, but other goals proved equally crucial. For Costa Rica, the trade agreement became instrumental in fostering key domestic reforms, modernizing economic and political institutions, and providing incentives for fair and sustainable development.

Nevertheless, the CAFTA-DR-U.S. experience also shows the limitations of FTAs. The agreement was not a sufficient vehicle to undertake all the items of the pending reform agenda for the Costa Rican financial sector, which included reforms well beyond the scope of an FTA, such as reforms of supervisory regulation and macroeconomic variables. Furthermore, despite its important merits, chapter 12 did not make possible the dismantling of all remaining barriers to trade in financial services in Costa Rica; in particular, branching and the lack of a level playing field between state and private banks are still unresolved issues.

In this regard, the CAFTA-DR-U.S. experience shows that FTAs cannot involve myriad highly politically sensitive reforms. In fact, one could say that the more politically sensitive the reforms are, the fewer of them can be enforced through commitments in an FTA. However, this problem does not diminish the significant value that an FTA may have as an instrument for governments to promote domestic reform. However, governments must use such trade agreements wisely. Any process of reform always faces resistance from vested interests and thus requires effective strategies to address such resistance.

A first lesson to be learned from the Costa Rican experience is that one of the key elements of a successful negotiation strategy, in particular in the case of smaller developing economies, is to prepare a roadmap for the negotiation process, attempting to anticipate from the outset the evolution of the different stages of the negotiation. In this regard, the best negotiation strategy is one that enables negotiators to have a predictable outcome. Thus, surprises should be avoided at all cost. Predictability is not easy to achieve in these contexts, particularly when, as for CAFTA-DR-U.S., negotiations at three different levels are entailed.

On the domestic front, three main levels of action exist, each entailing specific challenges. Within the government, the major challenge is to ensure a monolithic and coherent position in favor of the negotiations. On the positive side, the Costa Rican experience evidences the importance of setting up a capable and cohesive team of negotiators representing different public institutions, with clear negotiation priorities and an effective strategy to achieve those objectives. On the negative side, the Costa Rican experience also illustrates the importance of having a coherent position among the different public agencies regarding the negotiations as well as the pivotal role that, at least in smaller economies, single actors play in these processes. The difficult political situation generated by the INS and the withdrawal of presidential support for the agreement show the damage that can be generated.

Another level of action is in the private sector. Here the main challenge for the negotiators is to gain the trust and confidence of private sector groups in the government's team and negotiation strategy. In the Costa Rican case, the close working relationship between the negotiation team and the private sector led to a successful negotiation outcome and secured the private sector's support later on.

Third, civil society has to be convinced of the benefits of an agreement as a whole. The Costa Rican experience shows that bringing civil society on board to support instruments that entail domestic change can become a difficult task, especially in a context in which, paradoxically, the antiglobalization network has become more international as well. Vested domestic interests can find in that network a formidable ally to resist domestic transformations. Thus, the Costa Rican experience clearly illustrates the key leadership role governments must play in guiding civil society to discuss, in a rational, objective, and calm manner, the important implications of trade agreements such as CAFTA-DR-U.S.

This task is not easy because the public debate around FTAs tends to become oversimplified and is often colored with emotional pseudo-nationalistic tones.

The Costa Rican experience further indicates the challenges that smaller developing countries face when negotiating with significantly more powerful trade partners. Major superpowers like the United States tend to design negotiation templates in accordance with their own negotiation objectives. This technique allows the superpower not only to respond to the interests of its domestic constituents but also to maintain a coherent framework of rules and disciplines and concessions vis-à-vis its trade partners worldwide.

In this context, when a smaller developing economy like Costa Rica deals with a superpower like the United States, the main challenge is to convince the latter to deviate from its negotiation template and to adjust it to the particular needs posed by the smaller economy's domestic context. Obviously, the task is not easy, not only because most countries negotiating with the superpower pursue the same objective, but also because any deviation from the negotiation template has the potential to become an inconvenient precedent for the superpower in future negotiations with more important trade partners.

Thus, smaller economies must be particularly persuasive, creative, and constructive in addressing their specific needs in the negotiation process. In this regard, one of the main challenges for negotiators from smaller economies is to establish a credible and professional working relationship with their negotiation counterparts. Such a relationship, in turn, requires not only strong arguments, but also sufficient preparation and the ability to transfer that into credibility and trust at the other side of the negotiation table. The Costa Rican experience in the CAFTA-DR-U.S. negotiations illustrates that despite the enormous differences in bargaining power when dealing with a global superpower, with adequate preparation smaller economies can find and take advantage of the limited maneuvering space to pursue their negotiation objectives.

Annex 7A: Principal Laws Governing the Financial Sector in Costa Rica

Table 7A.1 enumerates the major laws governing Costa Rica's financial sector.

Table 7A.1   Principal Laws Governing the Financial Sector in Costa Rica

Name of law	Number	Date
Principal laws		
National Insurance Bank (Banco Nacional de Seguros)	12	October 30, 1924
Organizational Law of the National Banking System	1644	September 26, 1953
Law on Cooperative Associations and Creation of the National Institute for the Promotion of Cooperatives (Instituto Nacional de Fomento Cooperativo).	4179	August 22, 1968
Organizational Law of the People's and Communal Development Bank	4351	July 11, 1969
Net profits on auctions of goods	4631	August 8, 1970
Law Regulating Financial Investment Companies and Special Nonbanking Credit Companies	5044	September 7, 1972
Law on the State Monopoly of Reinsurance	6082	August 30, 1977
Law on the National Housing Finance System	7052	November 13, 1986
Law on Modernization of the National Financial System	7107	November 4, 1988
Law Regulating Financial Intermediation by Cooperative Organizations	7391	May 27, 1994
Private Supplementary Pensions Scheme and Reform of the Law Regulating the Stock Exchange and the Commercial Code	7523	July 7, 1995
Organizational Law of the Central Bank of Costa Rica	7558	November 3, 1995
Related regulations		
Regulations on the formation, transfer, registration, and operation of financial groups		January 29, 1998
Regulations on monetary policy		June 1, 1998
Regulations on exchange operations		October 10, 1998
Law on Worker Protection	7983	February 16, 2000
Law Regulating the Stock Market	7732	December 17, 1997

Source: World Trade Organization Secretariat.

Annex 7B: Chapter 10 (Financial Services), Chapter 11 (Cross-Border Trade in Services), and Chapter 12 (Investment)

Article 12.20 of the financial services chapter defines *financial institution* as any financial intermediary or other enterprise that is authorized to do business and is regulated or supervised as a financial institution under the law of the CAFTA-DR-U.S. country in which it is located. Thus, a financial institution is not defined in terms of the activities that an enterprise carries on; rather, it is defined in terms of how it is regulated in the country in which it is located. Therefore, two enterprises with identical activities need not be treated the same.[44]

Chapter 12 does not, however, cover laws of general application that affect the ability of investors of other CAFTA-DR-U.S. countries to invest. A law in the Dominican Republic that restricts investment by a non-Dominican in a business that is not a financial institution is covered by chapter 10, even if an investor of another CAFTA-DR-U.S. country is a financial institution. However, if the Dominican law restricting the ability to invest is directed at non-Dominican financial institutions, it is governed by chapter 12 and not by chapter 10.

Just as chapter 11 covers measures of a CAFTA-DR-U.S. country affecting cross-border trade in services, chapter 12 covers cross-border trade in financial services. Based on GATS, the definition of *financial service* is stated in article 12.20: "any service of a financial nature. Financial services include all insurance and insurance-related services, and all banking and other financial services (excluding insurance), as well as services incidental or auxiliary to a service of a financial nature."

An important aspect is that the definition of financial service is not linked to the definition of financial institution. Thus, a service provided by a financial institution has to be "of a financial nature" to be a financial service. A financial service need not be provided by a financial institution because a financial institution is defined in terms of how it is regulated and not in terms of what it does. Many companies whose primary business has nothing to do with financial services nonetheless provide financial services to their customers by way of loans or other credit facilities to enable them to buy their products.

In chapter 12, the concept of cross-border trade in services is identical to that used in chapter 11, excluding commercial presence from the definition because it is regulated by the chapter on investment. Thus, *cross-border trade in financial services* comprises the provision of financial services (a) from one CAFTA-DR-U.S. country to another (cross-border trade, or mode 1 under GATS); (b) within a CAFTA-DR-U.S. country by one of its nationals or enterprises to a national or enterprise of another CAFTA-DR-U.S. country (consumption abroad, or mode 2 under GATS); or (c) by a national (that is, an individual) of one CAFTA-DR-U.S. country within another CAFTA-DR-U.S. country (movement of natural persons, or mode 4 under GATS).[45]

For example, the cross-border financial services provisions of chapter 12 would cover Guatemalan measures affecting the ability of a financial services provider in the United States (whether or not regulated as a financial institution) to provide financial services to customers in Guatemala, or to a U.S. national, such as a financial adviser, to provide services within Guatemala. Chapter 12's cross-border provisions would also cover Costa Rican measures affecting the ability of a financial services provider in Costa Rica to provide financial services to customers in Costa Rica who are U.S. or Guatemalan nationals or enterprises.[46]

Standards of Treatment and Protection

Given the different application of chapter 12 with respect to investment in financial institutions, on the one hand, and cross-border trade in financial services, on the other, the standards of treatment and protection included in the chapter can be divided into three main categories. First are provisions that apply to cross-border trade in financial services exclusively; second are some standards of treatment and protection that apply only to financial institutions, investors, and their investments in financial institutions of a CAFTA-DR-U.S. country; and third are those provisions of general application that apply to both cross-border trade and investment in financial institutions.

Cross-Border Supply of Financial Services

With respect to cross-border trade in financial services, among the most important obligations assumed by the parties are those included in article 12.5 of the agreement.

They entail two specific obligations for the contracting parties. First, with respect to cross-border supply of financial services, chapter 12 obliges the contracting parties to provide national treatment only to those services explicitly listed in an annex. In this sense, for modes 1 and 4 of cross-border supply, chapter 12 is based on a positive list approach.[47] Contrary to NAFTA, CAFTA-DR-U.S. does not set a horizontal standstill with respect to all cross-border trade in financial services. With the exception of the services bound in annex 12.5.1, no obligation limits CAFTA-DR-U.S. countries from introducing more restrictive measures to the cross-border supply of financial services.

The second obligation provided by article 12.5 regarding cross-border trade in services applies to all financial services—but with respect to consumption abroad (mode 2 under GATS). It requires that each CAFTA-DR-U.S. country permit persons in its territory and its nationals to purchase financial services provided by financial services providers in the territory of other CAFTA-DR-U.S. countries. However, the provision explicitly states that under this mode of supply, services providers of one country are not allowed to do or solicit business in another country. Thus, for instance, Costa Ricans will be able to make deposits in banks overseas or will be allowed to buy insurance policies from services suppliers located abroad. The only limitation will be that to render these services the foreign services suppliers will not be able to solicit in Costa Rica.[48]

Standards of Treatment and Protection Applicable to Financial Institutions, Investors, and Their Investments in Financial Institutions

In comparison to the commitments related to cross-border trade in financial services, the commitments included in chapter 12 with respect to investment in financial institutions are significantly broader. Among the most important provisions are the following.

National treatment. The provision on national treatment as included in article 12.2 of chapter 12 entails the obligation of each party to provide to investors of other CAFTA-DR-U.S. countries, investments of those investors in financial institutions within a CAFTA-DR-U.S. country, and financial institutions of other CAFTA-DR-U.S. countries treatment no less favorable than it accords to its own financial institutions and to investments of its own investors in financial institutions in like circumstances. These obligations cover measures affecting the establishment, acquisition, expansion, management, conduct, operation, and sale or other disposition of financial institutions and investments in financial institutions within a CAFTA-DR-U.S. country.

One of the main issues of contention during the negotiations was whether the obligation of national treatment would apply not only at a federal but also at a state level. Countries such as El Salvador and Guatemala were interested in allowing their banking groups to penetrate the U.S. market to serve their Salvadoran and Guatemalan communities. Providing best-in-state treatment would have prevented the United States from applying the home-state rule that traditionally has applied to some financial services, and under which states can discriminate against banks established in other states of the American union. For instance, a bank established in Florida may not receive in California the treatment granted by the state of California to California banks, but rather the less favorable treatment granted to banks from Florida. For Salvadoran and Guatemalan banks, this rule could act as a barrier to entry and doing business across the whole U.S. market. In the end, CAFTA-DR-U.S. does not derogate from the latter. Thus, article 12.2 sets out rules relating to the application of these principles to state measures. This provision is best explained by an example.

Consider a Salvadoran financial institution with operations in the United States. If the Salvadoran financial institution is located in a state, the state must accord to it treatment no less favorable than the U.S. financial institutions located in that state. If the Salvadoran financial institution is not located in that particular state but is located in other states, the state must accord to it treatment no less favorable than that accorded to U.S. financial institutions in like circumstances. If the laws of that state prohibit U.S. financial institutions established in other states from establishing in that state, the same measure could be applied to the Salvadoran financial institution. If the Salvadoran financial institution is located in that state and in other states as well, the state must accord to it treatment no less favorable than that accorded to U.S. financial institutions in like circumstances. If the operations of a U.S. financial institution within that state are restricted because of its presence in other states, the same restriction could be applied to the Salvadoran financial institution. The effect of these provisions is that U.S. states may maintain restrictions on interstate branching as long as they are maintained on a nondiscriminatory basis.

Market access for financial institutions. Article 12.4 of the chapter carries an obligation quite similar to that included in GATS article XVI. Pursuant to article 12.4, the CAFTA-DR-U.S. countries assume the obligation to refrain from imposing any of the quantitative restrictions listed in the provision. Thus, the provision applies horizontally on the basis of a negative list approach, in principle allowing the parties to list all nonconforming measures.

Protection provisions imported from the investment chapter. A third category of provisions protecting investors and their investments in financial institutions covered by chapter 12 is incorporated from chapter 10. This category comprises articles on expropriation and compensation, transfers, investment and environment, denial of benefits, special formalities, and information requirements. Furthermore, investor-state dispute settlement procedures are adopted, which enable an investor to submit a claim to arbitration in case the host state breaches some, but not all, of the obligations in chapter 12.

Because chapter 12 applies to investment in financial institutions, the incorporation of these provisions from the general investment chapter becomes key to fostering investment in financial services. In fact, the inclusion of clauses on protection, such as expropriation and compensation and, more important, the guarantee pursuing enforcement of investor rights against the host state through international arbitration, are key instruments to providing the kind of certainty and predictability investors require to undertake business activities on an international scale.

New financial services. Article 12.6 requires a CAFTA-DR-U.S. country to permit financial institutions of other CAFTA-DR-U.S. countries to provide any new financial services that it permits its own financial institutions. New financial services are those that are not being rendered in a relevant market and will be determined in accordance with the host country's laws and regulations. The CAFTA-DR-U.S. country may determine the institutional and juridical form through which the service is provided and may require that authorization first be obtained.

Senior management and boards of directors. Article 12.8 rules out requirements for financial institutions to engage individuals of any particular nationality as senior managerial or other essential personnel. However, the provision permits nationality or residency requirements for the boards of directors.

Payment and clearing systems. Article 12.13 sets out the obligation of CAFTA-DR-U.S. countries to provide national treatment (a) to those financial institutions of another party established in their territory with respect to access to payment and clearing systems operated by public entities and (b) to official funding and refinancing facilities available in the normal course of ordinary business. However, as explicitly stated in the text of the provision, the obligation is not intended to confer access to lender-of-last-resort facilities existing in the host country.

General Standards of Treatment and Protection
The following standards are applicable both to cross-border trade in financial services and to financial institutions, investors, and their investments in financial institutions.

Most-favored nation. Article 12.3 sets out an MFN obligation analogous to those in the investment and services chapters. It obliges the parties to accord to investors of another party, financial institutions of another party, investments of investors in financial institutions, and cross-border financial services suppliers of another party treatment no less favorable than that it accords to the investors, financial institutions, investments of investors in financial institutions, and cross-border financial services suppliers of any other party or of a nonparty in like circumstances.

However, article 12.3 also includes an important qualification that is very similar to a provision that appears in the GATS Annex on Financial Services. A CAFTA-DR-U.S. country may recognize prudential measures of another country. Such recognition can be unilateral, achieved through harmonization or other means, or based on an agreement or other arrangement. If such recognition occurs, the CAFTA-DR-U.S. country according it must give a CAFTA-DR-U.S. country to which recognition has not been accorded the opportunity to demonstrate that its prudential measures are comparable and should also be recognized. The latter country must be provided with an opportunity to negotiate accession to the agreement or arrangement or to negotiate something comparable. However, the obligations do not extend beyond this opportunity.

The effect of these provisions is that CAFTA-DR-U.S. countries may enter into arrangements with nonparty countries respecting prudential measures without being bound to accord comparable treatment to other CAFTA-DR-U.S. countries. This provision may be of particular importance for countries such as the United States, which condition the establishment of foreign financial institutions in their territory on compliance with numerous regulatory and prudential requirements.

Transparency. Article 12.11 includes transparency rules with respect to the publication of measures. The transparency provisions require each CAFTA-DR-U.S. country, to the extent practicable, to notify all interested persons of measures of general application that it proposes to adopt and to allow an opportunity for comment. The provision also refers to applications for the provision of financial services. Regulatory authorities have to make requirements for completing applications available to interested persons and, on request, advise applicants of the status of applications. Decisions on completed applications must be made within 120 days, and the applicant has to be notified promptly. If the decision cannot be made within 120 days, the regulatory authorities must inform the applicant.

Finally, article 12.7 provides that nothing in chapter 12 requires a CAFTA-DR-U.S. country to furnish confidential information or information on the financial affairs of individual customers.

Self-regulatory organizations. Article 12.12 states that self-regulatory organizations—usually stock exchanges in some countries—to which financial institutions or cross-border financial services providers belong or in which they participate must observe the obligations of chapter 12.

Domestic regulation. Inspired by the contents and rationale of GATS article VI, article 12.14 of CAFTA-DR-U.S. provides that except with respect to nonconforming measures listed in annex III of chapter 12, each CAFTA-DR-U.S. country must ensure that all measures of general application to which the chapter applies are administered in a reasonable, objective, and impartial manner.

Exceptions. In addition to the rules and disciplines discussed in this annex, chapter 12 contains a series of provisions that clarify that the goals of trade promotion and liberalization of the agreement cannot be pursued at the expense of other key public policy objectives. In particular, chapter 12 includes five different exceptions, which, in turn, can be classified in two categories. First are those exceptions that can exempt the CAFTA-DR-U.S. countries from complying with any of the obligations of the chapter, and second are those that can be invoked to avoid compliance with obligations contained in chapter 12 and other chapters. Among the first category of exceptions, chapter 12 includes three relevant provisions.

The first relates to public retirement plans or systems of social security. Article 12.1, paragraph 3, explicitly states that chapter 12 does not apply to measures adopted or maintained by a CAFTA-DR-U.S. country related to activities or services forming part of a public retirement plan or statutory system of social security or of public financial resources. However, the same provision clarifies that chapter 12 will apply if the CAFTA-DR-U.S. country allows any of these activities or services to be conducted by its financial institutions in competition with a public entity or a financial institution. In the particular case of Costa Rica, the pension system is based on three pillars: first, the basic state social security program (managed by the CCSS); second, the fund of obligatory pensions; and third, voluntary complementary pension schemes. Although the first pillar remains reserved for the state, the second and third pillars are open to competition, both among the diverse state financial groups and the private sector. Chapter 12 thus applies to the second and third pillars of the pension system.

The second exception relates to the possibility of limiting transfers under certain circumstances. A CAFTA-DR-U.S. country may be authorized to prevent or limit transfers by a financial institution or cross-border financial services supplier if it does so through the equitable, nondiscriminatory, and good faith application of measures related to maintaining the safety, soundness, integrity, or financial responsibility of financial institutions or cross-border financial services suppliers.

The third exception within this category aims to safeguard regulatory power by stating that those measures consistent with CAFTA-DR-U.S. may not be constrained by any provisions in chapter 12. In particular, this provision applies to measures on deceptive and fraudulent practices and default on financial services contracts. However, the precondition is that the measures adopted do not arbitrarily or unjustifiably discriminate.

The second category of exceptions included in chapter 12 are those that can be invoked not only to evade obligations of the chapter, but even to evade rules and disciplines set out elsewhere in the agreement. This category comprises two exceptions.

The first is the exception on prudential measures. This provision states that nothing in chapter 12, chapter 10 (on investment), chapter 13 (on telecommunications), chapter 14 (on electronic commerce), and article 11.1.3 of chapter 11 (on services) prevents a CAFTA-DR-U.S. country from adopting and maintaining reasonable measures for prudential purposes. These measures include those to protect investors, depositors, financial market participants, policyholders, policy claimants, and persons to whom fiduciary duties are owed. They also include measures to ensure the "integrity and stability" of a country's financial system.

The second exception relates to monetary, credit, and exchange rate policies and provides that nothing in chapter 12 or chapters 10 (on investment), 13 (on telecommunications), or 14 (on electronic commerce) and article 11.1.3 of chapter 11 (on services) applies to nondiscriminatory measures of general application taken by any public entity in pursuit of monetary and related credit policies or exchange rate policies. This exception, however, cannot be invoked against the obligations on performance requirements under article 10.9 of the investment chapter or with respect to the obligations on transfers under articles 10.8 or 11.10 of the investment and services chapters, respectively.

Commitments of Liberalization

General aspects. In addition to the rules and disciplines included in chapter 12, the CAFTA-DR-U.S. countries undertook commitments to ensure effective access of financial services suppliers into each other's markets. For instance, all parties undertook commitments regarding portfolio

management services. Furthermore, all the parties undertook the commitment to provide expedited availability of insurance services.

In addition, all CAFTA-DR-U.S. countries bound all their measures
falling within the scope of the chapter that do not conform to the obligations of national treatment, MFN, market access for financial institutions,
and top managerial personnel. Table 7B.1 shows the number and type of
reservations each country undertook in the context of the chapter 12
negotiations. The number of reservations taken by each party does not
necessarily correspond to their importance in terms of the real effect
such measures may have on market access for financial services. Indeed,
a single measure may have a more significant effect than several other
measures together. However, given the architecture of chapter 12, under
which the obligations of the chapter apply to all measures except those
explicitly listed in the annex, and subject to the caveats explained before,
one can, in principle, infer that the higher the number of nonconforming
measures, the more hurdles foreign suppliers may face when competing
in the domestic market of the respective country.

Table 7B.1 reveals several important findings. First, the obligations to
which CAFTA-DR-U.S. countries made fewer reservations were those on
senior management and cross-border trade, where some, but not all, of the
parties have nonconforming measures or wanted to safeguard their discretion to adopt future nonconforming measures.

Second, the obligation that generated by far the highest number of reservations was market access, mainly because article 12.4 obliges the parties to
refrain from restricting or requiring specific types of juridical forms through

**Table 7B.1   CAFTA-DR-U.S. Countries: Reservations to Obligations under the
Financial Services Chapter, Including Nonconforming Measures and Future
Measures**

Country	National treatment	MFN treatment	Senior management	Market access	Cross-border trade	Total
Costa Rica	4	0	0	3	0	7
Dominican Republic	1	1	0	6	0	8
El Salvador	7	6	1	7	0	21
Guatemala	3	0	0	3	2	8
Honduras	4	2	1	8	0	15
Nicaragua	3	0	1	5	1	10
United States	11	5	3	10	3	32
Total	33	14	6	42	6	101

Source: CAFTA-DR-U.S. Annex III.
Note: MFN = most-favored nation.

which a financial institution may supply a service in their territories. Because most countries require financial services suppliers to establish a particular kind of legal entity to enter the market, market access was, not surprisingly, the obligation from which CAFTA-DR-U.S. countries most often sought relief. Third, table 7B.1 shows that the country with the fewest reservations to chapter 12 was Costa Rica, whereas the United States demanded by far the highest number of nonconforming measures.

Given the use of the negative list approach, chapter 12 of the agreement clearly represents an improvement compared to the GATS commitments assumed by the parties at the World Trade Organization. A relevant question to ask, however, is to what extent the commitments undertaken by the CAFTA-DR-U.S. countries in chapter 12 in fact represent a liberalization of trade in financial services and to what extent they just reflect the legal status quo in place before the negotiations started.

Given the progress most countries had achieved in unilateral reforms, the overwhelming majority of commitments were not particularly problematic for any of the Central American countries or the Dominican Republic. In fact, despite a limited number of exceptions, they could comply with most of the obligations of chapter 12 without any reform of their domestic laws and regulations.

Because Central American countries had a relatively open financial system even before the negotiations started does not mean, however, that CAFTA-DR-U.S. did not entail further liberalization of trade in financial services. In fact, contrary to negotiations in other contexts, CAFTA-DR-U.S. is an example of an agreement that did entail additional liberalization commitments for most of the countries involved—with the exception of the United States.

With the obligation to open its state monopoly on insurance services, Costa Rica clearly undertook the greatest liberalization commitments. However, all the other Central American countries also assumed commitments that implied reforms of their domestic legal framework for financial services. Those commitments were centered in two main areas: portfolio management services and branching in the insurance sector.

Regarding portfolio management services, the Dominican Republic, El Salvador, Honduras, and Nicaragua had no laws regulating collective investment schemes. Thus, most of these countries undertook the obligation to enact legislation within an agreed time.[49]

Furthermore, as mentioned previously, one of the key objectives of the United States in the negotiation was to provide its banks and insurance companies the possibility of establishing branches in each of the Central

American countries. Before the negotiations started, the Dominican Republic and all of the Central American countries, with the exception of Costa Rica, already allowed foreign banks to open branches in their territories, subject to certain conditions. However, practically none of them allowed insurance companies to do so. Thus, insurance branching became one of the main issues of discussion. Because of the negotiations, branching in insurance will be allowed in all of the CAFTA-DR-U.S. countries within a certain period. To reach a balanced outcome, the host country will be able to enact domestic legislation subjecting branching to solvency and integrity requirements.

Commitments of liberalization on insurance services undertaken by Costa Rica. For Costa Rica, the liberalization effects of CAFTA-DR-U.S. are limited to the insurance sector,[50] leading the country to open its state monopoly, which has been in force since 1924. In chapter 12, Costa Rica undertook two broad obligations.[51]

First, by no later than January 1, 2007, Costa Rica was required enact a law regulating the insurance sector, which will entail the establishment of a modern and independent regulatory authority with adequate legal powers,[52] legal protection, and financial resources.

Second, Costa Rica must gradually allow insurance services providers to compete effectively, on a nondiscriminatory basis, to supply insurance services. Such a process will start when CAFTA-DR-U.S. enters into force by allowing certain insurance services to be supplied on a cross-border basis and will conclude with the authorization of insurance services suppliers to establish commercial presence in Costa Rica, no later than January 1, 2008, for all noncompulsory insurance, and no later than January 1, 2011, for all insurance services. Costa Rica will also allow insurance services suppliers to be established through any juridical form, including branches, subject to the prudential solvency and integrity requirements that Costa Rican authorities may demand.

Currently, Costa Rica is in the process of discussing the legislation to comply with these commitments. It is, therefore, still too early to describe the specific features of the future regulatory framework, but some key policy decisions have already been made. First, the INS will clearly not be privatized. Thus, the INS will have to compete on equal footing with private services suppliers in the insurance market. This change will entail a major internal reorganization of the INS. Second, the superintendent agency regulating the insurance sector will be framed, as are the other supervisory bodies in the other sectors of the financial system, under the aegis of CONASSIF. One of the aspects being discussed is whether SUPEN will be reorganized to accommodate the supervision of pension funds and insurance services. The implementing legislation is expected to be approved together with CAFTA-DR-U.S. no later than early 2007.

Notes

1. At the time this chapter was written, CAFTA-DR-U.S. was still under discussion at the Legislative Assembly in Costa Rica. The agreement has since been approved and is in the process of being implemented.

2. Regarding the offshore banks in the country, the same document states, "Unlike the more typical offshore systems, Costa Rica's offshore banks are licensed in foreign (mainly Caribbean) jurisdictions but conduct most of their deposit-taking and lending activities with Costa Rican residents and are, therefore, fully woven into the country's domestic financial and economic activity" (IMF and World Bank 2003, 5).

3. As will be discussed further, Costa Rica had a poorly regulated financial system that was heavily distorted by state intervention in the economy as a whole and in the financial sector in particular. At least in qualitative terms, the reform process has been significant and has entailed deep transformations in the domestic financial market.

4. The Law of the Private Regime for Complementary Pensions, No. 7523 of July 7, 1995, not only created SUPEN but also authorized the creation of private schemes for complementary pensions and individual savings. The latter aimed to provide beneficiaries with coverage in addition to the traditional state social security scheme, which is mostly administered by the Caja Costarricense del Seguro Social, the Costa Rican Social Security Institution. The main regulations on insurance activity in Costa Rica are the Law on Monopolies and on the National Insurance Institute (Law No. 12) and the Law on the Monopoly of Reinsurance (Law No. 6082). The only exceptions were life insurance services rendered by the teachers' life insurance society (Sociedad de Seguros de Vida del Magisterio Nacional), a mutual society that already existed at the time the monopoly was established in 1924.

5. Given the INS monopoly of insurance services, traders are authorized only to commercialize INS insurance policies.

6. Investment funds, in domestic or foreign currency, also reveal an excessive concentration, both in terms of administered assets and number of clients. There are, though, differences between the national and foreign currency concentration ratios. Although state banks continue to dominate in the local currency market, private banks tend to dominate in dollar-denominated funds.

7. This fact does not mean, however, that all banks are treated identically under Costa Rican law. State and private banks do not operate on a level playing field.

8. Calculations are based on information provided by banking groups to SUGEF.

9. For reasons of external competitiveness, Costa Rica's exchange rate policy has, since the early 1980s, been implemented on the basis of an exchange crawl, with the rate of the crawl being regularly adjusted to compensate for differentials of past inflation rates between Costa Rica and the United States. Such a regime has enabled Costa Rica to avoid large real exchange rate overvaluations, currency crises, and sharp nominal exchange rate adjustments. However, by trading short-term real certainty against long-term nominal uncertainty (through the systematic targeting of the real exchange rate, rather than inflation), at the end of the day, the regime has, in fact, promoted dollarization in the financial system. See IMF and World Bank (2003, 12).

10. The principal regulations governing the Costa Rican financial system, the stock market, and pension schemes are listed in annex 7A.

11. To date, MOUs have been signed with Colombia, the Dominican Republic, El Salvador, Honduras, and Panama.

12. In 2005, six financial groups subject to supervision by SUGEF had banks domiciled overseas. Total assets of these foreign entities reached US$1.72 billion, an amount equivalent to 70 percent of total assets of the local banks that are part of those financial groups.

13. As has been recognized by the IMF and World Bank (2003, 6), this situation "hinders the reliability of financial statements and, by allowing regulatory arbitrage, could undermine the effectiveness of prudential oversight. In addition there were some supervisory weaknesses in the part that was supervised, particularly as regards the quality of information on asset quality and verification." In 2005, a new bill was introduced in the Costa Rican Legislative Assembly to reform the Organizational Law of the Central Bank. Five specific aspects were addressed in the bill: (a) it gives SUGEF the necessary authority and faculties to ensure effective consolidated supervision of private and public financial groups and the offshore banks of which they are part, (b) it creates a more stringent regime of sanctions, (c) it establishes an administrative procedure for the compulsory liquidation of entities supervised by SUGEF, (d) it promotes the legal protection of supervisors, and (e) it updates the Credit Information Center to make it a more useful instrument for managing credit risk.

14. Since 2001, a bill has been in the Legislative Assembly to create a deposit insurance scheme for private banks. Yet this bill, like many others, has stagnated in the Legislative Assembly because the country's heated political debate regarding the state's role in the economy has not allowed the process of financial reform to continue at the same pace it had during the 1990s.

15. Thus, all other credit institutions fund themselves with other services, such as certified deposits and loans.

16. Private banks must maintain a minimum balance of loans to any state bank equivalent to 17 percent of deposits of its total acceptances with terms of 30 days or less, after deducting the related reserve. The state banks compensate private entities for the use of these resources paying a rate of interest equal to half the basic borrowing rate set by the BCCR or the monthly LIBOR rate. Alternatively, private banks must establish at least four agencies or branches providing basic banking services, both lending and borrowing, in the relatively less developed regions of Chorotega, Pacifico Central, Brunca, Huetar Atlántico, and Huetar Norte. In this case, they have to maintain a balance equivalent to at least 10 percent of deposits, after deducting the reserve relating to total deposits with a 30-day term or less, in credits for development programs determined by the executive power. These credits must be placed at a rate not higher than the basic borrowing rate of the BCCR for its placements in colons or the monthly LIBOR for resources in foreign currency.

17. These measures include the enactment of a new monetary and exchange rate regime, fiscal strengthening, measures to decrease dollarization, and recapitalization of the central bank.

18. The introduction of fully consolidated supervision and regulation of financial groups, the strengthening of the supervision of onshore banks, and the introduction of prudential buffers are measures falling within this second category.

19. Improvements in the tax code and the legal, accounting, informational, and contract enforcement infrastructure are measures falling within this third category of reforms.

20. CARICOM comprises 15 Caribbean countries: Antigua and Barbuda, The Bahamas, Barbados, Belize, Dominica, Grenada, Guyana, Haiti, Jamaica, Montserrat, St. Kitts and Nevis, St. Lucia, St. Vincent and the Grenadines, Suriname, and Trinidad and Tobago.

21. These regional trade agreements have been instrumental not only in promoting increasing flows of intraregional trade, but also in allowing the Costa Rican manufacturing sector, which in the past was inward looking and focused exclusively on national markets, to gradually become part of the export sector. Moreover, these agreements have played an important role in attracting efficiency-seeking FDI, which, in turn, has played a pivotal role in the gradual industrialization of Costa Rican exports. Furthermore, these agreements have been key for promoting intra–Latin American investment and the emergence of an increasing, yet still limited, number of Costa Rican multinationals. From a political perspective, these agreements have been a mechanism for constructing political alliances favoring—or at least not opposing—further trade liberalization initiatives. In the case of Costa Rica, regionalism has been particularly useful in gradually incorporating the traditionally inward-oriented

manufacturing industries into the exporting sector. For a detailed explanation of the political economy of trade integration in Costa Rica and other Latin American countries during the 1990s, see Echandi (2001). Investment in financial services is granted host-country standards of treatment and protection only after such investment has been admitted in accordance with the host country's domestic legislation, which may vary from time to time.

22. See table 7.4 for the Costa Rican commitments under GATS.

23. As noted previously, an important feature of the process of financial reform in Costa Rica was that the gradual opening has been implemented following a nondiscriminatory approach on the basis of nationality. Thus, foreign ownership within the Costa Rican financial system has increased simultaneously with the growth of private sector participation. The need to level the playing field in the financial sector in Costa Rica is more a matter between state and private financial institutions rather than between national and foreign financial providers.

24. Public Law 98-67, title II, 97 *U.S. Statutes at Large* 384 (1983).

25. The Dominican Republic had not joined the negotiation by then. It became a party to CAFTA-DR-U.S. in 2004, after the main text had been negotiated between the Central American countries and the United States, and it acceded into the agreement after the conclusion of bilateral negotiations with all the parties involved. The accession of the Dominican Republic into CAFTA-DR-U.S. was possible because the country had already negotiated an FTA with the five Central American countries in 1998.

26. As previously mentioned, the Dominican Republic negotiated bilaterally with each of the parties after the main text was negotiated.

27. The Central American countries jointly negotiated an FTA with the Dominican Republic and another with Chile. In addition, El Salvador, Guatemala, and Honduras jointly negotiated an FTA with Mexico, and Costa Rica and Nicaragua negotiated bilaterally. Costa Rica also negotiated an FTA with Canada (while the other four countries negotiated a treaty jointly) and a bilateral FTA with CARICOM. Moreover, Nicaragua negotiated a bilateral FTA with Taiwan, China.

28. *Side room* is the term used to refer to a consultation mechanism by which the government consults with the private sector and civil society. During each round of negotiations, and in some countries before and after negotiations as well, government officials personally briefed private sector and civil society representatives on the specific topics that were addressed in each negotiation session. The term *side room* derives from the fact that such consultations are usually held in the same building where the negotiations take place but in a room other than the negotiation rooms.

29. The Costa Rican position is explained in further detail in the next section.

30. El Salvador and Guatemala were interested in allowing their financial groups effective access to supply financial services for the millions of Salvadorans and Guatemalans residing in the United States. Salvadoran and Guatemalan banks thought U.S. law contained a series of measures that acted as barriers to the establishment of their commercial presence in several U.S. states. Within this context, the financial groups in those countries saw in the CAFTA-DR-U.S. negotiation an opportunity to relax those measures affecting their entry. The problem was that the relaxation sought by those financial groups entailed reforms to U.S. federal and state laws, an outcome that the United States was not willing to accept.

31. Unlike other countries that have also negotiated with the United States, such as Chile and Colombia, Costa Rica did not consider restrictions on capital controls and cross-border investment management services for pension funds controversial issues. Since the 1990s, Costa Rica had liberalized its capital account, and BCCR authorities thought that in the event of a critical situation on this front, limiting capital flows would have harsher effects on the Costa Rican economy than using other policy means. Moreover, Costa Rica has historically not experienced any recurrent or significant problems with short-term capital inflows. Portfolio management services were not controversial either, because the existing Costa Rican legislation did not prevent local investment or pension funds from subcontracting those services abroad, as long as the local entity remained accountable to Costa Rican supervisory authorities.

32. Contrary to other developing countries, Costa Rica had, since the 1940s, successfully developed a welfare state that led the country to remarkable social achievements. In areas such as health, education, and life expectancy, Costa Rica has reached standards typical of developed countries. However, huge public debt and chronic fiscal deficit have decreased Costa Rica's capacity to finance social spending. Public unions and left-wing political parties have attempted to take advantage of this situation to associate the market-oriented reforms started in the 1980s—and, in particular, the attempts of several governments to open the various state monopolies—with the dismantling of the welfare state.

33. Participation by the INS in the CAFTA-DR-U.S. rounds at an early stage of the negotiations would have been counterproductive. It would have sent the wrong signal, both on the domestic front and to the United States, that the government was perfectly willing to discuss trade in insurance services. Although the INS did not participate in the initial negotiation rounds, COMEX established contact with the highest authorities of the INS to keep them informed about how the negotiation was evolving.

34. In 2004, the former executive president of the INS publicly announced that he was considering running for president in 2006. In the end, he did not.

35. Costa Rica concluded the negotiations in January 2004, one month later than the other Central American countries. In December 2003, when the negotiations were originally scheduled to conclude, Costa Rica and the United States were still far from agreeing on a package that was acceptable to both parties. Agriculture, textiles, and services were the three main areas where significant disagreements persisted. To avoid becoming an obstacle for the negotiations between the United States and the other four Central American countries, Costa Rica opted to leave the negotiating table in December 2003. Relative to its Central American neighbors, Costa Rica had the most complex internal political dynamics. It was the only country of the region that still had state monopolies, several of which would have to be opened as a result of the negotiations. Moreover, the political forces resisting market-oriented reform—in particular public unions—were stronger and better organized in Costa Rica than in other Central American countries.

36. All these factors were of key practical importance for the dynamics of the negotiations between a small country like Costa Rica, on the one hand, and the United States, on the other. As a global trader, the United States had developed a template for its FTAs, including the financial services chapter. U.S. negotiators often perceive any deviations from the template as a hassle, not only because such deviations can become a precedent for future negotiations, but also because such deviations may entail new consultations with domestic stakeholders. Within that context, the main challenge for a negotiator from a small country is to make the U.S. counterpart understand why and how the U.S. government has to deviate from its main negotiation template. Such a decision is not typically made by the negotiator at the table, but rather by higher political authorities. Thus, in practice, no consultation at the higher level will ever take place if the U.S. negotiator at the table does not believe and understand the reasons given by the small country.

37. Among the areas for research and analysis were the legal framework for financial services in Costa Rica and the United States, including recent jurisprudential developments and bills under consideration in both legislatures; identification of pressure groups in both Costa Rica and the United States, paying particular attention to the insurance and banking sectors; analysis of the legal texts of each financial services chapter negotiated by the United States in each of its FTAs, paying particular attention to NAFTA and the most recent negotiations with Chile and Singapore; analysis of U.S. commitments under GATS; analysis of any comments that U.S. financial businesses had expressed about the Costa Rican financial sector; analysis of reports of major international organizations on the Costa Rican financial services framework; and a series of studies on the particular strengths and weaknesses of the insurance monopoly in Costa Rica.

38. Contrary to other Latin American countries where the ministry of finance led negotiations of the financial services chapter, in Costa Rica, COMEX led

the negotiations. This role was never a contested issue within the Costa Rican government. Three factors explain this scheme. First, traditionally, COMEX, the BCCR, and the other institutions involved in the financial sector have enjoyed excellent coordination and a good working relationship. COMEX has traditionally relied on the expertise of the specialized agencies when dealing with financial services issues, either when negotiating at the World Trade Organization or on trade-related internal matters. In addition, from the outset, the presence of all the institutions involved as part of the negotiating team was a given. Thus, the specialization argument in favor of handing coordination of the negotiations to the Ministry of Finance or the central bank never was raised. Second, given that COMEX oversaw all the other negotiation tables, COMEX's coordination of the financial services negotiations seemed convenient to facilitate a coherent and adequate balance of the country's interests as a whole. Last, although the other institutions involved in the financial sector had a very capable and specialized staff in their respective fields, they were less familiar with international trade negotiations and the technical trade and investment law concepts and jargon. Thus, one of COMEX's main tasks was to train the staff members of the other agencies.

39. Despite the limited reforms, the financial sector has clearly seen itself as one of the winners of CAFTA-DR-U.S, mostly because of the anticipated increased demand for financial services from the expansion in economic activity, greater FDI inflows, and greater trade in services. Moreover, the financial sector also favored the better investment climate fostered by the disciplines included in the agreement.

40. Article 10.2, paragraph 3, of CAFTA-DR-U.S. provides that the chapter on investment does not apply to measures adopted or maintained by the parties to the agreement to the extent that those measures are covered by chapter 12. Article 11.1, paragraph 4(a), provides that the chapter on services does not apply to financial services as defined in chapter 12.

41. The positive effect of CAFTA-DR-U.S. should be measured not just in terms of its contribution to new financial liberalization. Clearly, binding the existing level of openness of the Costa Rican market for financial services is an important outcome of the agreement. Such binding should have a positive effect in terms of predictability and security and should thus help attract-and maintain-foreign investment.

42. Some Costa Rican think tanks have started to work with the Costa Rican government to prepare an impact analysis of the opening of the insurance sector. One of the important aspects already found is that, for its income level, the density and depth levels of the Costa Rican insurance market are low. Such findings suggest that the opening of the insurance market should have a positive effect on improving those indicators (see Arce 2005).

43. According to Promotora de Comercio Exterior de Costa Rica (the Foreign Trade Promotion Office of Costa Rica), the preferential access Costa Rican exports have enjoyed in the U.S. market since the 1980s through the Caribbean Basin Initiative has played a key role in attracting this export-oriented FDI into Costa Rica.

44. Thus, a financial institution is one that in principle is supervised. Following this logic, given that insurance is not supervised in Costa Rica, one could argue that the INS is not a financial institution. However, one of the main obligations undertaken by Costa Rica under chapter 12 is to set up a supervisory authority for insurance by January 1, 2007, thereby making it a financial institution in the sense of the agreement.

45. This definition includes, in principle, e-finance. In this regard, article 14.2 of the e-commerce chapter explicitly clarifies the following: "For greater certainty, the Parties affirm that measures affecting the supply of a service using electronic means fall within the scope of the obligations contained in the relevant provisions of Chapters Ten (Investment), Eleven (Cross-Border Trade in Services), and Twelve (Financial Services), subject to any exceptions or nonconforming measures set out in this Agreement, which are applicable to such obligations."

46. The following example may be useful to illustrate the scope of application of chapter 12. Consider a company that has its principal place of business in Costa Rica and leases automobiles in Nicaragua. If the company operates a car rental business, where a customer rents a car for a short period of time, the service being provided is unlikely one of a "financial nature." It is a transportation service rather than a financial service, and measures affecting the cross-border provision of such services would be covered by chapter 11 rather than by chapter 12. However, suppose that the Costa Rican company leases automobiles on a long-term basis and the customers leasing the automobiles are fully responsible for repairs and maintenance. The leasing company is providing its customers with an alternative means of borrowing or financing the acquisition of automobiles and, as such, is providing a service of a financial nature. Measures affecting the cross-border provision of these services would be covered by chapter 12 and not by chapter 11. An automobile leasing company operating in Costa Rica is not "regulated or supervised" as a financial institution and, therefore, is not a financial institution. Measures affecting investments in such a company by U.S. and other Central American investors and their investments would be covered by chapter 10 and not by chapter 12.

47. Under annex 12.5.1, all CAFTA-DR-U.S. parties undertook basically the same commitments to permit and provide national treatment to two kinds of services. First, regarding banking and other financial services, the commitment allows the provision and transfer of financial information and financial data

processing and related software, as well as advisory and other auxiliary services, excluding intermediation, related to banking and other financial services. Second, regarding insurance services, the parties committed to allow the cross-border supply of insurance of risks related to maritime shipping and commercial aviation and space launching and freight (including satellites), goods in international transit, and reinsurance and retrocession, as well as the supply of services auxiliary to insurance and insurance intermediation, such as brokerage and agency.

48. *Solicitation* will be defined in accordance with the terms of each country's laws. In Costa Rica, a Web page is not considered public solicitation. However, direct e-mails sent to customers may well be considered as such. In any case, given the territorial nature of the laws in Costa Rica—as in most other countries of the world—citizens may be free to conduct business abroad in accordance with the host country's laws.

49. The Dominican Republic and El Salvador undertook the commitment to enact that legislation no later than four years after CAFTA-DR-U.S. enters into force.

50. Indeed, besides insurance, the agreement does not entail any reform of Costa Rica's legislation on financial services.

51. For a detailed study of the commitments assumed by Costa Rica in the insurance sector, see chapter 12's annex 12.9.2., section H.

52. In this regard, chapter 12 explicitly states that the regulatory authority must act consistently with the core principles of the International Association of Insurance Supervisors.

References and Other Resources

Ángulo, José. 2004. "Décimo informe sobre el estado de la nación en desarrollo humano sostenible: Informe final—Principales cambios en el sector financiero costarricense, 1985–2003 [Tenth report on the state of the nation regarding sustainable human development: Final report—Principal changes in the Costa Rican financial sector, 1985–2003]." Estado de la Nación, San José, Costa Rica.

Arce, Gilberto. 2005. "Mercado de seguros en Costa Rica: Un análisis económico [Insurance market in Costa Rica: An economic analysis]." PowerPoint presentation, Academia de Centroamérica, San José, Costa Rica.

Bolaños, Rodrigo. 2003. *Reforma financiera en Costa Rica: Los grandes temas de la agenda para el inicio del siglo XXI* [Financial reform in Costa Rica: Major agenda items for the beginning of the 21st century]. Documento 5. San José, Costa Rica: Academia de Centroamérica.

Delgado, Félix, and Miguel Loría, eds. 2004. *Eduardo Lizano: Escritos sobre reforma financiera* [Eduardo Lizano: Writings on financial reform]. San José, Costa Rica: Academia de Centroamérica.

Echandi, Roberto. 2001. "Regional Trade Integration in the Americas in the 1990s: Reflections on Some Trends and Their Implications for the Multilateral Trade System." *Journal of International Economic Law* 4: 367–410.

González Vega, Claudio, and Thelmo Vargas, eds. 1993. *Reforma financiera en Costa Rica: Perspectivas y propuestas* [Financial reform in Costa Rica: Perspectives and proposals]. San José, Costa Rica: Academia de Centroamérica.

IMF (International Monetary Fund) and World Bank. 2003. *Costa Rica: Financial System Stability Assessment.* IMF Country Report No. 03/103. Washington, DC: IMF.

Jiménez, Ronulfo, ed. 1998. *Estabilidad y desarrollo económico en Costa Rica: Las reformas pendientes* [Stability and economic development in Costa Rica: The pending reforms]. San José, Costa Rica: Academia de Centroamérica.

———. 2000. *Los retos políticos de la reforma económica en Costa Rica* [The political challenges of economic reform in Costa Rica]. San José, Costa Rica: Academia de Centroamérica.

Lizano, Eduardo, and Grettel López, eds. 2003. *Economía costarricense y el Tratado de Libre Comercio con los Estados Unidos* [Costa Rican economy and the Free Trade Agreement with the United States]. San José, Costa Rica: Academia de Centroamérica.

———. 2005. *La economía costarricense y la evolución del sistema financiero en el 2004* [The Costa Rican economy and evolution of the financial system in 2004]. San José, Costa Rica: Academia de Centroamérica.

Ministerio de Comercio Exterior. 2003a. "Tratado de Libre Comercio entre Centroamérica y Estados Unidos: Posición nacional [Free Trade Agreement between Central America and the United States: National position]." San José, Costa Rica.

———. 2003b. "Volúmen 6: Información y consulta a la sociedad civil en el proceso de negociación del Tratado de Libre Comercio Centroamérica–República Dominicana–Estados Unidos [Informing and consulting with civil society in the process of negotiating the Free Trade Agreement between Central America, the Dominican Republic, and the United States]." San José, Costa Rica. http://www.comex.go.cr/publicaciones/PublicacionesTodos/USAv6Informacion.pdf.

White House, Office of the Press Secretary. 2002. "President Announces Step to Expand Trade and Create Jobs." Remarks by President George W. Bush to the World Affairs Council National Conference, Organization of American States, Washington, DC, January 16.

Index

Boxes, figures, notes, and tables are indicated by *b*, *f*, *n*, and *t*, respectively.

ECO-AUDIT
Environmental Benefits Statement

The World Bank is committed to preserving endangered forests and natural resources. The Office of the Publisher has chosen to print *Financial Services and Preferential Trade Agreements: Lessons from Latin America* on recycled paper with 50 percent postconsumer fiber in accordance with the recommended standards for paper usage set by the Green Press Initiative, a nonprofit program supporting publishers in using fiber that is not sourced from endangered forests. For more information, visit www.greenpressinitiative.org.

Saved:
- 11 trees
- 3 million Btu of total energy
- 1,015 lb. of net greenhouse gases
- 4,887 gal. of waste water
- 297 lb. of solid waste

green
press
INITIATIVE

www.ingramcontent.com/pod-product-compliance
Lightning Source LLC
Chambersburg PA
CBHW061001280326
41935CB00009B/786